D1395259

CREDIT CONTROL IN BOOM AND RECESSION

By the same author and from the same publishers

CREDIT RISK AND EXPOSURE IN SECURITISATION AND
  TRANSACTIONS

HOW TO HANDLE PROBLEM LOANS

THE MEDIUM-TERM LOAN MARKETS (*with J. A. Donaldson*)

THE TREATMENT OF INTANGIBLES

UNDERSTANDING CORPORATE CREDIT

Credit Control
in Boom and Recession

T. H. Donaldson
Managing Director
J. P. Morgan, London

First published in Great Britain 1994 by
MACMILLAN PRESS LTD
Houndmills, Basingstoke, Hampshire RG21 6XS
and London
Companies and representatives
throughout the world

A catalogue record for this book is available
from the British Library.
ISBN 0-333-58667-0

First published in the United States of America 1994 by
ST. MARTIN'S PRESS, INC.,
Scholarly and Reference Division,
175 Fifth Avenue,
New York, N.Y. 10010

ISBN 0-312-10642-4

Library of Congress Cataloging-in-Publication Data
Donaldson, T. H. (Thomas Hay), 1936–
Credit control in boom and recession / T. H. Donaldson.
p. cm.
ISBN 0-312-10642-4
1. Credit control. I. Title.
HG3705/D66   1994
658.8'8—dc20   93-31231
                                                 CIP

© T. H. Donaldson 1994

All rights reserved. No reproduction, copy or transmission of
this publication may be made without written permission.

No paragraph of this publication may be reproduced, copied or
transmitted save with written permission or in accordance with
the provisions of the Copyright, Designs and Patents Act 1988,
or under the terms of any licence permitting limited copying
issued by the Copyright Licensing Agency, 90 Tottenham Court
Road, London WIP 9HE

Any person who does any unauthorised act in relation to this
publication may be liable to criminal prosecution and civil
claims for damages.

11 10 9   8   7   6   5   4   3   2
05 04 03 02 01 00 99 98 97 96

Printed and bound in Great Britain by
Antony Rowe Ltd
Chippenham, Wiltshire

LEEDS BECKETT UNIVERSITY
LIBRARY
DISCARDED

LEEDS METROPOLITAN
UNIVERSITY LIBRARY

1701470146
B33BL
4413414 29.7.96
658.88 DON
31 JUL 1996 £40·00

To my wife, Natalie

Contents

1 Introduction

CREDIT CONTROL/STRATEGY: A SUBJECT FOR RECESSION ONLY?

During recessions many bankers with experience of bad loans are asked to speak at seminars. Almost invariably the subject includes some reference to lending strategy in a recession.

Many, including the author of this book, make the point that a strategy for recession starts during the preceding boom. In recession, banks find out whether their strategy and controls are sound. But the decisions which influence the answer were taken several years before, perhaps in full boom, or even in the early stages of the upswing. If lenders are to avoid excessive bad debts (they cannot avoid them all), the crucial time is well before the recession starts. A recession tests the quality of loans. The homework which decides whether they pass or fail was done, or not done, well before.

In many ways a recession is the easiest time to make a credit decision. The bad news is out. If the borrower cannot cope with adverse conditions, this is obvious, and the bank does not lend voluntarily. Conversely, a company which survives at the bottom of the recession has a proven strength.

We must not exaggerate this of course. For one thing, who knows when we are at the bottom of the recession? And the resilience may be more apparent than real. Never the less, the point is valid.

Conversely an upswing, even before a full boom, helps weak companies to cover their weakness. Loss of market share is less likely if your competition is producing at full capacity, and less damaging – as well as less obvious – in an expanding market. Failure to control costs is less dangerous with high volume. And so on. But to conceal weaknesses does not make them less real. Indeed, if companies conceal weaknesses from themselves, they are even more dangerous.

In summary, the time to hone credit controls and lending strategies is well before a recession. To leave it until then is almost invariably too late. A bank's options in a recession are mainly confined to damage limitation.

CREDIT/LENDING: PART OF A GREATER WHOLE

Credit Control is part of lending strategy, which is part of a bank's overall business strategy. The business strategy in turn results from many factors which can change, but usually do so slowly. These include the bank's existing organisation: its branch network; its customer profile; whether it is purely a commercial bank or has elements of investment banking, universal banking, and so on; whether it is domestic or international; what is its home base, and many other factors.

Important among these are the skills and training of its current staff. A strategy which requires them to do more than they are trained for or to change their approach can work, but only if it takes account of, and covers, these weaknesses.

It follows that no book can prescribe a strategy which most banks can follow slavishly. Rather, it can describe the various possible approaches to each aspect, their strengths and weaknesses, and how they fit – or do not fit – with other aspects of strategy. It can highlight the requirements – training and systems-support to mention two – which each approach implies; and discuss what they mean for different functions in each strategy. Only a bank which knows its own business – the types of client it has and wants, the risks it is or is not prepared to take, and the return it expects from them – as well as its structure, can make the decisions. And this too must fit in with the branch structure, the quality and training of people, the access to new types of people, etc. And even when all this is known, it is not cast in stone. As the bank changes and develops, so it must review and update its lending strategies, refresh its controls, modernise its training. Most often this is an evolutionary process, but sometimes requires more conscious and even dramatic action.

There are, however, a few general policies which apply to all banks in all parts of the cycle. We will merely state them here but discuss them at the appropriate stage of later chapters.

- Any credit strategy which makes growth in the loan portfolio a key objective is dangerous. The more rapid the target rate, the more dangerous. Growth can be a desirable side-effect of sound policies, but not their primary aim.

- Getting the pricing right is critical to long-term profits and to avoiding bad debts.

- Credit decisions which ignore the ability to monitor the particular loan are likely to be bad decisions.

- Lending in a boom, with everybody else, is highly risky. This is true whether the boom is a general economic one, or is confined to one industry or type of lending.

- The relationship between marketing and credit is critical.

- Credit control systems which underestimate the importance of monitoring have a huge hole in them.

- It is vital to keep the decisions on provisioning entirely separate from decisions as to how best to recover a problem loan.

CREDIT CONTROL DEFINED IN ITS DIFFERENT ASPECTS

All aspects of credit control are interlinked. At the same time, however, there are different phases which can be fitted together in various ways. It makes the discussion clearer to break it into parts even though this may sometimes involve an element of repetition. There are various ways we could break it down, but for the purposes of this book we have chosen four main sections, although even these have some subsections.

Analysis, Presentation and Decision

These three together decide the quality of the original decision, and therefore play a major part in the success of the strategy. A purist might question whether some banks actually perform a worthwhile analysis on many of their credits. Others would find it hard to distinguish between analysis and presentation; certainly they can be done by the same person, or combined in the same discussion in a way which makes it hard to tell where one starts and the other ends.

Never the less, some form of analysis, formal or informal, in depth or superficial, is done before any credit decision. A good credit strategy will ensure that the analysis covers the right subjects with the necessary skill. It will also aim to avoid overkill on the simpler credits, since good analysts are expensive.

Equally, whatever the forum for taking the decisions, decision-makers rarely ask for their own approval. Someone has to take the view that 'this is something the bank should do' and initiate the process which leads to a decision. And either the same someone or another has actually to present the proposal to the decision-maker. While the analyst can present, or the presenter also do the analysis, the functions are separate and it can be unsound to mix them.

Finally, both the format for taking decisions and the people who take them have to be chosen carefully. There must be a system to communicate policies, and changes in them, to these decision-makers. The bank must have a general consensus on the approach to credit. Failing that, the decision-makers may be constantly at loggerheads with the marketers, or worse still, overruled by them.

Structure of a Loan

An important factor in any lending strategy, and system of credit control, is the bank's attitude to the structure of the loan or other facility. While the individual decisions must take into account the facts of each case, there must be an underlying approach to structural matters. For it to work, everybody involved, not just the decision-maker, must be aware of it and understand the rationale behind it, so that they can judge how to apply it to each case; they must be able to defend it in negotiations with the client, and even educate the client beforehand.

Structure has several aspects.

Short, medium or long?

The maturity of the loan can range from on demand to ten years, or sometimes longer. Making sure that the bank tailors maturity and amortisation to the expected use of the funds and source of repayment is a critical part of credit control. If the bank classifies a facility as short term, the use and source of repayment must be short term, not just the form of the facility. Lending medium or long term without recognising it is one of the classic errors of banking. It changes both the time-span, and usually the source of repayment: from assets realised in the normal course of business to cash flow. There is thus a real danger that the whole of whatever analysis has been done is based on the wrong premise.

Where the bank is lending medium term, the question of amortisation is critical. This is partly a question of emphasis – how far will the bank insist on amortisation – and partly one of detail. Any amortisation is almost certainly better than none; but amortisation which is tailored to the purpose for which the loan is used, and the source of repayment, is best. Management must always ensure that the bank has a clear policy and that everybody involved understands it and can explain it to the borrower.

Covenants and other protection

Much the same points apply to covenants. They are a key aspect of medium-term lending. Their understanding and proper use is an important part of the training of lending bankers, and is critical to the quality of a medium-term portfolio. Covenants play two main roles. Non-ratio covenants – negative pledge, dividend restraint, alienation of assets are leading examples – prevent the borrower taking specific actions which might damage the lenders' interests. Ratio covenants – minimum current ratio, maximum debt to worth, interest cover and cash flow cover are among the most common – perform two roles. They provide a monitoring tool, as the bank sees the margin of compliance contract, expand or remain stable and a protective tool if the covenants are actually breached.

A bank which consistently allows borrowers to avoid covenants, or accepts only weak ones, faces unnecessary problems when borrowers deteriorate. And some inevitably do, even if they stop short of complete collapse. Equally, a bank which rigidly insists on the same ratios for all borrowers will miss some good business, and still face most of the troubles of a bank with no ratios. Often its rigid covenants will not meet the requirements of the particular case.

Thus again, training bankers to understand and sell covenants is critical. Decision-makers must know which covenants to choose, and when to achieve the objective of a covenant in a different way, so as to enforce the bank's policy with minimum loss of good business.

Security

Security is often a vital part of the structure of a loan, particularly, but not only of a medium-term loan. Security is, however, even more often an excuse for not thinking the credit through. The fixed and floating charge in the United Kingdom is a particularly bad example of this.

It may be the word itself that is at fault. Security gives a suggestion of safety, while in fact secured loans are in general at least as risky as unsecured ones, and often more so. We start from the position that the reason we need security is that the loan is unsafe without it. Obviously, there are some exceptions to such a sweeping generalisation, but they are too few to weaken it.

So perhaps we would do better to refer to collateral. The key point is that it should support a well analysed loan, but only will if it itself is well analysed and fits the overall purpose. Collateral is dangerous if it is seen as a substitute for analysis and strict credit control, rather than as part of them.

Few bankers admit, even to themselves, that they are substituting collateral for analysis. Rather, they indulge in a form of sloppy thinking that amounts to the same thing. There is therefore a real management task in overcoming this tendency, made worse in some banks by a long-standing emphasis on the importance of collateral that tends to obscure the dangers of taking it without thinking it through properly.

Documentation

Every credit facility needs to be documented. For overdrafts and other short-term facilities the documentation may be simple. For unsecured medium-term loans, it can range from the eight- to ten-page letter to 100+ pages for a complex syndicated loan. Secured and project loans can be even longer.

A loan agreement is normally drafted by lawyers, and may in some cases be largely negotiated by them as well. The banker must be in charge of the process, however, or he may find that legal bills sky-rocket, negotiations with clients become acrimonious, and the final document bears little resemblance to what bank and client thought they had agreed. Even if they avoid these mistakes, bankers and lawyers often forget that the prime purpose of a loan agreement is as an operating document. It is true that, at worst, the parties may end up in court, with a judge interpreting the agreement. It is desirable to avoid this by making the agreement legally clear. On the other hand, the clerks in the bank's and borrower's back offices are going to be making payments and performing other functions regularly throughout the life of the loan. If it is obscurely worded (in terms of clerical understanding, not that of a High Court judge) they will make mistakes in the operation. The prospect of this should worry everybody at least as much as that of a judge misinterpreting the agreement.

Management must allocate responsibility within the bank for negotiating documentation, and train those who do it; and inculcate standards and communicate policies. Not all documentation covers strictly credit points. The treatment of withholding tax, for instance, is important to banks and borrowers, and can cause deep and sometimes bitter disagreement between the parties. But the bank also needs to have clear policies on things like grace periods for payments of principal and interest, cross-default and such items.

Training

All aspects of credit require training. But the nature of the training and who receives it will vary with the other factors.

Where a generalist recommends and follows credit, he or she must have appropriate training. The level will depend, in part, on the depth of the responsibility, in part, on the support the generalist receives. Where most of the credit is covered by specialists, they must have a different level of credit training, and perhaps a career structure, to ensure that the depth of knowledge and judgement needed is always available. If only a few people have the specialist knowledge, the bank must not allow them to be diverted to more glamorous tasks.

Training in analysis is just as important as training in making decisions, but different in form. Making decisions requires knowledge of analysis, but also requires judgement of risk which comes more from common sense and experience.

The art of presentation is different again, but can only flourish if credit skills are combined with balanced judgement.

Computers

Computers are helpful, even critical, to several aspects of credit control. They allow bankers to spend time on marketing and other duties as well as the aspects of credit that the computer cannot do.

Computers have two major drawbacks. First, they are too often programmed by people who understand computers but not business, and used by people who understand business but not computing.

This creates a very real risk that they are programmed to do the wrong thing; or that while correctly programmed for use by a computer buff, they do not give a banker the service he needs. The validity of the phrase 'user friendly' depends heavily on who the user is.

The second drawback is that the computer sometimes becomes too useful. The obvious example is its use to prepare forecasts. A good program enables us to spew out figures and makes it easy to forget that they are merely the output. The quality of the forecasts does not depend on the arithmetic, but on the thinking about the business, the risks and other aspects which goes into generating the figures. There is a growing tendency for younger bankers to think that a computer run is an analysis when it is nothing of the sort. 'Garbage in, garbage out' or GIGO is too often forgotten.

MANAGEMENT ATTITUDES AND CULTURE RULE ALL

Credit consciousness can only come from the top. But it must be more than a statement, it must be an attitude which pervades all management's thinking. Only in this way will it permeate down to the levels where, in practice, the mistakes are made or avoided. And to be more than a statement, it must show in management's actions. Depending on the style of the bank, it may be more stick or more carrot, but it must be clear to everybody what the stick or carrot are for, and both must be credible.

Management must therefore be prepared to authorise expenditure on systems, both hardware and software; to countenance headcount levels appropriate to the needs; to avoid senior bankers who become so absorbed in marketing and generating revenue that they think credit no longer matters; or, if that is how management wants them to think, it must cover credit in some other way. If the bank uses credit specialists, management will need to think carefully about their career structure and reward; failure to do this may leave credit as a second-class career staffed, if not by failures, at least by people who are seen as second to the deal getters. Above all, banks need to recognise that a credit specialist may avoid a $10 million bad loan, or reduce the probable loss from $10 million to $5 million. The value to the bank of this is probably greater than that of the revenue earner who brings in fees of the same size. In particular, the deal that brings in $1 million in fees sometimes creates the possible $5 million loss. The reward here is too often for bringing in the deal rather than saving or reducing the loss.

On the other side, it is easy to have a credit control that is so uncommercial that the bank turns away good business. Indeed, there is a history of banks swinging from one extreme to the other. In boom times, when sound credit control is most important, it is overruled by marketing considerations. Then when the boom turns to recession and bad debts proliferate, the bank instals rigid and impracticable rules. When in turn these lose good business the bank swings back to being too permissive. Getting the balance right through the whole economic cycle is critically important.

It is also vital to have sound systems, both computer systems and in the wider sense, and procedures. Without these even the best management intentions will not be translated into action. But managements must recognise that systems and procedures depend on people to work them. They will only do this effectively if they believe in the systems, and this belief depends on top management sharing it, and demonstrating that continuously.

CREDIT CONTROL COVERS MORE THAN JUST LENDING

Credit has always covered more than just loans. However, with the development of new products and the breakdown of the distinctions between investment, merchant and commercial banking, the non-lending aspects of credit are more important than ever before. They range from areas such as counterparty credit in forward exchange, swaps and other products; settlement risk in many products and markets; underwriting risk in loan syndication and bond distribution; credit risk in a wide range of traded debt instruments, from commercial paper to thirty-year bonds, senior or subordinated.

Many of the considerations raised by these types of credit parallel those in lending, and this book will therefore concentrate mainly on lending. However, there are some types of credit which are different to lending; sections within chapters, and some chapters, deal with these.

Part I

Analysis, Presentation and the Decision

2 Analysis

THE TYPE OF ANALYSIS

Credit analysis can take several forms. Management needs to think carefully about which type it wants before it can decide how to provide it. The first question is exactly what to analyse. A bank can analyse the borrowing company, the transaction, the security, or all three, but it needs criteria to choose which.

Analysing the Company

There are two main approaches to analysing companies. The choice each bank makes may influence the decision on whether, and if so how, to analyse the other aspects. The approaches can be mixed in various ways and usually are, but the underlying attitude is often more black and white than the detailed practice.

Liquidation or 'gone concern' analysis

The older approach, which tends to foster reliance on security, is liquidation analysis, sometimes called 'gone concern' analysis. It analyses what the bank expects to recover from the assets in liquidation. It recognises that they will rarely fetch book value, and therefore assesses their forced-sale value. Because other creditors will also be trying to recover their debt, it encourages an emphasis on taking maximum security to ensure that the bank ranks ahead of those creditors.

This approach has two weaknesses. First, it wrongly assumes that the source of repayment is assets in liquidation. They may well be a second way out, in emergency, but they are not the expected source of repayment. No bank makes a voluntary loan expecting its borrower to liquidate and repay the loan in that way. The expected source of repayment is normally: either cash flow from operations; or the realisation of assets in the normal course of business, very different to liquidation. It must surely make sense to analyse first the expected source of repayment. It is useful to know that if this analysis turns out to be wrong, the liquidation value gives a second hope of recovery.

13

Secondly, to rely on security may be sound where it is the expected source of repayment; to do so otherwise is unsound. In theory, there is no reason why taking security where the bank does not expect to realise it should conflict with analysis of the expected source, often cash flow. In practice, it clearly does. Indeed, the great fear is that bankers take security as a substitute for analysis, rather than in support of its results. Management of any bank should aim to prevent this. And while much of the answer is cultural, some of it comes from the form of analysis used.

Cash flow or 'going concern' analysis

In most manufacturing and commercial companies the expected source of repayment is cash flow, and the value of most assets arises from the cash flow they generate. However, cash flow analysts recognise that there are more demands on cash flow than just debt service; some of these demands are essential to ensure the continuing ability to service debt. Some also arise from the needs or strengths of the balance sheet. Cash flow analysis therefore focuses on the balance sheet as well as the profit and loss, but the emphasis is on the latter.

Cash flow analysis fosters understanding of the nature of the business; the competitive and other features which affect it; the risks which threaten it and the factors which can increase or protect against them. Finally, it recognises that the cash flow to pay off debt is generated over time, and in the future; it thus involves an attempt to forecast the future, in outline at least, and to assess the probable path, the range within which cash flow will lie in normal circumstances, and the factors which can throw an otherwise reasonable forecast off course. In brief, it calls for a deeper understanding of many aspects of a company's business than does liquidation analysis. This requires more sophisticated bankers, analysts or both; more computers and better software; and it engenders a better understanding of risk among all concerned. It also has some marketing advantages, since clients are often impressed by the interest in their company.

Analysis should take account of the economic cycle. While it relies on historic data to establish trends, it also tries to assess the impact of future developments on those trends. Economic growth is an important factor; in cyclical companies their relationship to it, or their separate cycle, are even more critical. The operative word here is 'should', however. Too often, analysts, who in many cases are bright but inexperienced, are carried away by the general euphoria in a boom.

Where a company expects sales to grow at 10% p.a. for the next ten years, and margins to be 25% more than they have ever been before, any banker will look at the impact of lower growth or margins. But a downside case that says sales grow at 5% p.a. for two years and then 10%, and that margins are only 20% higher than ever before, may not meet the point, particularly if the company can only start to repay debt in the fourth year even on its own case. An experienced, and perhaps less marketing-oriented, banker may need to say 'Wait a minute. We are two-thirds or more through a boom. What happens if the downturn comes earlier than expected? Or is more severe than you allow for when it does come? Run me a case with sales down 5% for the first two years, and margins 10% below their present level until the fourth year. Then convince me either that they can pay off the loan even then or that the risk is so small that we can afford to take it.'

The author of this book has been on both sides of that argument; as a young man ridiculing it, and as an older credit officer upholding it against ridicule. The argument has saved many banks millions of dollars over the years, but only where they have people able and willing to make the argument; and where these people hold the right positions and visibly carry management's support.

The time to be most cautious in analysing a company is when it seems to be doing best. At the bottom of a cycle, it is easy to see the problems. This does not excuse us from careful analysis, but it reduces the chance that we miss hidden weaknesses. Analysing a company in the upside of the cycle carries the risk that favourable conditions temporarily conceal weaknesses. The losses banks record in a recession are rarely the result of decisions made during the recession, but usually of mistakes made well before it began. The aim of credit control in general, and analysis in particular, must be to ensure that the bank makes as few such mistakes as possible. The control of euphoria is a critical aspect of credit control, and a forward-looking analysis, properly used and supported, is a vital tool.

The depth of analysis

Management must also decide what depth of analysis it wants, and in what circumstances. This affects computer costs, and analytical headcount.

A simple but effective analysis in three or four pages will look at the business in general terms, the balance sheet structure, the cash flow and perhaps a source and reconciliation of funds. It will relate cash flow to debt service and other known and projected needs, and assess the viability of the company on that basis. It will look forward only in the most general sense; the ability of current levels of cash flow to service debt, for instance, tells you something about the likely future trends, but not in great depth. This does not need computers, extensive forecasting or industry knowledge.

Banks can, without computers, prepare detailed forecasts; indeed Robert Morris Associates, an American trade association for lending officers, used to provide its members with a form to standardise the process. Doing it by hand is excellent training. It helps to understand the interaction between the balance sheet and profit and loss, and between accrual accounts and cash generation. There is a strong argument that no banker should forecast on a computer before doing several hand-prepared forecasts. However, the process is cumbersome; it is not practical for all cases, and it does not allow a flexible range of sensitivity analyses.

The computer gives the power to run the arithmetical forecasts quickly; to run as many cases as are needed to explore the various risks and opportunities in depth. But it requires management to invest in:

- personal computers for the analysts, possibly linked to a central computer;

- the software, which may be developed in-house or bought as a package;

- training analysts in computers, or computer experts to understand financial analysis, and produce programs that work.

All this is becoming less costly as more people use PCs as a matter of course.

The danger of the computer, however, is that it makes life too easy. The ease of computer runs may make inexperienced bankers put too much weight on what comes out, and not enough on what goes in. The easier it is to use computers, the more important it is to remember GIGO – garbage in, garbage out. Thus training has to cover more than just the use of the computer; it has to cover all aspects of analysis, and above all the basis on which to develop assumptions to feed into the computer.

The forecasts are thus of most value if industry expertise is available. This may mean industry analysts; or industry experts of other sorts who are available to credit analysts to provide the basis; or experienced analysts to do detailed investigations of industries with which they are not closely familiar before concentrating on the analysis. Or some other combination.

All of these affect cost and the organisation of the analytical effort, discussed in more detail below. Banks also need to match the analytical effort to the pattern of their loan portfolios. A British clearing bank with over 1,000 domestic branches and tens of thousands of small local companies may apply one set of criteria to them and another to the major multi-nationals to which it lends from its head office. It will need systems which can differentiate between the analytical and other needs of the two types. A merchant bank, or a major wholesale bank, which lends much larger relative amounts to fewer borrowers can afford a single system, as sophisticated as its portfolio justifies.

Since some of the benefits of the computer also apply to the monitoring of loans, Chapter 7 will cover those aspects. Here it is worth making two points. Both are heavily reinforced by the experience of many banks in the 1989–93 recessions in various countries.

First, while the individual risks are small, the cumulative amounts can be massive. For instance, in May 1992 Barclays Bank said that 44% of provisions were for loans under £100,000. Thus, analysing small companies must be cost-effective; but the emphasis must be on effectiveness as well as on cost.

The question 'Can we afford to spend so much on credit control?' is thus best answered by another: 'How can we afford not to do so?' The losses reported by a wide range of banks in North America, Japan, Britain, Scandinavia and to a lesser but growing extent Continental Europe, cover the whole spectrum. There have been large individual losses to what had been thought first-class borrowers; there have been huge losses lending to small business and individuals; there have been losses on all types of both secured and unsecured loans.

Any bank with a well-spread lending portfolio will take some losses, and more in a recession. But the contrast between the least and most successful banks suggests that the size of recent losses for the worst hit is well beyond any 'inevitable' level. Spending more money on credit control alone might not have changed this, since much of the problem is one of attitude and management culture. On the other hand, the attitude which avoids loss will probably also accept the need to spend money to do so. And if even 10% of recent bad debts could have been saved by better analysis and monitoring (the costly parts of credit control), the cost would have been recovered many times over.

Analysing the Collateral

There are several types of secured loan; their nature often decides that of the collateral. The two together will decide the type of analysis required. It is as important to analyse the collateral as it is to analyse an unsecured borrower. Indeed, in many cases a prime reason for taking collateral is that the borrower is too weak to borrow unsecured.

The fixed and floating charge

This phrase covers loans where a bank takes security on all or most of the working assets of a cash flow borrower. It refers to the English legal mechanism for doing so, but the underlying idea exists in most countries, although the legal form it takes may differ.

The assets charged gain their main value from the cash flow the company generates, or in other ways related to the success of the company. If the company fails the assets are at worst almost worthless, at best lose substantial value. The analysis of the collateral then focuses on two main aspects: how much independent value does the collateral have in liquidation, and how much flexibility does the bank have to realise on the collateral without precipitating liquidation?

The collateral under a fixed and floating charge usually consists mainly of three types: receivables, inventory and fixed assets. Sometimes, of course, there will be cash and short-term investments or trade investments; or intangibles such as brand names or patents. These may have a value in liquidation, or may be valuable only so long as the company is solvent (see T. H. Donaldson, *The Treatment of Intangibles*, Macmillan, 1992). The first part of the analysis should then take each main type separately.

Receivables   The analysis of receivables in liquidation has several main aspects. First, how concentrated is the risk of customers failing to pay? Secondly, how many different customers are there, how large is each and how does the cost of collection relate to the likely recovery? Thirdly, what risk is there that customers will refuse to pay for non-financial reasons, such as the need for continued servicing or product enhancement? Clearly collapse makes either impossible, although sometimes there may be alternative sources of servicing. Also, many of the same questions as we would ask of a going concern: how good is the credit of the obligor? is there any right, such as set off, which would interfere with our claim? and so on.

There are cases where receivables are collected in full in liquidation, but usually collection becomes more difficult and losses greater. Only with an understanding of the product, of why customers buy it and what follow-up they expect, can the bank make a realistic advance assessment. Of course some of this comes from the main analysis of the borrower; the quality of receivables, for instance, is a key element in cash flow lending. The danger to avoid is failure to analyse the cash generation because the loan is secured, or the value of the collateral because that is not the expected source of repayment.

Inventory Again, we need to know, from a different angle, much of what we would need in a cash flow analysis. What is the nature of the inventory? How much is finished goods, how much work in progress, how much components or raw materials? Is the finished inventory held against firm orders, and perhaps unsaleable if the orders evaporate? Or is it a popular consumer item that can be sold at face value out of liquidation? The same sort of questions about work in progress: can we use it for other products or sell it to another manufacturer of the same product, or is its only value as part of the end-product? And with raw materials, similar questions.

Fixed assets We need, increasingly, to look for possible costs in the collateral. The obvious example is pollution, where foreclosure, or the mere fact of a pledge, may make the bank liable for clean-up costs. Legislation threatened in other countries might extend this liability. The costs attached to arresting a ship are another example.

Where there are no disadvantages to taking a charge on fixed assets, banks still need to analyse their positive value as security, and how far that value might decline in liquidation. Again, much of the analysis is related to the cash flow analysis. How specialised or flexible is the asset? how tied to the particular product or useful in a range of products? and so on.

This analysis is not difficult, although occasionally it will require some specialist knowledge. Rather, the analysis will often show that the factors which undermine the cash flow, and require reliance on collateral, also undermine the value of the collateral. Too often, whether consciously or not, banks take a fixed and floating charge to avoid the effort of analysing the company. If they analyse the security instead, this will often show clearly why they should have analysed the company.

Some bankers believe that a fixed and floating charge allows them to realise on the collateral before liquidation. To support this, banks need to analyse whether they can realise the collateral without precipitating liquidation.

Look again at the three classes of asset, given that no bank thinks of realising its collateral while the company is doing well. We assume that the loan, and the collateral realised to pay it, are substantial in relation to the borrower.

Receivables are the life-blood of a company. To borrow against them is a timing and liquidity adjustment, not a genuine raising of new money. When a company borrows against its receivables, it brings forward its cash inflow, to the moment of invoicing, when the receivable can be sold or pledged, instead of when the receivable is collected. At collection the proceeds which would otherwise have been a net cash inflow repay the related debt; new receivables which can repeat the process create continuing ability to borrow. This change in timing can be of great value; but to realise the collateral reverses it. To call in a loan and collect maturing receivables to pay it destroys the company's cash flow for the collection period. A company whose condition justifies calling in the loan is unlikely to survive the collection period, so that a decision to call is tantamount to bankrupting the company.

Much the same point applies to inventory and fixed assets. Sometimes a company will have one or the other surplus to immediate requirements. Sometimes it can realise on them, repay a modest loan without damaging the company's ability to operate. More often, and certainly with larger loans, to seize all or most of the inventory leaves a company unable to continue. This is even truer of the company's main factory or office, although where a company has a variety of smaller fixed assets, it may survive the loss of some of them.

Lending, against a fixed and floating charge, to a cash-flow-based company, thus exposes the bank to most of the risks it would face if unsecured. If analysis shows a high-risk loan within the acceptable range, it may well then be sound to take a fixed and floating charge on the assets, and thus reduce the probable loss in the worst case; it makes no sense to take such a charge where you reject the cash flow risk. Equally, to lend against a charge without having analysed the borrower gives no idea how much the bank must rely on the collateral. Only if analysis shows that the assets covered by the charge have real value in liquidation does it give enough reassurance to lend. In other cases, analysing the collateral will push the bank back towards analysing the company, which it should have done in the first place.

An important part of credit control, therefore, is to ensure that the bank never takes collateral as an excuse, even unconsciously, to avoid analysis. The collateral should either result from the analysis of the borrower, or should be analysed itself, often both.

In a boom, it is too easy to assume that assets will always face a seller's market. In a slump, the factors that effect their value relate to the business, but values are lowered further by the general lack of confidence.

Self-liquidating, short term

There are two main types of self-liquidating security. Both repay the loan in the normal course of business, without damaging the borrower's ability to continue to operate. Or they do if genuinely self-liquidating, which is why they need to be analysed.

One form of self-liquidating security is financed on an item-by-item basis. Commodity lending is one example, where a cargo of cocoa beans is purchased in Ghana using a bank loan or letter of credit. When the cocoa arrives in England and is sold to a chocolate manufacturer, the proceeds of the sale pay off the loan with a profit left over for the commodity trader. The analysis here is of the value of the cocoa, the risks of resale, or of failure of the buyer to pay, and hedges against, for instance, price or currency fluctuation. Since banks often finance a series of transactions rather than a single one, the analysis may need to focus more on the company's ability to handle such deals than on the details of each. Either way, the bank must understand the risks, how the company manages them, and how the collateral ties that management to the bank's need to minimise risk.

The other main type of short-term self-liquidating security relates to fluctuations in financing need. The easiest to describe, though by no means the only one, is the seasonal fluctuation.

For instance, up to 75% of a toy manufacturer's sales come in the two months before Christmas. It probably starts to produce for these sales in the summer; the resulting inventory turns to receivables as the goods are delivered to the stores. Once Christmas is over and the stores have paid their bills, receivables, in turn, drop sharply. The best way to finance this build-up and run-down is temporary borrowing, perhaps on overdraft or some form of bill finance. Often the bank takes no security, but a floating charge on inventory or receivables may be sensible in marginal cases. Either way, the source of repayment is the goods produced with the initial borrowing; and it comes by realising those assets in the normal course of business. This does not mean that all toy companies are asset-based; they generate cash flow, and can use it to repay debt raised to build a factory. But this aspect of their operation is asset-based and can be financed accordingly.

Whatever the exact nature of the loan or borrower, a bank which lends against security needs to analyse it and the company. It must make sure that the loan is genuinely self-liquidating without destroying the company. Taking a charge then merely ensures that what should happen does happen.

Thus, a key aspect of credit control is the recognition that to lend secured without the appropriate analysis is even less sensible than to lend unsecured without it.

Self-liquidating, long term

Long-term self-liquidating liabilities are a slight misnomer. Never the less, there are longer-term transactions which, while not self-liquidating in the traditional sense, fit the concept. Some ship-loans repay the borrowing used to purchase a ship with earnings from a long-term charter. The loan may be tied to the terms of the charter; or the life of the loan may be shorter than the charter, with repayment of the remaining amount depending on the value of the ship, which in turn is based on the ship's ability to generate further charters.

The same approach can be taken with an office-building, except that its life is usually longer. It is thus rarely let at an initial rent which will repay a bank loan in the time-span banks require. The rental arrangements vary from country to country, but the source of repayment of the bank loan will rarely be the rental income directly; it will rather be the capital value of the property, which in turn will largely reflect the cash flow – its quality, reliability, growth prospects, etc. The actual source of repayment will be the proceeds either of the sale of the property, or its long-term refinancing. Although a ship may generate enough cash flow to pay off the financing, often it also looks to capital values based on cash flow as the source of repayment.

In both cases, and others, banks obtain independent valuations. In both cases, however, any valuation can change with circumstances. Unless the bank analyses the cash flow and related factors, it will never know how likely such a change is, or what could cause it. Equally, where the source of repayment, or part of it, is cash flow the bank must analyse it. A ship charter gives different degrees of security depending on: whether it is bareboat, voyage or time; the skill and reliability of the operator; the margin of revenue over costs; the escalation factors in the charter; and the adequacy of the insurance cover, to mention a few factors. And the value of the charter depends critically on the financial strength of the charter party, and the contractual strength of the charter.

Much the same principles apply to property cash flow, with allowance for the different nature of the asset. In neither case is it enough just to take a valuation and lend a given percentage of it. It may be simpler to write the loan agreement that way, but to do so without analysis is dangerous, and will cost money surprisingly often.

Here again, values which look unquestionable in a boom can look very different at the bottom of a recession.

Other asset-based borrowers

There are other asset-based companies which often borrow secured, such as leasing and finance companies, and others where the security is a financial contract, or a portfolio of them, over the underlying assets.

A leasing company is one example. The goods leased can vary from small consumer goods to major capital items. Where the security is leases on £1 million computers, the loan may be tied into a specific contract which is self-liquidating in the medium term; or there may be a portfolio securing a larger loan. The leases may be full payout, in which case the analysis focuses on: the lessees' credit standing; opportunities to cancel the contract, following any failure by the lessor; the prospect for reletting or selling the equipment if the original lease fails.

Where there are more than a few contracts involved, and more so with small ticket items, the thrust of the analysis changes to: the policies the leasing company uses to generate the leases; credit standards in selecting lessees; credit controls once leases are on the books; identification and control of arrears; documentation; ability to avoid having leases broken, etc. The greater the number of leases the more statistical and systems-oriented the analysis becomes.

Some leases are only partial payout. Here the same considerations apply to the period covered by the lease, plus the need to assess residual value. The main factor is usually the probability of renewing the lease, or of placing the goods elsewhere. A particular focus of this analysis is the risk factors which can undermine the normal expectations about reletting the equipment. The classic case of failing in this analysis is Lloyds of London, who insured lenders to companies leasing IBM computers against failure to relet. Unfortunately, IBM introduced a new range which made the ones Lloyds insured obsolete, and Lloyds faced claims beyond anything anticipated. This was not a lender's failure, but the example is sound.

This section aims to illustrate the areas that need analysis, and typical aspects of the analysis. This in turn should reinforce the basic point that analysis is a critical part of credit control, and that secured lending requires more, if sometimes different, analysis than unsecured. It emphasises that asset values decline more than proportionately in a downturn, whether general or specific to the particular asset. Assessment of future change is therefore a critical and often neglected aspect of all analysis. In 1973, for instance, a question about the impact of a 25% fall in value of a specific property seemed overcautious. Just over a year later the property had lost 50% of its value, with no buyers.

Thus analysis of collateral is a critical part of credit control. Ensuring that it is done, and taken seriously, is an important management function. Many bad loans have resulted from banks taking the word 'secured' to mean 'safe'.

Asset-backed lending

Asset backed differs from strictly corporate lending, in that the basis for the loan is usually the assets, plus credit enhancement. Never the less, the underlying need to analyse is similar, even though it takes a specialised form.

Take mortgage-backed as an example. The basis of the loan consists of a portfolio of mortgages, plus credit enhancement. For high-quality performing mortgages, the enhancement may take the form of an equity cushion of 2–3% of the face value of the mortgages. Before the 1989–92 housing slump in the UK it was reasonable to believe that this would absorb any likely level of losses. And this may still prove to be right, despite the unprecedented fall in house prices, if the basis for selecting the original mortgages was sound, the amounts lent against them were conservative, and the monitoring controls were fully adequate. Only careful analysis will tell banks whether this is so when they lend, and remains so thereafter.

Most mortgage lenders set a maximum of 75% of the appraised value of the house. Most also impose a maximum multiple of earnings, perhaps 3–3.5 times, perhaps with an additional allowance for second income for a couple. The two controls combined should ensure that the borrower can service interest and principal, failing which, the lender can sell the house and recover everything. But in competitive markets, the temptation to lend say 80%, or 4 or more times income, is great; after all, the economy is booming and both house prices and incomes rising fast.

Where companies lend higher percentages, or give fixed rate or low-start mortgages, as a conscious policy the credit enhancement must be greater. It may apply to the individual mortgages; for instance, some companies will lend over 75% only against an insurance policy covering any loss arising from selling the house at between 75% and 100% of the mortgage valuation. Or the enhancement may cover the whole mortgage pool. Or the equity contribution may be larger, or there may be subordinated debt in the securitisation vehicle. They absorb the losses, if any, and allow the senior, and highly rated, tranches to be repaid. Or there may be a special liquidity facility which allows the senior notes to get their interest on time. This covers, for instance, a timing difference in the receipt of interest from the mortgages and the payment to the noteholders.

Interest is both the major source of revenue, and the major cost, for many asset-based or backed companies. Lenders need to analyse interest risk carefully. Inept management of interest or currency risk can create huge losses even where the vehicle's credit risk is sound. If credit losses are added to interest rate losses, the combined loss is often fatal.

Much the same analysis, adjusted for the nature of the asset, applies to other asset-backed vehicles: credit card receivables, car loans, etc. In most cases the individual assets are too small to allow a lender to analyse each in detail. He must rely partly on statistical analysis – of lending policies, the mix of maturities, arrears expected and achieved, etc. – and partly on the systems used to implement the policies. In both cases, much analysis relates to the quality of management, which is critical but less subjective than in some types of analysis.

Analysing the Transaction

In straightforward unsecured lending, the analysis of the transaction is normally straightforward. An overdraft, or even a medium-term amortising loan, does not require detailed analysis. Indeed, in considering basic points like the reason for the loan and the source of repayment, bankers will analyse the transaction without realising that is what they are doing. For these purposes a loan secured by a fixed and floating charge counts as unsecured, since the collateral has little relation to the nature of the transaction.

With self-liquidating security, the transaction and the security will often be closely linked. The cocoa from Ghana demonstrates this. In a slightly different way so does the seasonal loan to the toy company. In both cases the analysis of the security carries with it the analysis of the transaction, and vice versa. Much the same is true of shipping and property loans, and of asset-backed transactions.

With complex loans, such as project loans, leveraged buy-outs (LBOs) or other highly structured loans, the analysis of the transaction is critical. However, the critical nature is usually fairly obvious, since without understanding the transaction, bankers cannot begin to develop the appropriate structure, security package, etc.

It is probably most important to understand the transaction, and easiest to overlook the need, where the credit risk is not a loan at all. Complex interest rate, currency or commodity swaps, for instance, are outside a credit specialist's day-to-day expertise. If he is asked to approve a ten-year swap and does so without understanding the nature of the risk, he may find it comes back and bites him very hard a few years later. With volatilities such as those shown in the September 1992 and July/August 1993 ERM crises, the bite may come in months, not years. The same point applies to a whole range of security-related credit risks: settlement, whether delivery vs payment or not; options on a number of underlying products; underwriting bonds or equities where the underwriting risk affects credit risk and vice versa, but they are not the same.

In summary, the simple answer to the question: 'When should I analyse?' is 'always'. The form of analysis needs to be tailored to the nature of the loan, or of the collateral where appropriate. But some form of analysis is critical. Unless bank managements recognise this, and spread the recognition throughout the bank, bad debts will proliferate in future recessions. And they will be most common in areas which were considered 'safe' enough not to need the rigorous analysis which would apply in obviously risky cases.

Analysis helps banks to avoid unnecessary bad debts; it may also help them take on good business. Just as many exposures look safe until analysed, so some look risky, but analysis suggests greater defensive value than shows to the superficial glance.

WHO DOES THE ANALYSIS?

Once a bank accepts the need for analysis, it must decide who should do it. This can be the banker, or a specialist analyst, or some combination. The analyst can be a full-time credit analyst, or can have a wider analytical brief. Or the analytical function can be part of an overall credit support role, such as the advances departments in UK clearing banks. The decision also has implications for how the bank staffs each section, for training, career paths and other aspects of personnel management.

The Banker as Analyst

In many banks, the banker was expected to understand credit and was trained in credit analysis. Whoever made the final decision (see Chapter 4), the responsibility rested with the banker. Even in banks which lacked the account officer concept, the branch manager, or whoever dealt with the customer, was expected to have basic credit skills.

Even before the rapid changes in banking over the last five years or so, there were drawbacks as well as advantages to this approach. The changes have added to the drawbacks and made this a less popular approach, although it still remains valid for some banks.

The traditional banker in this context was first and foremost a lender. This was his main function and his bank's. He also sold related products such as current accounts and time deposits, money transfer, payroll, foreign exchange, collections, etc. But even these mostly carried with them a credit element, and they tended to follow the lending relationship rather than the other way round. Of course there were exceptions; never the less, as a generalisation, credit was at the centre of the job description for mainline bankers until the mid-1980s. Either they saw it as what they did, or they saw it as central to their ability to do what they did.

Not all bankers, even if they had a basic understanding of credit, were necessarily good analysts; this takes a certain type of mind. Secondly, because analysis was only a part of their function, even analytical bankers were less well practised than full-time analysts. At best the analysis took them longer, and at worst their analysis was below the standard of which they were capable given more practice. Then again, the banker had demands from other customers to meet. Unless the workload was tailored to allow time for it, analysis might become the residual task, done only when more pressing concerns allowed. And where a rapid decision was required on a new customer, or one which had not been recently analysed, the banker's ability to drop everything and concentrate on one analysis is limited. Other clients do not accept 'Go away, I'm busy', even when put more tactfully.

Even before the rapid changes of the 1980s, some banks relied to a greater or lesser extent on specialist analysts. This tendency has grown as the role of the banker has changed. The development of products half way between investment and commercial banking, such as floating rate notes or swaps; the general tendency for the distinction between investment banking and commercial banking to blur; the increasing tendency to see bankers as salesman of financial products, rather than as skilled judges of credit; all these and other factors have made it harder for management to expect, or bankers to deliver, a high standard of credit analysis.

In addition, the blurring of the distinctions has made some bankers more of an adviser to the company, selling the bank as a whole, and not any specific product. In this case, the banker may wish to sit, so to speak, on the customer's side of the table, advising the customer as to what he should expect to be able to borrow, on what terms. This role may not combine well with asking difficult questions; or negotiating tough amortisation or ratio covenants which the analysis shows to be necessary, but the borrower does not want to meet. This aspects affects the whole role of the banker in credit control, not just in analysis.

This is not true in all banks, and has been carried to less extreme levels in some than in others. Never the less, in banks which previously relied entirely on bankers for analysis, it can leave a gap. Indeed, as we shall discuss in later chapters, the gap may not be confined to analysis, but may cover all aspects of credit control. It is vital in these cases that management recognise the gap and fill it early rather than late. The bad debt record of a wide range of banks in the 1989–93 recessions suggests that this may not always have happened.

There are, of course, advantages as well as disadvantages to having the banker analyse his own credit. First, he should know the company better than anybody else in the bank. The banker can therefore be surer, faster, that he has the information needed for a full analysis; conversely, if he knows that he will have to analyse the company, he has more incentive to obtain that information. Indeed, one of the traditional and sound arguments for making the banker the analyst is to ensure a feeling of responsibility for the credit.

Good credit understanding and analysis can also be a useful marketing tool. Indeed, as we shall discuss in more detail in Part VI, marketing and credit are closely linked. A banker who understands the company's business, and whose analysis gives him credibility within the bank can develop a level of confidence in his customers that nothing else can give. Conversely, someone who clearly does not understand the customer carries less credibility.

In brief, the changing patterns of banking and the changing role of the banker are shifting the balance of this argument. Managements need to be sure that this shift has not eroded the traditional quality of credit analysis.

The Specialist Analyst

Banks can use several types of specialist analysts, in different ways. Which they use may depend as much on the historical background of the particular bank as any obvious logic, or right or wrong way of doing it.

Banks must decide whether to use pure credit analysts, or a wider definition which covers equity, merger and acquisition, and bond analysis as well. They may use industry analysts, whose main expertise is in their knowledge of a particular industry, or analysts whose main knowledge is of credit, or some mixture; or specialist analysts for all loans or borrowing customers. If they do not analyse in all cases, they must be clear about how to decide which warrant them and which do not. They may rely, in part, on outside rating agencies, or generate ratings of their own.

The relationship between the analysts and the bankers carries opposing dangers: if the relationship becomes too adversarial, bankers may try to find ways round using the analysts; if it gets too friendly, analysts may lose their objectivity, which should be one of their main advantages.

Another is more organisational. Its importance will vary depending on the branch structure of each bank. Should banks have analysts based in all or most branches or concentrate them at regional or head office level?

Before getting into these points, perhaps we should just summarise the advantages of any type of specialist analyst. Some of them are the other side of the disadvantages of having the bankers analyse. The specialist has fully honed skills and no prior commitments which prevent him devoting full-time to a particular analysis in an emergency. He has time to learn about the industry, and may be an expert in it. Finally, he has no marketing reason to want to see a particular result to the analysis, nor a deep enough involvement with the management to colour his views. The fact that he can be objective is one of the most important points, and one management must work to retain.

What type of analyst?

The pure credit analyst is most likely in a commercial bank, or one with a strong commercial banking background. His skills and focus will be credit-oriented and he will be used to analysing ability to repay and the structure of borrowing. He may pay more attention to balance sheet analysis, as a second way out, than most of the other types of analyst. There will be no question of Chinese walls between him and the necessary information and no reason to withold information, or restrict direct contact with the company. Nor will he often have a vested interest in arguing for or against a particular company, since he will never have decided to lend or made a strong recommendation to a customer to buy.

Banks from an investment banking background may have developed the analytical capacity more to help sell public securities, whether debt or equity. They will take a shorter term view, and focus more on the impact of credit on the price of the security than on long-term ability to repay. This is even truer of equity analysts. Either type will be debarred from confidential information which a lending bank might expect to see for at least the longer term and more difficult loans. They can come over the wall for specific transactions, but clearly that is not practical very often. Moreover, they may see their first duty as to their salesmen and their customers and be reluctant to give credit the immediate attention lenders always think it deserves. And while they should be objective, it is not always easy to reverse a view when customers have acted on the previous view.

This sell side analysis can provide considerable value, but often more as a background aide to the banker's own analysis, than as a full credit analysis. Except in rare cases where the analyst comes over the wall, he will not see forecasts, divisional breakdowns and margins, or other information which banks request before lending. And his focus will be different. Never the less, he may have a knowledge of the company, its industry background, competition, products, etc., which will be invaluable to whoever analyses the credit. Even if the industry analyst cannot see the answers, he can advise what the questions should be, and what looks like a good or bad answer.

Within the above, there may be specialisms within the specialism. For instance, some US commercial banks have long been allowed to underwrite municipal bonds, although barred from underwriting corporate bonds or equity. They have built up analytical skills which may be transferable internationally where banks lend direct to similar borrowers.

Investment managers mainly analyse equities, although they also buy some bonds. The analysis has a different slant to the sell side analysis, often longer term. They sell their own ability to choose, and adjust, a portfolio which best meets stated criteria, rather than the merits of a particular share. The quality and objectivity of analysis can be an important factor in achieving success, as well as an important marketing tool. However, the Chinese walls have probably been in place between commercial banks and their investment management arms for longer than anywhere else. This can make it hard to use the investment analysts on the lending side.

Merger and acquisition (M&A) analysis looks at the company first as if it were debt free, and then values the equity in the light of the actual debt. It also seeks anomalies in value. Where the market has underpriced a company, there is often an opportunity to bid at an attractive price. Here again, though, there are confidentiality problems, since M&A activity is often highly sensitive, and best restricted to a need-to-know basis; apart from price sensitivity in a public company, a leak might allow competitive bidders to move early, upset the unions or, where a subsidiary is for sale, the management of that subsidiary. And companies may open their books and hearts to their M&A advisers about things they may not want their lenders to know.

While all these analysts use the same basic tools, they do so in different ways to achieve different objectives. The pure credit analyst is interested in the margin of error; whether the cash flow (or asset base, where appropriate) will pay off the proposed loan, and others, and with how much margin. Provided there is an adequate margin, he or she need not strain to be precise, but is concerned with what might undermine earnings or cash flow.

The analyst also looks at the balance sheet structure and asset base to assess the second way out. In other words, this is more of a downside analysis.

Equity analysts look more at the upside. Of course they look at the downside too, but their risk reward bias is different. A lender shares the downside only beyond a certain stage, and shares none of the upside; a shareholder shares fully in both, but usually buys for the upside. Equity analysts focus mainly on the upside, and usually specifically on earnings per share or, in some markets, dividends. In either case they are concerned to estimate the exact level of earnings in the next few years, and usually less inclined to forecast beyond that. Also equity analysts, probably wrongly, pay little attention to the balance sheet.

M&A analysts do look at the balance sheet, but more as a possible store of hidden value, than as part of an analysis of how much cash the company will generate or absorb in the future.

Rating agency analysts will be closer to bank credit analysts in their approach, and sometimes with more information than banks can obtain. It may make sense therefore to rely on these ratings rather than insisting on in-house analysis, up to a point. There are, however, several drawbacks to exclusive reliance. One is that outside the United States only a few companies are rated. Secondly, the ratings tend to change too slowly after the event. Thirdly, relying on a rating agency gives no feel for what went into the rating and therefore no assistance in monitoring or marketing. Ratings, however, help to make a quick decision on a well rated company, and to decide where to put the main analytical effort.

There are thus drawbacks to relying on analysts whose main job is not bank credit. A banker doing his own analysis may find it useful to tap in to the knowledge of any one of these analysts. And they all may have useful insights.

The Chinese wall problem is currently of primary concern to banks operating in countries where the insider trading and conflict of interest laws are furthest developed. However, these laws tend to spread to other countries; and even those banks which can ignore the problem at home have to take it more seriously overseas.

Given that credit analysts are best suited to credit, banks' investment management operations probably need different analysts as well. Banks risk ending up with three, four or more analytical functions, often duplicating each other's efforts and possibly confusing the client and damaging the marketing effort.

To be cost effective, banks need to find ways of reducing duplication without impairing the value of the analysis. There are no hard and fast rules on this, since this is a relatively recent problem with which banks are still wrestling, where they have recognised it at all. However, some ideas are possible; some of them may apply to getting the best results in areas other than credit as well.

A bank can have a few specifically credit analysts, who can tap into work done in other areas. An industry specialist based in a sell side equity unit should make the output freely available to the credit analyst, who could also consult on specific points where necessary. (The Chinese wall need not restrict the flow of information from outside the wall to inside it, only the other way round.) The occasional situation where the need for industry expertise on a project was greater than this might still arise; as long as it was genuinely occasional, the analyst could come temporarily over the wall for the life of that one project.

Equally, what analysts write for public consumption about shares or bonds should be available to the credit analyst. As sometimes happens, where the public analyst publishes the bank's own rating of an issue or borrower the credit analyst can use this as a basis for his own judgement, and to decide how much effort to put into independent analysis.

We need to separate research and analysis. What we have so far called analysis contains an element, sometimes a major one, of research. Indeed, many banks refer to the function as research rather than analysis. It may, for the reasons given, be impractical to have all the different types of analysis done by one group; this does not preclude having most of the research done centrally, and then used by the different types of analyst. In some cases the sell side research will not be enough for the credit or M&A analyst. More often it will, and even where it is not, it will be a foundation on which the credit analyst can build.

Allocating the analyst's time

Given the existence of specialist analysts, of whatever type, the question arises as to how to use them. They can supplement the banker's work, either in stipulated conditions or on request; instead of the banker in certain types of project; or all the time, in which case we need to specify when we analyse and in how much depth.

The criteria must be clear and well enforced. Perhaps that all new borrowers should be analysed by the specialist; that all proposals that increase the bank's total exposure to a borrower, or group, by more than X million should require an up-to-date analysis; that any borrower rated below Y should require a new analysis annually; and that either the banker or a credit officer with overall credit responsibility can ask for an analysis at any time.

This assumes that the banker is capable of, and expected to do, some analyses; and that it is a sensible use of his time in at least some cases. We therefore need guidelines as to when the banker is insufficient, which should be independent of any individual banker's wishes. The analyst, or the head of the unit, should be able to decide to analyse any name he sees fit, whatever the criteria, and whether it is a new loan, declining existing credit or just one that has not been looked at closely for too long.

Where the banker does no analysis, then by definition the specialist must look at everything. The temptation to impose a cut-off point for size is dangerous. Although for a large bank $5 million, and for a small one $100,000, may seem too small to justify the cost, they do not look so small when they are lost unnecessarily. In terms of interest earnings to replace them, or fee business which the analyst could be helping to win, they look enormous. Equally the argument may be that we do not need to look at subsidiaries, provided we have looked at the parent. This again can be a recipe for bad loans where the parent support is not clear-cut, or its credit is suspect.

Banks should, therefore, look at everything, but not necessarily in the same detail. It may be cost-effective to adjust the depth of analysis to the requirements of the client or transaction. If a AAA rated company asks for a £10 million overdraft, a glance at its ratios should be enough to establish that the rating is justified; provided, of course, the system generates the ratios quickly. To lend the same company £500 million for ten years requires a deeper analysis, because even AAA companies can decline over that period. To lend a medium-sized unrated company even £10 million for five years requires an understanding of its business which only fairly intensive analysis can give. And as discussed in Chapter 7, analysis as part of monitoring can be even more selective.

Analysts should not be judged on the depths of their analysis or indeed, purely on written analysis, but on the quality of help they give to bankers. A ten-page memo weeks after it is needed is no help; two pages, or even an oral briefing, before the decision may be invaluable.

The analyst's role

The tone of the analysis is important too. It should probably be mildly critical, given the point about downside analysis made earlier. The aim should be to highlight weaknesses, without underplaying strengths; to present an analysis which is constructive, but looking for unacceptable risk. If it cannot find it, the credit is more likely to stand up. This requires careful balance; if the tone is too critical, it will appear destructive. The aim is rather to test, to probe, without destroying or weakening. Moreover, a good

analysis gives a sound basis for monitoring; by highlighting the weaknesses and risks, it helps to identify areas which need to be monitored most
carefully. Analysis should also be positive in the sense that it looks for
good points to balance or protect against the weaknesses. The best analysts
take pleasure in enabling the bank to do business with companies which
look weak, but where the analysis uncovers hidden strengths; and in
preventing the bank lending to apparently strong borrowers with hidden
weaknesses. Furthermore, they make sure the bankers know this.

This slightly critical approach also encourages the banker to understand
his credits better. He must feel that he has to make a positive case, not rely
on the analyst to make it for him; and that he will be allowed to do so.
Bankers should not feel that the analysts are there to prevent business, or
that they use their greater skill to overwhelm the bankers' arguments; they
may then try to go behind the analyst's back, or just give up trying to do
any business which involves credit.

On the other hand, if the analyst is too positive, the banker may rely too
heavily on him or her and not provide the check based on close knowledge
of the borrower which an analyst cannot always give. The best results will
come from the combination of analytical skill and relationship knowledge,
each applied from a basis of independent thinking. Creative tension is
good, but too much or too little tension can offset some of the benefits of
independent analysis.

The other reason for wanting a little tension is to avoid the analyst
ending up in the banker's pocket. Sometimes the natural next step in the
analyst's career is to be a banker; sometimes the banker's input into performance appraisal is critical. In either case, there is a risk that the analyst
loses some of his or her independence, and writes what the banker wants
rather than what he believes. Management must always be aware of this
risk. The culture must make everybody reject this type of pressure.
Management must also recognise that career prospects can make even the
best analyst lean unconsciously. It is up to management to see that the
structure as well as the culture avoids this risk.

Where to put the analyst

The analysts' physical location also needs thought. The exact answer will
depend on the answers to all the other questions, as well as the nature of the
bank and its branch network. There are some considerations which are
relevant whatever the particular bank.

Where practical, the best place for the pure credit analyst is close to the
borrower. A domestic bank, with a dense network, can put analysts in

regional headquarters, which will usually be within an hour or two of any borrower in the region. This combines nearness to the client with another aim, critical mass. An analyst working alone is cut off from the interplay of analytical discussion, has no safety valve if the workload becomes temporarily excessive, and risks going native and losing independence. It is better therefore to have at least two analysts on any location, and more are preferable.

Thus international banks, with widely spread networks of small branches, must choose between having many small units close to the borrower, and fewer, more centralised ones further away. Given language, accounting and regulatory differences, neither is entirely satisfactory, and the choice is a difficult one.

In some other types of analysis, the balance may be different. Equity analysts probably need to be closer to the stock-market, and its sources of information. Probably, too, industry analysts need to be more centrally located, since their industry may be too scattered for them to be close to all of it. If their written material is an important input for the credit analysts this may partly offset the disadvantages of being too far from the centre and allow that balance to change.

3 Presentation

DISTINGUISH BETWEEN PRESENTATION AND ANALYSIS

One person can combine presentation and analysis in the same memorandum. Or they can be entirely separate. Either method can be correct, but combining them runs some risk of confusion.

Analysis starts from a neutral position, and remains neutral throughout – or should. The analyst absorbs information and analyses it to come up with a view. This may be a view as to the risk rating, or as to whether the risk is acceptable in light of the particular proposal. But either way, the analyst's job is to provide source material to help other people make the right decision. An analysis is not therefore a decision document, although it is one which should help with a decision.

Presentation starts where analysis leaves off. It uses the analysis and information on the profitability of the relationship and the return on each transaction, as a basis for recommending a decision. The presenter is a decision-maker, and often a sponsor, in a way the analyst can never be. The presenter says, in effect, 'I have decided that the bank should lend on these terms. I need your approval to carry out this decision, and these are the reasons why I think you should give it to me, and the weaknesses and risks I have taken into account in coming to my view.' Or that is what this book believes he should say.

The presentation must not be a selling document, nor present an unbalanced position; it must cover the weaknesses and risks as well as the strengths, and balance them. This balance is critical to good credit decisions and control. Unlike the analysis, a presentation is therefore a decision document.

Where, as in many banks, the presenter and analyst are one, he can certainly analyse and present in one memorandum. To do so, however, runs the risks of confusing the two, so that the analysis is, or seems to be, twisted to fit the desired conclusion. A bank which allows combined analysis and presentation therefore needs to see that its people are trained to make this distinction.

COMBINE THE TWO, OR SEPARATE THEM?

Despite the above, it is often cumbersome to separate the two tasks, particularly where the banker, who is the natural but not only person to present, is also expected to analyse. Where the banker analyses and presents, it will be difficult to insist on separate memoranda.

The arguments in favour of having the banker do both assume that he is a competent analyst; given that, he knows the borrower better than anybody else in the bank, and can combine analytical skills with knowledge of the company. In addition, the banker is most likely to understand the risks and benefits to the bank and the risk reward ratio, and is also well placed to judge the profitability of the relationship and whether the transaction will improve it.

However, that raises a difficulty. Some bankers are pure marketers, whose prospects are closely tied to doing deals; often, credit quality is secondary to the revenues, and bonuses, they expect. To have this banker analyse and present, risks an unbalanced view and in due course, a high level of credit losses. Moreover many bankers now are marketers not so much of products but of the bank's breadth of expertise, and ability to advise clients on the best approach to solving problems. They want, and managements want them, to be seen as on the client's side. This does not fit with the questioning needed to assist the analyst, or to come to a favourable conclusion; nor with the difficult negotiation of conditions which the presenter often requires to enable him to recommend the facility internally. Some of this may not matter if the analysis is separate, and an executary unit carries out the detailed negotiations and documentation.

If the banker is not going to present, there are four alternative approaches: the internal advances approach, the credit as a product approach, the product approach, and the ladder.

Internal Advances Department

This could also be called the credit or loan department, or credit administration. Its function is to handle all the internal aspects of credit: analysis and presentation; administration of the facility; checking of collateral, and so on, once the loan is made. It rarely involves direct contact with the borrower, except at a mechanical level. In some banks the senior members of this department also have quite large lending authority.

The department, however, has no real incentive to sponsor the transaction or the borrower/counterparty. The client is not the department's client, nor the transaction their transaction. Their function, unless management makes great efforts to avoid this, is mechanical. It becomes a question of filling in forms correctly rather than assessing risk. Even where the system requires a recommendation from the advances department there is no necessary feeling of sponsorship.

Sponsorship is critical to good credit control. Of course, it can degenerate so that the sponsor fights the client's battles regardless of merit. That is a risk which management must guard against. Positive sponsorship implies responsibility: to satisfy oneself that the client and transaction both fit the bank's policies; that the information is adequate for the decision and that future information will allow full monitoring; the acceptance of the obligation to monitor, and most importantly to act if the monitoring shows anything untoward.

The sponsor is not necessarily the presenter, but if the presenter is the advance department, it may well mean that nobody acts as sponsor.

Credit as a Product

This approach may seem similar to the advances approach, or to the product approach. In fact it is distinct from either. It is a recent development in response to changing circumstances, and is most likely to appear in banks moving from pure commercial banking business closer to investment banking, while retaining the ability to lend. It recognises that the senior banker now sells many more products than he did as a commercial banker; or perhaps sells the bank and advises the client on which services best fit its specific needs, such as equity, a bond issue, a private placement or bank debt; or which combination of them. He can then bring in the appropriate product specialist to advise on the details; or he can bring in several to discuss the best combination.

Until recently, the banker would have been the credit product manager, advising on and negotiating the terms of the bank debt portion of the package. In many, perhaps most, banks he still does. But some banks, following the logic outlined above, are treating credit as a separate product. There are groups of credit specialists who follow the credit of clients, market credit to them when appropriate, negotiate the terms and monitor the credit once granted. They may also manage the whole credit portfolio; i.e., the return (on equity, assets or otherwise) on the portfolio as a whole, and keep the portfolio balanced, with no excessive concentrations in high-risk areas, and so on.

Where such a unit exists, it will naturally present the credit. There may be an analytical unit within the product group, which will provide the analysis. However, each bank will organise this differently, and in some cases the analyst/presenter/sponsor will be the same.

However the group is organised, its main features are its direct involvement, its marketing responsibilities, and its clear sponsorship role.

It will call on the client, alone or with the account officer, to discuss all forms of credit extension; negotiate the terms directly; draft, or supervise the drafting of, the loan agreement or other documentation; work with the client to syndicate the transaction; and monitor the credit as well as the transaction.

In the marketing role, a specialist group may be better able to argue in favour of the most appropriate form of credit; may be able to explain more convincingly the credit standards on which all banks should insist, and which, when well judged, are as much in the borrower's interest as in that of the bank.

Sponsorship may mean the overall sponsorship of the client as a borrower, although probably this should be the account officer's role. More probably therefore it means sponsoring the particular form of loan, as being appropriate to the client's needs, properly priced and structured, and of an overall standard with which the bank can be comfortable.

The Product Approach

For products other than loans, there is an argument that the product specialist should present and sponsor. For instance, few lending bankers understand all the implications of a complicated synthetic asset transaction; or the credit risk of lending stock or bonds, and so on. Some bankers suggest that the product specialist, who knows the product, and often the client, better than the banker ever can, should present and sponsor.

A drawback is that the product specialist rarely has any interest in, or knowledge of, credit. However well he knows the product, the product specialist is poorly placed to assess the credit risk, or to explain it. Secondly, his interest is to do the deal, not to make fine credit judgements. Product specialists often push too hard for credit approval. To give them the power to recommend approval directly to the decision-maker may add to that tendency.

Moreover many product specialists are reluctant to take this responsibility. They regard credit as someone else's problem; if they can persuade, or sometimes pressure, someone to approve the credit even wrongly, they can take their profit without concerning themselves with whether it is wise.

This is perhaps the best argument for requiring product specialists to sponsor, especially, clients with which the bank does little or no other business. These are probably with financial institutions or intermediaries, including many types of broker, who either provide no current financial

statements, or only obscure ones of little analytical value. The factors
deciding the counterparty's creditworthiness will thus be matters such as:
personal integrity (even more critical than usual); effective back-office support avoiding losses through poor administration; tight risk management;
skill in judging the particular market; ability to focus and avoid risks
outside the area of expertise.

A normal banker may have little ability to judge how these factors apply.
Moreover, normal financial analysis will not identify warnings of trouble.
The most effective form of monitoring for this type of credit is often from
the market. Traders can tell whose paper is trading at a discount, and why
the market will only pay the lower price (although the market is not always
right, it is unwise to bet against it); traders or salesmen can tell if the counterparty is taking extreme positions; traders and salesmen can tell whether
the back office is competent and up to date, and so on.

Banks risk having the knowledge which would enable them to foresee a
problem in a place where it does no good. They need to move information
from the product specialist to the credit specialist who can make the decision to cut exposure. There are several ways of doing this, some of which
will be discussed in other parts of the book. One way, however, is to make
the product specialist sponsor the client. He does not approve the credit, or
even write the credit presentation. Rather, he certifies that the client is honest and a serious business; that the transactions with the bank fit his normal
business; and that the sponsor will keep an eye on future dealings and
report anything unusual. The sponsor may do this alone or in conjunction
with a presenter. Either way, he accepts a degree of responsibility which
product people have not often accepted in the past.

The Ladder

With a ladder, the initial presenter does not make the final presentation.
Where the presenter is in a branch it may not be physically possible for him
to present to a committee in head office. He may present to his senior, who
in turn presents it to the committee. Or he may present it to a colleague in
head office who takes it to the senior who in turn goes to the committee.

Some banks deliberately encourage the ladder, perhaps by making the
branch office go through a regional headquarters, which will then present
to head office. This can be a serious mistake, made worse if each new inter-
mediary rewrites the presentation memo; the one the committee sees may
bear little resemblance to the original. Even where this is not so, there is a
real risk in having someone who does not know the credit, or feel any
responsibility, present it for decision.

This may sometimes be unavoidable, but it can be made more or less damaging. It is best to use the original presentation in the final decision; at least then the committee sees what the banker closest to the credit thought. Among other things it can judge how well the banker understood the credit. Where a more sophisticated banker rewrites, he may conceal the weaknesses of the branch. Senior management may then fail to recognise this weakness and therefore to correct it. Moreover, an important factor in many credit decisions should be 'how well can we follow this?' Since the answer depends heavily on the local branch, its understanding of the credit is relevant to the decision. But the ladder makes this quality harder, sometimes impossible, to judge.

In some banks, the ladder is hierarchical. Only a senior executive is fit to go in front of the committee, even where the presenter is in the same office. This is a serious mistake even if the senior uses the original memo by the first presenter; worse if he rewrites it or speaks without reference to the original written one. One senior banker who participated in this process commented that he did not need anything from the banker: 'If I do not understand the credit, I should not recommend it.' In one sense this was admirable, but in wider senses it was short-sighted and dangerous, as are other aspects of the ladder.

First, in cutting the committee off from the banker, he removed a valuable source of answers to questions on management, the local labour pool, and similar items. Secondly, he robbed the banker of responsibility for the recommendation. Thirdly, he missed a chance to expose the banker to the credit committee. Hearing the questions seniors ask, and the factors they take into account when making a decision, is excellent training for a young banker.

Training is, however, not the main point. To obtain the best credit judgements, banks need to combine credit experience with on-the-spot knowledge of the borrower, counterparty and transaction. The ladder gets in the way of this combination.

STANDARD FORMAT, OR PRESENTER'S CHOICE?

Banks need to think quite carefully about the form they want a written presentation to take.

A standard format provides an agreed basis, so that everybody can know where to find what they want. It ensures that nothing, or nothing crucial in most cases, will be left out. And it is easy for an inexperienced banker, even a trainee, to fill out.

That is also a major argument against a standard form, which applies equally to analysis and presentation. A form requires little thought to fill out, and only a limited knowledge. The most important aspect of credit control is the quality of the thinking about both the individual credit and the approach to credit risk. A form which kills the need for thought is thus counter-productive.

Moreover, there are so many different types of company and of transaction that no form can accurately cover them all. To attempt it puts the presenter into a strait-jacket which preludes original thought about the credit. To kill the need for thought is bad enough; to kill the possibility is worse.

A standard approach is never the less possible. A good presentation consists broadly of two aspects: an expression of opinion, and the facts to support it. Weak presentations have many faults, but probably the two most damaging are to present either opinions with no factual back-up, or facts with no indication of what points they illustrate.

A standard approach to presenting the facts may therefore be acceptable, even where an outright form is rejected. Even here, however, we need to be careful. If facts exist to support opinions, we cannot tell what facts we need to use until we know what opinions we want them to support. So the standard approach to presenting facts should not mean that the facts themselves are standard. Put another way, if we use ratio analysis, we should present the ratios in tables covering five years, with the earliest year always on the left, and standardise how we express them and what we call them. If some parts of the bank say debt to worth, some leverage and so on, nobody is quite sure whether the expressions mean the same thing, or whether we are using them to present different concepts. Nor does it matter if we use debt to worth or a reciprocal ratio, so long as everybody in the bank uses the same one and knows what it means.

It does matter if we insist that the presenter discuss debt to worth as the main ratio in all cases. This undermines the ability to present a company where other ratios are a better guide to financial health. In an international bank it also ignores the vagaries of accounting in different countries, which make some ratios meaningless and the information used to calculate them unreliable.

We thus seem to have ruled out forms and restricted the use of formats. What then can we offer to help bankers provide a useful presentation and decision-makers to get value for them?

The answer can only come after we have considered what we want the presentation to achieve.

This falls into several parts:

- to set out clearly the nature of the decision which we are asked to take;

- to assess the risk and why, and on what terms, it is acceptable; where appropriate, to describe protections against specific aspects of risk, such as covenants, security or amortisation;

- to review the compensation, to be sure it meets our risk/reward criteria;

- to assess the impact of this facility, or of our failure to provide it, on our relationship with the client, and on our strategy for managing that relationship;

- to try to ensure that the facility and borrower fit within our overall portfolio and credit policies, including any concentration concerns we may have.

Naturally the importance of each of these will vary from case to case, as will the need to deal with each. Never the less, a presentation which leaves the reader unsure as to the writer's view on any of these has failed.

The presentation should meet all the above aims as briefly as possible without excluding relevant information or views; the readers are usually busy, and a ten-page memo when the relevant information could fit better into two pages is wasteful. Moreover, a ten-page memo when two pages is sufficient means that the writer has included much irrelevant material, making one wonder how much relevant material has been omitted.

There are, of course, arguments in favour of particular approaches, which the author has covered in his *Understanding Corporate Credit* (1983). The purpose here is more to set out what the approach should achieve, than what it should be.

Any memo advocating a decision should specify first what the decision is, and the key factors which affect it. There is a view, especially from recent graduates, that we should know what the arguments are before reaching a decision. This partly confuses analysis with presentation, partly represents the academic influence. But we are not taking academic decisions here, but real ones. If we are to judge whether the arguments justify a loan, we first need to know whether the loan is for £100,000 or £100 million; for one year or ten, and so on.

Thus despite what was said earlier about flexibility, it is probably better to insist that the first item in any presentation be a statement of what the proposal is. At this stage, however, it should confine itself to just enough to enable the reader to assess what follows. Secondly, given the need for

44   *Analysis, Presentation and the Decision*

sponsorship, the presenter must make his own view clear. In most cases this should be a positive recommendation.

But we also need to encourage the presenter to choose what is important in the proposal, to make him distinguish the critical from the routine; and again, to save the decision-maker reading pages of irrelevant – or at best low value – material.

Thus a section, perhaps called 'Rationale' or 'Reasons for Recommendation' or something else to taste, makes sense in most cases. To get the maximum value from it, banks, and senior bankers in particular, must insist on rigorous standards. The role of such a section is to highlight – briefly – the factors which the presenter believes are key to the decision. In a simple decision for a small amount, this may be the whole presentation. In more complex cases it will set the scene for the main presentation. Once it has identified the key points on which to base the decision, the rest of the memo should fall naturally into shape in justifying the points. Here again rigour is required to turn 'should' into 'does'. But the more closely the main memo follows the factors set out in the rationale, the more important it is that the rationale actually focus on the key factors.

Throughout presentations, but particularly in the Rationale, balance is crucial. A presentation must never be a selling document, but present all aspects of the case fully and draw a fair conclusion. If banks allow presenters to sell the credit, rather than present it, the quality of thinking about credit, and in the end the quality of credit on the bank's books, will deteriorate. Indeed, there is no surer recipe for bad debts than a bank which allows credit decisions to be ruled, or even over-influenced, by marketing considerations.

The dividing line between influence and over-influence is critical, and is discussed in Chapter 5; banks which get it wrong face heavy bad debts.

Returning to the Rationale, then, it can come in various forms, but it should highlight clearly the key relevant issues. These should include the company's strengths, but also its weaknesses; the risks which could undermine the strengths, and any protections the company has, or the bank can create, against those risks; the reward the bank expects, and the extent to which rewards other than direct earnings on the facility are certain, prospective or outright speculative; and the extent to which those rewards are a direct rather than indirect result of the positive decision.

We then have two sections; one describes the purpose and nature of the facility, the other the key factors in the decision. For a simple decision, these two may even be enough. For a more complex one, they provide a framework for the rest of the memo.

What goes into the framework is a matter for each bank, or better still each individual presenter. Banks can, and should, train bankers how to recognise, organise and present the factors which the Rationale has highlighted. We can give them tools such as the intelligent use of a Background section, what its aim and contents should be; or how to relate financial figures to the nature of the company's business, and assess which are the critical ratios for different types of company, and so on. But if we eschew the use of prescribed formats, bankers will have their own way of thinking about credit, and presenting it. Each must be able to choose how to give their own view, if the view is to have any value: whether to have sections on Operations, Background, Management, Competition, etc. Indeed whether to have sections at all or write an essay; whether to use bullet points to summarise strengths and weaknesses; whether to use tables and if so what to put in them, and so on. Each must also understand the credit and the facility well enough to judge whether it is asset-based, to be repaid from liquidation of assets in the normal course of business; or cash-flow-based, with cash generation either from the use of the loan or more generally as the expected source.

In summary, no form and little format; but an organised way of thinking which helps the presenter create a coherent and balanced picture. In this way, the decision-maker can concentrate on the points critical to his judgement, rather than spending hours trying to find out what are the factors which should be considered.

4 Who Makes the Decision?

INTRODUCTION

All banks have rules as to who can take credit decisions. They should be clear and specify levels of authority; numbers needed to make the decision; whether authority is cumulative, pooled or individual; whether authority relates to the transaction or total exposure, and any special requirements for specific types of credit exposure. Some banks use a separate structure for counterparty – or Treasury or investment banking – credit; this chapter will deal mainly with plain lending authority, with specialised requirements for counterparty or products covered in Chapter 6.

The choices for traditional credit fall into three pairs, although they can be mixed in various ways. They are:

- committee authority or individual authority;

- centralised or decentralised;

- specialist or generalist.

The mixtures include committees exercising decentralised authority, individuals exercising centralised, as well as vice versa in each case; committees of generalists or of specialists; committees in branches, individuals in head office and vice versa and almost any other combination.

The combination reflects several aspects of the bank and its business; the way it trains its staff and allocates responsibility; and its desired risk profile. Since these change over time, any system should be updated regularly. While some aspects of change can be introduced *ad hoc*, each bank should occasionally review the whole system. This could, for instance, be a useful project for somebody approaching retirement, who has experienced most of the possible combinations, understands how the bank works, and being on the way out with honour, has no axe to grind.

ASSESSING THE ADVANTAGES AND DISADVANTAGES

Some choices follow naturally from aspects of a bank's nature. Small banks, for instance, may still have the partnership ethic, whether or not they are actually partnerships. This makes a committee the natural vehicle for major decisions. Or there may be legal requirements, as in Germany, which require centralised decisions.

Where there are no such prerequisites, however, banks should consider the strengths and weaknesses of each approach, and the situations in which they work best – or worst. Only comparing this assessment with the actual circumstances establishes the combination suited to each bank.

Committee or Individual?

In outline, the arguments in favour of a committee are the arguments against individuals, and vice versa.

A committee at its best provides collective wisdom and cross-fertilisation. It protects against the risk of an optimist or pessimist frequently making unsound loans, or turning down good ones. It brings to bear a variety of experience, knowledge and temperament. It encourages discussion, perhaps the best way to test a proposal. It raises points in different forms and allows everybody to view them from several aspects.

All this can, but does not always, happen. If there is free discussion with no bias in favour of senior or opinionated members, then the full advantages may follow. The committee may, however, be dominated by one member, senior or merely vocal; or, more dangerously, using the committee as a vehicle to push pet theories or obsessions. These may lead to argument for, or against, a transaction on specious grounds, but which still carries the day.

More importantly, a committee dilutes responsibility. A dominant character can impose his will on it, but still not accept the blame for wrong decisions. A presenter can, whether consciously or not, abdicate responsibility; it is easy to feel that the committee knows best, and if you can persuade it that the loan is sound, then it takes the responsibility. This is a risk with any form of presentation, but a greater one with a committee. An individual will ask questions and put points directly to the presenter, who must answer them and in doing so accept responsibility for the answers. The committee may discuss among itself, rather than with the presenter.

Individual authority, on the other hand, relies heavily on the individual. If it is widely distributed, this means relying on the judgement of many different people, which requires confidence in the training and quality generally, plus sound controls to catch any slippage. If that confidence is justified, decisions flow from a variety of sources, which reduces the chances of the same mistake being often repeated. This has some of the advantages of cross-fertilisation available from a committee without the disadvantages.

If individual authority is concentrated, the need to be sure of the individuals' quality is greater; on the other hand, it is easier to make this assessment confidently about two or three people than about twenty or thirty, let alone several hundred.

One major advantage for individual authority is speed. A committee – which may in some cases be the board of the bank – meets only at set times. If these are infrequent, there may be a mechanism for calling *ad hoc* meetings, but it will often be difficult to be sure that you can do so, and may take several days in some cases. A specialist should be available at all times, but at worst, more readily so than a committee.

Perhaps we should define 'individual authority' a little more closely. There are variations which are fairly close to an informal committee, just as some committees react more like a group of individuals.

Few banks formally allow one lender alone to decide. In most, at least two signatures are required. In some, however, the authority of the senior decides the amount that the two can approve. In others, the authority is cumulative, so that two lenders each with authority of $5 million can together approve $10 million, three $15 million. The process is limited; a loan of $25 or $50 million may require a signature with authority above $5 million. Some banks have different powers as well as varying limits within each category; for instance, in some banks an original life of more than ten years may require the most senior category, regardless of amount. Or the limit may differ depending on the rating applied to the credit. One bank gives its second category a limit several times higher for names rated investment grade than for names not so rated; and greater authority where renewing a short-term facility than when approving a new facility.

Lending authority can be aggregated or disaggregated. Disaggregated authority applies the limit to the facility alone; aggregated authority applies the limit to the total exposure. To give examples: if Mr A has disaggregated authority of $10 million, he can approve a $5 million facility to Company B regardless of other exposure; with aggregated authority, if existing exposure is above $5 million, the new facility would exceed Mr A's limit. A different version of the same approach allows increases in total exposure of say 10% to lower levels of authority.

There can be other limitations on individual authority. Some banks require that at least one of the lenders approving some specialised borrowings should be a designated specialist. Specialities covered may include property, securities business, commodities, energy, media and telecommunications, and highly leveraged transactions (HLT). Some banks also allow different authority for a lender to approve his own client than someone else's.

Centralised vs Decentralised

The choice whether to centralise decisions, or if decentralising, how far, should depend on the structure of the bank, the skill of bankers outside the centre, the nature of the client base, and the need for swift decisions. In fact, however, it seems to be more closely tied to nationality than to anything else. The Americans clearly decentralise most, though with wide variations. The British seem to delegate next, although much less than the Americans. Continental Europeans are more variable, but on the whole centralised, while the Japanese hardly decentralise at all and then only to expatriate Japanese.

There is also a tendency to recentralise when experience is bad. This begs the question of whether the bad results are due to decentralisation or to other weaknesses in the bank's credit structure.

Outside the situation of each bank, the arguments for and against centralisation balance the benefits of local knowledge against the skill and experience available at the centre. There is also an argument about control, but this is more questionable, as discussed later in the chapter.

Of course, centralisation is not an all or nothing question. It may be perfectly sensible to say, in effect: 'I trust local branch managers to have a clear idea of credit, and reasonable judgement, but not to take decisions which, alone or cumulatively, might threaten the bank's future. I will therefore delegate authority only within limits.' Even where the local branch has the basic skill to analyse the credit and present it, it may not have the experience to judge the risk. Or the branch may deal mainly with small clients, which require one type of skill, but have a few larger ones which require different experience. In those cases it may well be sound to allow the branch to decide the smaller amounts and require higher authority for the larger ones.

Generalist vs Specialist

The third question is whether the decision-maker should be a generalist or a specialist lender.

In traditional commercial banks, credit was the main product sold to corporate clients. It was therefore an inherent part of the job for any banker; credit judgement was never the only attribute of the banker, but no banker could rise very far without it. In the broadest terms, therefore, credit judgement went with seniority. In some such banks, there were specialist credit functions (such as the advances departments in the UK clearing banks). Often, however, these were not staffed by true specialists, but rather by up-and-coming bankers taking a few years to hone their credit skills, before moving up as generalists.

Where the structure of the bank and its business still follows this pattern, there is good reason to stay with the generalist. However, many banks, not just those moving towards investment banking, have broadened their product range far beyond credit. Bankers market such a wide range of products, or play such a different role with the client, that they no longer have the time to understand credit in depth. Indeed, their career path may have excluded credit altogether. Many branch managers, at least in overseas branches of international banks, are M&A specialists, exchange dealers, swap traders, bond underwriters, salesmen or administrators by training. As a result, seniority and credit judgement have lost their connection.

This does not prevent generalist bankers working under these non-bankers, and exercising credit skills; nor change the arguments in favour of making bankers responsible for credit. The advantages of putting knowledge and responsibility together remain. There are risks, however.

If the manager has no credit knowledge, it is hard for him to judge whether those who do have credit knowledge are using it effectively. There are ways round this which do not involve specialists; the second or third in command may be a banker with the requisite knowledge and take on this task, for one. And many banks have credit review units. These units can, in theory at least, soon identify failures in credit standards. Nevertheless, this puts the manager in a weaker position. This weakness is compounded if, as often happens, the second in command has reached the position because of marketing or other non-credit skills. Even among those who are bankers, credit skills may no longer be commensurate with seniority.

There is a strong feeling among experienced bankers that account officers must accept the responsibility for the risks related to their accounts. This book shares that feeling, but recognises that it can be a snare for the unwary. Banks can allow credit standards to slip in too many ways; any of them make leaving the credit responsibility with the banker a recipe for disaster. The bank's credit training may no longer meet traditional standards; or the bank may define the banker's role in a way which makes credit unimportant; it may reinforce this by rewarding for everything but credit skills. In these circumstances it is no surprise if bankers pay little attention to credit.

Thus, each bank must constantly review the structure of its business, the demands it puts on its bankers, the training it gives them, the way it rewards them and the support available. If this review convinces management that its bankers can take credit seriously, then relying on generalists may still be the best way of managing credit. Even where, as discussed later in the chapter, there is some mixture of specialist and generalist, the weight put on the generalist, both as decision-maker and in presenting credits to the specialist when the system requires it, can be greater.

Conversely, a bank which has allowed its generalist credit management to slip has a problem. The answer may be to give more or even complete authority to specialists. But this does not happen in a vacuum. If the bank has worked solely through generalists in the past, it may not have a ready supply of competent specialists. Perhaps the bank can turn selected generalists into specialists, but this can also have disadvantages. The best bankers were probably good judges of credit, but also better at other aspects of banking than their competitors. There are two probable objections to making them credit specialists: first, if credit has become less important than it used to be, why take your best people away from revenue-earning jobs? Secondly, will they accept a job which may well be seen as a dead end? If they will, perhaps the credit culture has not slipped as much as in some cases.

Even where the bank overcomes the initial problem, however, there may still be a longer term structural problem. This applies even more where the bank accepts credit specialists who were recognised as less high powered. This need not mean they are poor judges of credit; even under the old regime some bankers were better at credit than at other aspects of banking. But because they had been seen as less than top bankers, they may carry less weight going forward; they are also often less well paid. This will become known, and if the climate is too revenue-oriented, the gap may widen. This will make the existing specialists less likely to stay in credit, and new recruits harder to attract.

When credit ceases to be a critical part of the skills and training of all bankers, banks may no longer have an internal source of recruits for the credit speciality. Therefore they need to develop a training pattern and a career path which ensures that the right people, with the right skills, are available to replace older, more experienced bankers as they retire. This raises a number of questions.

Do they have a programme for credit specialists, or give everybody the same basic training with modules for different product skills, including credit?

Do they treat credit as a product, through which people rotate as they do with other products? Or is the product so critical that once a specialist always a specialist? Or a mixture of both?

Where reward is revenue-based, how do banks reward credit enough? If they do not, credit may attract only less successful types, who carry less weight. This runs a cumulative risk. Even if the initial credit specialists are competent, their lesser weight means that credit standards may be over-ruled by marketing and other considerations. This will make it even harder to attract competent replacements; the less competent they are, the less weight they carry and the harder it is to attract even semi-competent people.

There are other ways in which banks move towards using specialists. Some after all have always done so; others are moving into aspects of commercial banking from an investment or merchant banking background, instead of the other way round. Those with no reservoir of trained judges of credit are forced to hire specialists from outside to set up the function. However, if they are to build on the initial hires, rather than always looking outside for replacements, they must answer the same questions about training, remuneration, career path and replacement outlined above. And to hire only outsiders means that the bank never develops an indigenous credit culture. Good credit control, while it requires many factors, requires the right attitude above all others. Attitude alone is not enough, but it is a long step in the right direction. The wrong attitude, or even just the lack of a positive attitude, can undermine everything else a bank does.

All these points are most relevant in a boom. In a recession bad debts rise and credit suddenly seems more important, particularly when bad debts are unusually painful, as in 1989–93. But the bad debts are unusually painful not just because the recession is severe, but also because so many banks allowed their credit standards to slip in the face of competition. As suggested earlier, credit control in a boom is more important and more difficult than in a recession. And a system that relies on specialists but does not support or encourage them is probably the worst of all.

Let us return now to the main questions. First, training. Part of the answer depends on the form training takes. Where it is all, or mostly, on the job, it certainly makes sense to rotate the credit specialists through many departments, even though these may not seem directly relevant. It is important for credit specialists to know, and be seen to know, as much as possible about the way the bank works: to know, because the bank must make commercial judgements if it is to prosper; be seen to know, because if credit-users believe that credit judgements are made in an ivory tower, they will not take those judgements seriously. The credit specialist must be seen to understand the pressures faced by colleagues; seen to be looking for ways to do the business they want to do, but safely; seen to be reaching for substitute proposals when the first idea does not work; only then, will colleagues accept a 'no' with good grace, rather than grouching or appealing over his head. Only then too will they – or at least may they – recognise that it is both their job and in their interest to understand what the credit specialist needs and to try to provide it.

Where the training is more structured and more formal, the same points apply, with the added advantage of the 'new boy network'. In a large bank, with branches in many countries, 'He was on my training programme' is a potent communications tool. More importantly, the wider the knowledge, the greater their value as credit specialists. To understand how a swap works helps to understand how it gives rise to credit risk; the more complex the swap, the greater the chance of hidden credit risk. A credit specialist can understand credit in swaps without being a swap expert, but an understanding of how swaps work, and how swap dealers use them, helps to separate the sound from the unsound risks.

Credit as a product, and the structure for handling it are discussed in Chapter 5. Remuneration is also covered in Chapter 5. The key point to focus on where credit is not treated as a product, and thus a revenue centre, is that good credit decisions contribute to revenues in several ways which are indirect, not obvious, but nevertheless real.

In summary, credit decisions are vital to the future of any bank with any size of loan portfolio. Credit judgement requires technical knowledge, but more than any specific knowledge, it requires judgement and common sense. It also requires an understanding of the commercial realities of the bank's business; an ability to match the need to avoid unsound credits against the risk of losing good business unnecessarily; the ability to make positive suggestions to improve poor credit proposals; the guts to say no in the face of 'All the company's other banks have agreed' or 'If we turn this down it will cost us a $1 million fee'; and equally the guts to say 'yes' to a difficult proposal when it has been well thought out and makes sense. Finally, it needs a feel for risk; where it exists, at what level it is acceptable, how to mitigate it, and when to reject it unequivocally.

Where generalists have the necessary knowledge and other characteristics, they are the best decider. Failing these, they may be the most dangerous. Perhaps most dangerous of all is the generalist who was trained in credit, but has moved away from it and never recovered the sense for risk. In these cases we need specialists, but perhaps ones who have been generalists, or in other ways have been exposed to commercial life and the needs and whims of clients.

FITTING THE AUTHORITY TO THE BANK

From the choices, each bank must select the combination which best fits its structure and business and the career patterns of its people. While each bank is unique, there are some general points.

A bank with no branches cannot decentralise. For a small private bank the choice between a committee and individual authority may also be easy. Since all the partners' funds are at risk, and since they all know the bank's business well, the partners are the credit committee and take all decisions of size. In an emergency, or for small amounts, one or two partners may represent the whole, confident that they know how their partners would react. Sponsorship comes from the partner responsible for the relationship whose own money is at stake; he will take it seriously. Even where the bank is not a partnership, the directors probably have a personal stake in the bank's success.

Where such a bank begins to go international, as some British merchant banks have done, it may have greater problems. The head of the office may argue that he needs to be seen to have authority to act alone. A British merchant bank, to continue the example, does not have the name recognition in America or Germany that it has in England. If it has to refer all decisions back to London, some clients may find this unacceptable; or at least it may be hard to refute the argument that they do.

This may seem a minor problem. The overseas office is not intended mainly to lend money, nor to have a large portfolio. Against this, the head of the office probably was not chosen primarily because he is a good lender. In addition, the office does not have the analysts and other credit support it needs to ensure sound lending. None of this may matter if in fact it makes only a few loans to blue chip names. The danger, however, is where the office cannot break into the blue chip names. The names it can break into may make the provision of credit a condition of doing other business; this is common practice in some countries. To lend money to lower rated names, opens a bank to risks which the partners in London may not fully recognise. Moreover, if the head of the office is desperate to generate the business promised, he may approve loans for that reason alone, without full consideration of the credit risk.

Thus for the small partnership bank, decentralisation carries risks that may not apply to a larger commercial bank.

Equally, centralisation in this situation carries risks. The partners are hundreds, if not thousands, of miles away. They may not speak the language; they may be unfamiliar with accounting and other practices; they cannot assess management or product, the requirements of the borrower's market, the competition it faces and so on, without relying on the branch. Indeed, one lesson is that half-hearted lending is always dangerous. Either lend in enough volume to justify skilled analysts, good lending bankers and at least one experienced senior lender, or do not lend at all. It is highly dangerous to make a few loans, as a by-product of other business and without the skills to assess the borrower or monitor it. A loan portfolio of $50–$100 million may not sound like much, and may not generate enough earnings to justify spending much following it. But even a single failure may eliminate the profits of a small branch for several years.

At the other extreme is the major retail commercial bank with hundreds, even thousands, of branches. These may be all domestic, or spread around the world. The domestic branches will include many whose business is mainly retail, but with some exposure to small business; some with retail business and a spread of small and medium corporate clients; and some with major multinational clients, perhaps mixed in with the other types. The international branches may include retail networks, or exposure to small business; more often, they are wholesale, although the size of the company they deal with varies.

The first question is whether to use the same combination with each type of branch. Retail and small business lending require different skills to major wholesale lending. Domestic borrowers all use the same accounting principles and operate under the same company, banking, security and insolvency laws. Overseas offices may differ in some or all of these respects and require specific local knowledge. Lending in New York is different to lending in Germany, which is different to lending in France, and so on *ad nauseam*. Different, that is to say, in detail. The underlying principles remain valid, but the knowledge needed to apply them differs.

As a result, the method of lending in a small branch may need to be different to that in a major branch. It may make sense to give the manager of a small branch authority to lend to individuals, sole proprietorships, farmers and shopkeepers. The manager should have the knowledge of the community, of the value of collateral where appropriate, and of the local pitfalls. He will lend too little in any one case to damage the bank if he makes a mistake.

The same branch manager, however, may handle corporate accounts with borrowing requirements from a few hundred thousand pounds or dollars to tens of millions. The skills which make a good manager and lender to grocery stores will be, at best, irrelevant; at worst, they will mean that he pays too little attention to the risks in lending to these larger companies. Here some centralisation of authority, even if at a regional level rather than at head office, makes sense.

Banks can centralise into the hands of a generalist or a specialist; to an individual or a committee, depending partly on the marketing organisation of the bank. If the branch retains responsibility for relationships with corporate clients, this may suggest a specialist. He will rely on the branch for the client contact, views of management, local developments and so on. The specialist can concentrate on reviewing the information, calling for whatever analytical support is required and leave the manager to develop the relationship. He then also relies on the manager to negotiate pricing and other conditions considered appropriate to the case.

Some banks, however, regionalise the relationships with companies above a certain size. Here the contacts at other than an operational level may not be with the branch at all, but with a corporate specialist in a regional headquarters, or a specialist business unit. Given training and experience, this unit may be the right place for authority to lend money to these clients. Its members have the day-to-day contact with management of the client, know its business and often have access to local knowledge. Giving this unit lending authority fits well with the traditional view that the account officer should retain the main responsibility.

Again, whether the bank gives authority in this situation to generalists or specialists, it still has to decide between individual and committee authority. Where the unit is large, with a range of experience, a committee may be sensible. It allows cross-fertilisation of views, may be good experience for junior members, spreads the knowledge of each client around the group. With a smaller unit, with one or two experienced members supported only by inexperienced juniors, individual authority may work better. In either case, too, it can be sensible to have gradations; give some individual authority even to the juniors, but put the larger decisions to a committee or to senior individuals. This allows small and routine matters to be dealt with promptly, and develops the experience of the juniors in taking decisions; at the same time it ensures that more important decisions get the attention they deserve.

Not all branches are small. Take a British clearing bank, with branches in large industrial centres. These may be run by a Senior Manager, and have several Managers or Assistant Managers who are more experienced than most managers of small branches. Some of these managers may handle only corporate clients, while others specialise in retail business.

The balance changes here. There is in the branch a cadre of experienced corporate bankers. The bank can put more authority with the client knowledge than with a small branch, because of the greater experience in the larger branch. Even if the training and other culture of the bank calls for specialist rather than generalist lenders, it is right to have the most senior specialist practical in such a branch. He or she will work with the client managers, and thus have the closest possible access to all their information. He will be better able to discuss with them the key points which decide whether the bank should lend; when it does, he can influence their handling of negotiations on pricing, structure, and so on, to ensure that the bank obtains full protection in each case. He will also be readily available to meet the client. This allows him to market the bank's credit standards, or educate the client in a particular requirement, such as covenants or amortisation, when appropriate.

The international branches may require different treatment again. The few with retail networks overseas may find the retail treatment fairly similar to that of a domestic branch network. Most banks, however, confine their international lending to wholesale clients; companies, governments and their agencies, and so on; or at least they aim to do so.

Lending in these conditions is often mainly to large companies in fairly large amounts; or at least to the largest companies in the country. In some countries, that may not be very large; in others the large companies may either not borrow very much or be well tied up by the domestic banks. The bank's credit strategy often assumes it will be lending only to large, highly rated companies. If it starts to lend to smaller ones, this assumption may be dangerous. If larger borrowers are simply not available, the bank should review whether it wants to lend at all; if it decides to continue, then it should review all aspects of its credit control, including the training and specific skills of the bankers involved. Only if satisfied that these fit the different type of lending it is doing, should it continue.

A wholesale bank, with few branches, can fall into the same trap overseas. At home its standing gives it ready access to major companies, but it may lack access in overseas markets. The temptation to go down-market for volume to cover the overheads, or to attract fee business, is great. It may be even more dangerous than with the retail bank, which does have experience of this type of lending somewhere in the bank. Wholesale banks may lack the expertise, and fail to recognise the need for it.

Moreover, wholesale banks generally have a better argument for decentralised lending authority than most other types of bank. The branches tend to be fairly large, and covering quite a large area. They will usually be staffed by experienced bankers, to make the impact needed on management of major companies. The argument put forward earlier about needing to be seen to be able to respond locally has greater validity than with a merchant bank.

These arguments are strengthened in the international field. The accounting standards, the amount of information available, the reaction to requests for security, for covenants, amortisation and other aspects of banking support, all of these differ from country to country. In some countries the differences are more of emphasis – Italy, Spain, France and Portugal, for instance. In others they are more fundamental. The US differs from all European countries, though less so from the UK than from Continental Europe; Britain and Germany have more in common than either has with the Latin countries in Europe, but still differ markedly, and so on. These differences are often so great, but sometimes so subtle, that they are almost impossible to understand from a distance. Moreover, because the American system is so much more open than most of Europe, it is harder to understand Europe from the United States than to understand the United States from Europe. Neither, however, is easy.

The differences relate to accounting and banking law, as well as to company and bankruptcy law, and to attitudes of both bankers and companies. In some countries, banks rely heavily on security, perhaps because they cannot get reliable financial information to allow sound analysis, perhaps from sheer laziness, or perhaps they lack the ability to enforce covenants and other protective methods needed for unsecured lending. In countries where this applies, banks may not develop the analytical tools for unsecured lending; companies are therefore often unused to the requirements, and unwilling to provide foreign banks with the basic tools to make unsecured lending sound. Equally, banks from such countries lending into countries where information and analysis plays a larger part in the decision, lack the skills, and often fail even to recognise the need for them.

All of this, plus the different attitudes to debt, the need to understand how the local government, and banks, react to the possible failure of important companies, argue in favour of decentralised lending authority. Banks must ensure that those who know the local environment take adequate account of it. It is damaging if a distant head office turns down sound loans because it does not understand the local environment. As head office finds it is unable to get any worthwhile business, it may then start to accept the local office's word, without surrendering the formal authority. This leads to the worst of both worlds. The people who know the market feel no responsibility; the people with responsibility have no way of exercising it soundly. A recipe for disaster. And yet a situation that many head offices will justify on the grounds of keeping control, instead of recognising that it is a formula for losing control.

Control is certainly necessary. Without it standards can slip in any market. The argument is that centralisation is not, in itself, a viable form of control and may actually cause loss of control. In any form of lending, control is critical; this is equally true whether the decisions are centralised, by committee and specialist or any other combination. Indeed we often see banks pulling authority back to the centre after a bad experience; and yet the bad experience is proof that the centre failed before, so why should giving it more authority change that?

Control relates, in fact, far more to training, to instilling standards, to ensuring that authority and responsibility are closely connected, than it does to centralisation. Given the training and standards, it must be better to put the authority in the same place as the local and client knowledge.

Sometimes that is not possible. A branch in a small country may not have enough business to justify the depth of experience to make large loans, or the infrastructure needed to assess and follow small loans. This may always have been true or may become true because of a change in the bank's approach to lending and to the market. If the types of client to whom the bank wishes to lend can borrow in the securities markets; and if they are so heavily solicited by other banks that they can borrow on ridiculous terms, then the bank should reduce lending and concentrate on other aspects. If this is in line with the basic strategy anyway, it may make even better sense.

Or a bank may wish to take lending authority away from the generalists, in line with a switch in their role, but not have enough specialists to put one in each branch; or enough lending business in each branch to justify the calibre of specialist the type of loan requires.

In either case, the answer may be regionalisation rather than centralisation. This is almost certainly true if the head office is in a different time zone. An American bank with a European branch network might well put full responsibility for all of the European branches in London, Paris, Brussels or Frankfurt. Equally, a European bank with a branch network in North and South America might want to have one or perhaps two regional headquarters to cover the business.

There are, of course, difficulties in regionalisation. Just because it is the regional headquarters, London does not lose all its differences to the European offices, and its pre-eminence may arouse jealousy. The cultural, legal and governmental differences between London and Paris remain hard to reconcile. But London is still closer to Paris than are New York, San Francisco or Tokyo. London and Paris can talk at all times of the day; a specialist or senior lender from London can get to Paris in a couple of hours. Some of these advantages may be reduced by technology, such as Concorde or the video conference. But the main point remains. A regional headquarters focuses only on the region, and can more easily overcome the regional disparities, than a worldwide headquarters whose focus is inevitably wider.

This section cannot list all possible combinations of lending authority. The combinations are myriad, and as said earlier depend as much on the culture of the bank as on other factors.

SUMMARY AND COMMENT

The precise combination of types of lending authority depends on each bank's circumstances. Nor can it be considered in isolation from the analysis and presentation, discussed in earlier chapters and further in Chapter 5.

Within these limitations, however, we can state some preferences, and point to advantages and disadvantages. Each of them depends to varying degrees on the people concerned being appropriately trained; conversely, before choosing a particular approach banks must ensure that the people expected to implement it have the proper training and other support.

Better to Decentralise

First, it is wise to decentralise lending authority as far as is practicable. Even where a branch lacks the expertise to handle large loans, it should have authority up to its maximum capacity, and management should look to increase this level if the branch's skill improves. This may be difficult if it means preferring some branches ahead of others; moreover the skill may be that of one or two people, rather than inherent in the branch structure, so that a reduction when they move on may damage morale.

Thus the urge to decentralise must be a tendency, rather than an absolute. Nevertheless, it is an important tendency for several reasons.

First, the bank needs to have the decision made by people who know the client and its environment. This may be less important in a domestic branch, but is important even there. Particularly with loans to small companies, local presence and the ability to pick up local news early can be critical to making sound loans, and to monitoring them.

Secondly, there is responsibility/sponsorship. A banker with no power to lend rarely feels the same responsibility for loans as for those approved locally; where the particular loan requires a higher authority, the recommending banker should also be one of the approving signatures. Even if lacking the full power to lend, he should at least be necessary to the decision.

Thirdly, there is the question of control. Many bankers who work in head offices believe that centralisation means control, and that looser control is the price for decentralisation. In fact, there are strong arguments that the reverse is true.

Two of the arguments relate back to the comments immediately above. If knowledge of the client and its environment is essential to sound decisions, removing the decision from the source of the knowledge weakens control. Taking responsibility away from the people who know the client and are best placed to gather and assess local knowledge also weakens control.

Thirdly, control before the fact means the setting and reviewing of standards; and of the way in which, or extent to which, people live up to these standards. But this, by definition, is not something head office can do to itself. Control in this sense comes from outside the body or person being controlled. But if head office takes the decisions, who controls head office? While one part of head office may control another, this is not always effective. The short answer to the question is then nobody. (There are various forms of after-the-fact control which we will discuss in the section on monitoring. But, while necessary and useful, they catch errors after they are made. True control prevents them being made; or at worst reduces the number of errors and their cost.)

Generalist Authority Better than Specialists, with Qualifications

There is no doubt that when the conditions are right, it is better to give authority to someone who knows the borrower thoroughly, and who feels responsible for the bank's overall relationship. This is usually the relationship manager, or account officer, who by definition is a generalist.

'When the conditions are right', however, is a vital qualification; the generalist must have the right training and clearly defined responsibility. Indeed, credit judgement in this case should be, and be seen to be, an important criterion for promotion and salary, bonus payments, etc.

These critical points are easily overlooked when the nature of the bank changes. It is easy to assume that because account officers have always been trained to understand credit, this training is in some way inherent in the job. It is in fact extraordinary, and alarming, how fast bankers trained in credit will change their attitude to it as their job changes. Managements often fail to recognise that they cannot place greater emphasis on some parts of the job without placing less on others. When more emphasis is put on marketing, less is put on credit, whatever management intends. There are several ways of dealing with this, but ignoring the problem is not one of them. To remove the responsibility from the account officer altogether may work, but loses the involvement of the person who is best placed to understand the credit, and to observe if it starts to deteriorate. A system which requires the account officer and a specialist to approve, so that neither can approve alone but either can veto, has some merit. So does some degree of authority for account officers, with specialist approval being required for larger amounts.

Whatever the precise form of lending authority, it is critical that the officer with the main responsibility for fostering the relationship have a feeling of sponsorship for his client. Lending authority is the best way of ensuring this where training and job description allow. Where they do not, it may be necessary to institute some formal system of sponsorship.

The reason for this is clear. Banks ultimately lend to people. Whatever the strengths or weaknesses of companies, they can be undermined, or offset, by people. Equally, these people will know better than any outsider whether business is good or bad, improving or declining. Some managements are deceitful, some are incompetent, some are secretive or too self-reliant to ask for help when they need it. Equally, others are quick to ask for help and make good use of it when offered.

Financial analysis of a company is crucial to good credit judgement and control, but alone it is not enough. Knowledge of the people is just as critical, in some cases more. And the trust of these people in the bank can be equally important. They must feel able to come to the bank for help without setting off a panic that will destroy them. Better still, they should believe that the bank can and will help them solve the problem; or, where a bank cannot help directly, that it will work to give them the time they need to solve it themselves.

A bank thus needs to satisfy itself that it is dealing with honest and competent people, who will tell it early about problems, and then be committed to work to solve them. The best defence for a bank against either deliberate fraud, or the resort to fraud in an attempt to hide failure, is not to deal with people who use it. Equally, a bank cannot always do much to help a company in trouble, even if the bank learns about it early. But often it can, and the chance diminishes with time. Moreover, where a company is beyond help, the sooner the bank realises this and moves to wind it up, the less the bank, and perhaps other creditors and even shareholders, will lose.

There are some banks who have so few clients that they can eliminate losses due to dishonest or secretive managements almost completely. Retail banks with thousands of branches and commensurate numbers of customers cannot hope to do so altogether; they can, however, reduce the percentage of this type of customer in their portfolio. These customers cause the most numerous losses, and the largest loss relative to the size of the advance, so that success or failure in this area is one of the largest factors in bad debt experience.

The relationship officer or the account officer has more contact with the borrower than anybody else in the bank; is the first line of defence against deliberately dishonest people, or weak people who fall into dishonesty in a crisis; and best able to recognise a mistake while there is still time. Equally, when the borrower's level of trust in the bank decides how he will react in a problem, it is these individuals whom the customer sees as the bank. For all of these reasons, the alertness of a bank's account officers to a company's management strengths and weaknesses, as well as management's trust in it, are crucial. While sponsorship alone will not guarantee that all account officers are alert, or lack of it that none of them are, it will tend to push them in the right direction.

Individual Authority Better than a Committee

An individual reacts faster than a committee, and is more likely to ask the right questions, and, above all, takes responsibility for decisions in a way no committee can. An individual can also ensure that the presenter or junior banker takes responsibility more easily than can a committee.

However, an individual with weak judgement can do serious damage to a bank's portfolio in a short time. Even an individual with fair judgement can be dangerous if he has a particular weakness which is important to the decisions actually faced; above all, where the marketing pressure to agree is great and he is too weak to resist it.

A committee, at least when functioning well, allows a cross-fertilisation of views which can be valuable. It is noticeable that members of a good committee strike sparks off each other and can come up with points of view that none of them would think of alone. Not all committees are good committees, however, and at their worst they can be an excuse for everybody ducking responsibility. This can lead either to no decision when one is needed – in effect, a decision not to lend without anybody ever consciously deciding that – or to a positive decision without taking into account the true issues.

In brief, the balance between committees and individuals depends much more on the people concerned than either of the other two balances discussed above. Given the right people, either can work well. If a bank does not have the right people, it is probably in trouble whichever way it goes.

5 Putting the Parts into a Coherent Whole

INTRODUCTORY COMMENT

Previous chapters discussed three factors which lead up to a decision to lend. This chapter will look at some general policies, mentioned in the first chapter, and then discuss ways to combine the structures into a coherent approach. As with the individual parts, no one combination works for all banks, and each must design combinations to fit with the rest of its business.

SOME PERMANENT DOs AND DON'Ts

Do Not Set Growth as a Main Aim of Lending Strategy

Control of credit includes saying 'No'. A strategy which requires growth weakens the ability to say 'No'. If growth is pre-eminent, the bad debts will increase; perhaps not immediately, but inevitably, because at times the best credit strategy will reduce the portfolio: when the economy booms, just before a probable downturn, or when competition pushes returns below economic levels, or when industries or regions face decline, or when available opportunities are unsound – as with the peak of the leveraged buy-out (LBO) boom. Often several of these factors work together. No strategy should require the portfolio to grow even when it is imprudent to do so.

At other times, a growth strategy will push bankers towards making loans they should not, or accepting pricing and other conditions that a sound policy would reject.

The policy is most dangerous from a small base, where rapid growth soon poses problems. These demand more rigorous controls, which it is rarely possible to instal until too late. However, even from a large base, keeping control of rapid growth is difficult, particularly when the climate is for growth rather than control.

Emphasis on growth has been a factor, often the major one, in most problems in bank loan portfolios in the past decade.

Make Sure the Price Reflects the Risk

Inadequate pricing often accompanies a growth strategy, but is dangerous in its own right. The right price depends on the risk, and failure to price adequately for higher risks is as serious a failure as general underpricing.

All banks, however sound their credit controls, have some bad debts. Banks which, from policy or lack of choice, lend to weaker credits have a higher proportion. The earnings on the sound bulk of the portfolio must cover these losses with sufficient margin. Loans must therefore be priced specifically in relation to their credit standing.

It is not just a question of profit, however; underpricing tends to increase the actual number of bad debts, in several ways.

First, where most banks do it, it tends to distort the capital structure of industry. All companies have a different optimum mix of sources of finance. If one form, bank debt, is consistently underpriced, companies will rely on it too much, and add to their risk of failure. For any one, the additional risk may be small, but cumulatively it can be large.

Secondly, if only a few banks price accurately, particularly for weak credits, they will lose the bidding on some loans which later they will be glad to have avoided. Credit control is not just a question of refusing to lend, but of refusing to underprice.

Thirdly, some companies may be encouraged to borrow too much and use the funds for unsound projects when money is cheap. Again, the risk in any individual case is small, but the cumulative risk is larger.

Chapter 18 will discuss pricing in more detail. It is a crucial part of the lending decision, and of credit controls.

Make Ability to Monitor a Critical Part of the Decision

Banks rarely lose money solely because the initial decision was wrong. Even with a bad decision, there is usually time to take preventive action to avoid or reduce the loss. Failure to monitor loses this opportunity. A decision which accepts an inability to monitor adds to the risk in any loan.

There are several reasons why a bank may not be able to monitor loans.

1. A general inability to monitor, lack of systems, controls, people, etc. This is a major weakness.
2. Specialised requirements for a particular type of borrower which the bank cannot meet. The specialist nature of the business may also make it hard for a non-specialist lender to understand. The best

answer then is not to lend; if there are overriding business reasons, be extra cautious.

3. A weakness in the banker or branch concerned. This is a management problem, to improve or replace the weak players, and meanwhile to lend carefully and ensure some form of extra support.
4. Refusal by the borrower to provide information or meet other conditions to make monitoring practical. This often reflects the market climate, and is then part of a wider problem; if the leading banks in a market do not insist, the quality of monitoring in general suffers, and bad debt losses rise.
5. Sometimes, the borrower cannot provide information, which suggests poor management or weak financial controls, which give little ability to react promptly to adverse trends. This is a recipe for a bank to lose money, since if the borrower does not know where it is going, the bank cannot.

Lenders Should Not Be Lemmings

Lending tends to go in waves, whether a general economic wave, or one related to a particular industry (property and shipping are two recurrent examples) or product/lending type (LBOs or LDCs).

The general economic boom breeds over-optimism and a tendency for banks to lend and companies to borrow most, just before a recession hits. Sales drop, but interest rates often do not, at least at first. Any bank should include in its credit controls a continuing review of the stage of the economic cycle. As a boom develops, banks should scrutinise all proposals closely; above all, ensure that all projections have a downside scenario which includes a recession. Also, it is here that pressure on pricing tends to be greatest; maintaining pricing in a boom can be a useful counter-cyclical tool.

Where the boom is more specific, the factors at work are likely to be only slightly different. Take industry lending first. There are always banks that have expertise in, say, shipping, a high-risk industry. The right skills can ensure sound loans, but those without should keep away. The risk, or the skill, makes shipping a high-rate borrower in normal times. When other loan demand is slack, or non-shipping margins unusually low, banks without the skill try to take advantage of the higher shipping rates – and force them down. These banks rarely recognise the need for skill, but instead rely on the 'security' of a ship mortgage. Rates in general come down, and many unsound propositions get financed. Perhaps the shipping banks manage to avoid the worst disasters, and perhaps those who come in earliest do so while most propositions are still sound. Those who come in just before the bubble bursts lose heavily.

This cycle, with minor variations, has occurred repeatedly in both shipping and property; and to a lesser extent in lending to finance and leasing companies. It happens most often with 'secured lending' when banks ignore the need to analyse the collateral thoroughly, but it can happen in almost any industry that becomes the fashionable growth industry of the moment. (What next? Cellular telephones? Cable TV?)

A sound credit control strategy will therefore focus on avoiding these obvious, but enticing, traps.

Where the industry or product is a new one, the process is similar, but the lesson harder to learn because the repetition is less obvious. Take leveraged buy-outs (LBOs). In the early days the concept was simple: take the right company, buy it with a lot of debt and a little equity, pay off the debt from sale of undervalued assets, better management of cash flow, or a bit of both, and the return on equity is sensational. Although the high borrowing added to the risk, careful analysis and good timing reduced the losses to a minimum. However, as banks scented the opportunity and rushed to lend, the best opportunities were gone and the demand for return on equity grew so that the balance between debt and equity deteriorated. Soon banks were looking for any opportunity to lend to LBOs, and the quality weakened further. Add a touch of recession, and you have a recipe for disaster.

In such cases the concept is theoretically sound but limited, and banks and investors in the early projects do well. The sufferers are those who join in just before the boom tops out.

Do Not Let Marketing Make Loan Decisions

The balance between letting marketing over-influence credit, and being uncommercial is a narrow one. Refusing to make good loans is, in the long run, almost as bad as agreeing to make bad ones.

There are several areas subject to marketing pressures, since a decision to lend has several parts to it. The most critical is whether the credit is good enough to lend on any conditions. If it is not, then marketing should never be allowed to persuade the bank to lend. The trouble is that the decision is rarely a clear 'yes' or 'no'. But it is critical that in the borderline cases the decision be independent of marketing, so that if the credit decision, after some agonising, is no, that is the end of it. Anything else leads to bad debts far higher than any profits that can be made on the lending, or from even the most profitable relationship in other areas.

Where the decision is borderline, or weakly positive, the bank can sometimes reduce the risk by security, amortisation, ratio and other covenants or some combination. Often the borrower resists them, particularly if it is a formerly sound credit which has deteriorated without recognising the implications. Often, too, the marketer will support the borrower.

Here the position is less than clear-cut. The borrower may accept the principle of covenants but argue against those proposed. For credit as well as marketing reasons the bank should take these arguments seriously – but not necessarily accept them. To some extent it is a question of degree. The principle of covenants, for instance, should never be sacrificed; but the correct level is a matter of judgement not fact. The point can be one of principle, or of commercial judgement in other areas, too. For instance, even the strongest credit should sign a cross-default clause, which a serious bank should never give up. To do so under marketing pressure undermines a critical protection. If, however, the argument is not whether there should be a cross-default, but exactly what it should say, there may be room to adjust the bank's position. The decision as to how far to go depends on a number of factors, but marketing can have a legitimate input.

Similarly with pricing: there is a level below which it is never right to go. But there is also a level at which it is right to consider other business. What these levels might be, and how to balance marketing against needed return are covered in Chapter 18. While it may in some circumstances be right to allow the marketers a say, the decision must be made by the credit people. They must be commercial enough to know when to adjust pricing for other than purely credit reasons; they must also be seen by marketers as being positive rather than negative. If credit becomes an obstacle that bankers must surmount, rather than a useful guide to sound business, credit standards will suffer. It is worth paying attention to marketing considerations, and sometimes modifying the full rigour of credit demands, if only to avoid that happening; or reverse it when it has happened.

FITTING TRAINING TO THE STRUCTURE

It is a truism that lenders should be trained in credit, but the different lending structures affect the type of training required.

Credit judgement requires a mix of formal training and experience; enough analytical training to understand the analysis, but not necessarily in the same depth as a specialist analyst. In the traditional structure discussed in earlier chapters, it was usually enough to have limited formal training at the beginning; the analytical and judgemental training came, with experience, on the job.

Where this structure remains, this approach to training probably still works. Arguably more rigorous early training and more frequent refresher courses than most banks use are desirable, but the basic approach is sound. It requires careful supervision by seniors to ensure that the juniors not only gain experience, but also learn from it. In particular, given that the best way to learn is from one's own mistakes, the seniors need to review and correct the mistakes to protect the bank and educate the juniors.

Other structures require different approaches to training. If the bank largely relies on specialist analysts, there is a multiple need to train the analysts and the bankers.

The analysts need training in analysis directed towards the banker's needs and to whom they will be comprehensible. Specialist analysts must avoid writing 'perfect' memos, regardless of time and value. The bank needs a memo tailored to specific needs where speed of response may be critical; it requires training and constant vigilance by management to ensure that practical benefit triumphs over perfectionism.

The bankers need training in understanding the analysis and sometimes correcting it where their knowledge of the company justifies this; judging the risk–reward ratio, and presenting the credit for a decision. The banker must be able to make an independent judgement of the credit, using the analysis as a tool, not a crutch. Given that even the best analysts are fallible, he must be able to argue with the analyst as an equal.

The banker must also present a balanced case, not a selling document; understand that it is as much in his and the client's interest to avoid lending where the borrower cannot repay as it is in the bank's. The banker must overcome the natural desire to do the deal regardless, and replace it with a desire to do only good deals, and to be able to tell the difference.

The decision-makers need to be trained in acting as umpire. There is often a need to balance the criticisms of the analyst against the belief of the banker in his client. Sometimes that belief is blind, based on ignorance of risk and unjustified trust in 'my friends'. But it may be based on a closer understanding of the people and strategy than the analyst can attain with his limited access to management. Judging which is the case and discounting for bias is often an important part of credit judgement.

All three need to learn to work together in their common interest rather than at cross purposes. Training the banker to recognise the value of the analyst; to introduce him to the client positively rather than defensively; to accept that his purpose is to find weaknesses, and that this is not a sign of hostility, but necessary to protect the bank, and often the borrower, from unsound risk. Recognise, too, that a risk identified is more easily avoided.

Training in other situations must be adapted to the precise needs. With 'Credit as a product', the account officer has no direct responsibility for credit decisions. He does, however, need to advise whether the client can afford to borrow and if so in what form; this requires an understanding of credit, and of what various types of lender demand, even if in less depth than where making the decision. It also requires an ability to absorb and explain the requirements to borrow in each market.

PUTTING THE PARTS TOGETHER

Earlier chapters have discussed the three aspects of the structure of credit decisions (analysis, presentation, decision) individually. In practice, they are a package, with each part needing to fit with the others to provide a coherent approach.

The Banker Can Analyse

Where the banker is expected to analyse and decide, the specialists are, to some extent, there to help carry out these functions, not to do the whole job for him. Banks must find the right balance between the analyst doing so much that the banker loses the ability, and having the banker decide when help is needed.

A truly independent analytical support must be able to decide which names it will look at, even when not requested. On the other hand, if a competent banker covers many small clients, it will be at worst, impractical and at best, expensive to analyse each name in full.

The choice of both initial and repeat analysis therefore should fall somewhere between a specialist analysis of every transaction, and analysis at the banker's request. The level can be set in one of several ways. Either all borrowers/exposures above a certain size require specialist analysis; or all first-time borrowers and all others which have not been independently analysed for a given time; or where there is an internal rating system, the decision as to what to analyse may be linked to that.

There should also be several people who can require analysis even where it is not compulsory. These include the account officer, who should be encouraged to call for help when he needs it; the analyst or head of the analytical group, who must, to be independent, be able to review any name which raises doubts; and perhaps the senior manager responsible for the business area within which the particular borrower falls.

Where the account officer is the main source of credit judgement, there is a temptation to give him a right of veto over which names the analysts should cover. This is a mistake. It undermines the analyst's independence; analysis is aimed mainly at names already identified as problems, or at least difficult credits, instead of being the tool to identify them as early as possible; as a result, it may overstress the negative aspect of the reviews, and make bankers reluctant to commission analysis for fear of the 'wrong' answer. Indeed, these points apply in all situations where specialist analysts work. There must always be a relationship manager who can choose to use the analyst as a tool to help with the decision, not as a crutch. The analyst's independent ability to review a name is critical, but should not make the banker feel that the analyst is trying to stop him doing business.

With a well-trained and competent banker, individual authority and maximum delegation works well. Given the training, the banker needs to have his sense of responsibility reinforced as much as possible. The power to take decisions, and to be held accountable for the result, is the best form of reinforcement. Naturally the level of authority must be tailored to each banker's experience and judgement. Even where the banker cannot alone approve a facility, however, he should be one of the necessary signers. If the banker recommends approval to an individual, and co-signs, it is harder to ignore the responsibility than for a decision by a committee of which he is not a member.

The Banker as Pure Marketer

Where the banker is a pure marketer, with little credit judgement, the analyst's role is even more important. He must analyse every name, because nobody else will. This puts much greater onus on him, and increases the need for management support. A pure marketer, with no pretence to understand credit, ought in logic to accept an adverse credit decision without argument. Marketing bankers and product marketers, with only a few honourable exceptions, resent being turned down on credit grounds, or told that they are underpricing for the risk. A banker with some credit judgement can understand the reasoning, but may not agree with it.

There must still be some discrimination in the depth of the analysis, and the costs involved. It does not make sense to spend $50,000 analysing a borrower, if the potential revenue is only $25,000. On the other hand, the exposure which generates $25,000 in revenue may run into millions. Unless the marketer recognises the costs involved in analysing, deciding on and then monitoring the exposure, he will always push for approval because he bears no cost but benefits from all of the revenue. Some banks are groping for ways of charging product areas for credit. If the product specialist or marketing banker has to pay the analyst – or more probably a specialist group including the decision-maker – for credit as he uses it, this should help to ensure that he only chases business with a fair prospect of providing the bank with profit, not just revenue.

The requirement for analysis must be flexible. The need for written analysis in every case is, on the argument put in earlier chapters and sections, paramount. It only makes economic sense, however, if the level and cost of the analysis is tailored to the size of exposure, the risk involved, and the revenue expected. Where the banker is able and willing to write the presentation, the simple analyses can be left to him, and often included as part of the presentation rather than done separately by a specialist analyst. Where the banker has no credit skills, the analyst must cover every name. However, his analysis can vary: a few lines for an overdraft to a highly rated or AAA (to use Standard & Poors terminology) name; two or three pages for a genuinely short-term facility to a lesser but straightforward credit; or, for a major five-year term loan, a detailed memo including projections, industry information, discussion of management, competition, possible changes in regulatory requirements and whatever else is relevant to the particular case. It is important to ensure that the analyst provides the right type of analysis for each situation.

Access to the client by the analyst is always important, as management is a key element in credit. Where the banker is credit conscious, his assessment of management may be more reliable than the analyst's; where the banker is not, it is vital that the analyst, and perhaps the decision-maker, make their own assessment.

Moreover, there is information which only management can provide. Part of this is financial; details of historical finances, cash flow and projections or sensitivity analyses. The same applies to details of items such as capital expenditures, new product launches, opening up of new geographic markets, and the reasons for these. All are items which can prove either a source of added risk or a protection against it, depending in each case largely on management. It is thus vital that the analyst have access to management, particularly when the banker can provide little aid, even second-hand. Equally, however, the introduction of an analyst who asks the wrong questions, or the right questions in the wrong way, can damage a good relationship. Although this happens less often than many bankers think, it still requires confidence between analysts and bankers if the analyst is to gain access.

Banks should never uncritically accept information from the company as accurate in all respects. In particular, they should carefully review any budgets or projections; banks often compare their own projections with the company's. Indeed, one way of assessing management is to compare its views with the bank's own. But while uncritical acceptance is wrong, there is no better source of information as raw material for analysis than the company itself.

The influence of bankers with no credit consciousness on the format for decisions is harder to generalise. On balance, it probably makes for more individual authority, and more decentralisation, but not all banks will see it that way.

The argument for individual authority is that the only people with capacity to decide are the credit specialists, and there are unlikely to be enough in any but the largest branches to form a meaningful committee. Thus unless the authority is heavily centralised, there is no option but individual authority. The argument for decentralised then relates mainly to job satisfaction and credibility. Given that the specialists are the sole source of knowledge and understanding of credit in the branches, they should be both high calibre and well perceived by clients and colleagues. But this does not fit with low authority. To obtain good people in the job, and make them credible, banks must give them authority; not unlimited authority, of course. A bank could take the larger loan decisions in a committee in head office or regional headquarters, and grant individual authority for smaller loans.

Credit as a Product

The approach of credit as a product contains both aspects discussed above to some extent. We have a group of bankers who, while not account officers in the full sense, play much the same role in regard to credit. As credit specialists, they may be more competent analysts than many old-fashioned bankers, and need less analytical support – although they will certainly need some. Conversely, they will be more capable of making decisions, and will see this as a more important part of the job, so that decision by committee or highly centralised authority will be less acceptable both in terms of job and client satisfaction. The extent to which this is true, and the availability of numbers for a committee will vary with the size of the branch, importance of lending in its range of products and so on. The general point remains, however.

SOME SPECIFIC FEATURES TO CONSIDER

In considering the overall situation, there are some points that need to be fitted in, but will depend more on the bank's general strategies and philosophies than on the precise combinations so far discussed.

Balancing Revenue and Cost Against Avoidance of Loss

The main purpose of lending is, naturally, to generate revenue. This can come solely from the loan portfolio, or can include other revenues which the willingness to lend helps to obtain. The latter is usually more subjective than the former.

Any bank can, in the short run, increase revenues by taking more risk. It can do this either by underpricing the risk, with the revenue coming more from volume; or it can do so consciously, taking additional risks that it understands and is paid for. Many banks mix the two; some unfortunately think they are doing the second when they are doing the first.

Equally any bank can, in the short run, increase the profit from a given revenue by cutting back on the cost of analysing and monitoring it.

Either or both of these strategies, if carried very far, will lead to a sharp increase in credit losses, and a reduction therefore in profits. In extreme cases, the losses can threaten the bank's survival.

Conversely, any bank can be so cautious in its lending that it never makes a credit loss, and practically never makes a loan. Unless lending is only a minor product, this too will have a severe impact on its profits. Or a bank can spend so much on analysing and monitoring every credit that the costs of doing so eat up all the revenues and there is little or no profit left, certainly not enough to provide a reasonable return on equity.

The revenue on lending is a tiny proportion of the loan. Therefore, one loss eats up the revenue from a much larger portfolio. On the other hand, the low revenue limits the cost a bank can absorb on each loan.

Again, part of the answer is volume. With a large portfolio, a bank can afford systems with a high fixed cost, but a low variable cost. With a low volume the fixed costs will kill the revenues.

Another part is pricing to reflect risk. A bank can justify a conscious decision to take higher risks by a higher level of expertise: in a specific industry such as shipping, where the recognised high risk allows a higher revenue to compensate; or a high level of general analytical and monitoring skill, used to earn the higher returns which riskier loans provide. Whether these banks absorb the losses, or avoid them by paying for greater skill to protect against losses, they need to be paid more than for less risky loans.

Banks must price their loans in accordance with the risk. This cuts both ways. In the long run, it can be as damaging to overprice good loans as it is to underprice weaker loans. The worst trap, which surprisingly many banks fall into, is to do both, so that they end up with a predominantly weak portfolio, priced as a higher quality one.

Banks must also adjust the cost of analysis and monitoring to the quality of the borrower. To spend as much effort on an overdraft to an AAA borrower as on a term loan to a BB borrower is to guarantee inadequate profits on the AAA, or take inordinate risks on the BB, or both.

In brief, the assessment of risk, and of the price and effort demanded by that risk, is essential. So is the reward potential. Banks must know the reward needed for the right risk–reward ratio, as well as the risk.

Avoiding Second-Class Citizens

In any bank, there will be glamour jobs. If these get out of proportion, others will feel that they are second-class citizens. This is always undesirable, but is worse when comparing credit specialists with bankers. If the revenue side gets too far ahead, the credit side loses credibility with a devastating impact on credit quality in the long run. If credit becomes too strong the banker can lose credibility with his client, or begin to believe that credit risk is something his bank will not take.

Finally, in banks which have not moved away from bankers with credit judgement, does this discriminate against bankers who have other skills? Or ignore their weaknesses in credit because they are important for those other skills? And if so, does this mean paying lip-service only to credit and getting the worst of both worlds?

Managing the Portfolio

The main discussion on the portfolio will come under monitoring, but managing it is more than just monitoring. Banks need criteria on concentration, maturity, level of risk, which are in everybody's mind in making the individual decisions.

Concentration is probably the single most important risk in a portfolio. Banks need rules to prevent too much exposure to a single name or related group or to a single country. Sometimes they may need to prevent too much exposure to a single industry – oil, shipping, property, for instance; or to a type of product such as highly leveraged transactions (HLT). They may also, depending on their business need to restrict exposure to a region (Latin America, say), or to countries dependent on a single product, such as copper.

Pricing is important in a portfolio, as is maturity pattern, balance between types and levels of risk, and so on.

Committees to manage some aspects of the portfolio, such as the balance between industries, may work better than committees for individual decisions.

6 Credit in Treasury and Capital Market Products

INTRODUCTION

Traditional commercial banks traded foreign exchange and had some other products which required credit. However, their corporate clients were the main users, apart from the interbank market, and they treated credit decisions on these products in the same way as loans. Moreover, few banks provided these products to counterparties who were not also borrowers, or at least potentially so. The main work in assessing the credit was thus already done; applying that judgement to the particular product was not difficult.

(Borrowing gives credit risk only to the bank. If the borrower fails, the bank loses money; there is no reciprocal risk if the bank gets into trouble. A counterparty arrangement is reciprocal. If either fails to deliver, the other will have to replace the transaction in the market, and may lose money doing so. Thus the counterparty risks a similar loss if the bank fails to the loss, the bank risks if the counterparty fails. The situation can be worse if one side delivers and the other does not, which is why delivery vs payment (DVP) is so important. Not all Treasury products are counterparty products in this sense, but most of them are. See T. H. Donaldson, *Credit Risk in Securitisation and Transactions*, Macmillan 1989.)

More recently, with the growth of new products, and the entry of many banks into products which were foreign to them, banks have dealt with a range of new counterparties. Many were not previously clients, or were non-borrowers. While all of the products contain a credit element, their main risks tend to be market or trading risks. The traders or salesmen in these products understand market risks, but have little conception of credit risk.

Equally the banking and credit officers found it hard to understand the products and their credit implications. Often, too, the counterparties showed special features which require a different analytical approach to that for manufacturing or commercial customers. Finally, the bankers saw little prospect of profit from these clients and were reluctant to spend the time needed to understand the credit. This led to what in

77

some banks were known as orphans: clients with whom one or two non-traditional areas of the bank wanted to do business, but where nobody was willing to understand the credit.

At the same time, in many areas where the bank had done business in a small way and taken the peripheral risk for granted, it has expanded the volume enormously. In these and the new products, banks found areas of risk they had not previously recognised, and others out of all proportion to their earlier levels.

This led to a recognition that new structures were needed to take care of these risks. The need had two facets: first, the banks had to identify, manage and control the risks, before some disaster struck them. Secondly, they had to assess the levels of risk accurately, to ensure that they avoided unacceptable risks, without over-estimating sound ones. Because the risk was often one of the difference between two amounts, rather than the whole amount, it was easy to inflate the risk and refuse to take it when the true risk was much smaller than appeared and well worth taking in view of the expected profit.

A simple example: a bank has bought $100 million of government securities from a broker. If settlement is DVP, the only risk is the amount by which the price of the securities may move between the date settlement should take place, and the date the bank finds out it has not and replaces them from the market. In many cases this will be as little as one or two per cent of face value. The difference between risking $1 million and $100 million to obtain the profit on the trade obviously makes an enormous difference. But unless the bank understands how the settlement system works, and that it is truly DVP, it may turn down a low-risk transaction, believing it to be high risk.

These problems call for two types of response. One is research to establish the true risk and thus quantify exposure. This decides the level of lending authority required to approve, the capital to be allocated, the pricing, the impact on total exposure to a client, and so on. The exposure is referred to by the Basle Committee as risk equivalent, and by some banks as loan equivalent. Whatever the name, understanding the concepts for each product and identifying the level of risk is critical to the health of the credit portfolio, and to the ability to trade soundly in these products.

The second response is to separate the credit management of these products, and clients which trade mainly in them, from the normal approval channels. Some banks have established units to do just this, and must define what they cover, decide what lending authority they need, ensure they are properly trained and set them to work.

WHAT SHOULD TREASURY CREDIT COVER?

There are two main separations, though they can be recombined in various ways. Banks can designate certain types of client which do mainly counter-party business. A specialist unit then handles all credit relating to these clients, even if the specific transaction is not a counterparty one. Or all counterparty transactions may require approval of a specialist group, regardless of the client.

Banks can also give authority to specialists in each product, alone or with a client unit, to approve all or certain credit exposures for the product. This leads to a series of 'Product Credit Officers', or different types of credit authority or both.

Following by Client

The analysis of some types of client differs from analysing a manufacturing company. Banks are an obvious example; they are also big users of coun-terparty products. Among other industries in this category are brokers of all types; asset and investment managers; pension funds and the investment side of insurance companies.

For many of these clients, particularly banks, the skill is in allocating credit, rather than making the initial credit judgement. Banks can decide annually what is the maximum total exposure they are willing to accept on other banks. But within whatever the total is how do you decide that Branch A should have x million in foreign exchange lines, while Branch B should only have $0.1x$ million of option facilities? This partly comes back to the question of loan or risk equivalents, but is also based on returns on capital. On this basis, some banks include sovereigns in this group.

We have three possible bases for including clients in this category: types of transaction; differences in analysis; and need to allocate. There is no necessary conflict between these criteria, but it helps to decide which is the ruling one. Without a clear standard, there are abiding doubts about where some clients belong, and some are rejected by everybody.

The differences in analysis fall into two areas. One, of which banks pro-vide the best example, covers technique and information. Banks are clearly susceptible to financial analysis, but are asset based and the analytical techniques reflect this. Asset-based borrowers should provide different information than cash-flow-based companies; details as to asset quality and the controls to maintain it, for instance. This is rarely available for banks; even US banks which provide the most information are hard to analyse. There are techniques other than pure financial analysis to overcome these drawbacks, including use of market information from traders and sales-men. A special unit can concentrate on the specific techniques, and keep in touch with market developments.

The second analytical difference is more dramatic. Many clients provide little or no opportunity for financial analysis. Either their position changes so fast that any financial analysis is solely or mainly of historical interest (stockbrokers, except perhaps the very biggest, are good examples); or they are dealing, often as agents, in amounts which dwarf any possible capital they would ever need. They could not borrow $100 million, but nor do they wish to; they can, on the other hand, buy and sell government or corporate bonds, whether for themselves or clients, in these amounts. The decision, if the settlement process is not DVP, may still be whether or not to accept a $100 million temporary exposure; if the relationship is active, it may be to accept a series of them so continuous that they amount to one long-term exposure.

It would be entirely wrong to accept this type of exposure without analysis, but the analysis is very different in type to that of a manufacturing company.

It starts with understanding the client's business and how the trans-action(s) in prospect fit in with it. The bank may know, to continue the above example, that the client acts as investment manager for a group of high-quality pension funds and comparable investors, and that the orders are placed on their behalf and funded by them. This does not remove all risk, but it starts to establish a reasonable presumption that the risk may be small. The bank may need to enquire into the legal claim, if any, against the funds for non-payment, and perhaps even to establish one. It will certainly want to get to know the managers of its clients to establish their trustworthiness, as well as satisfying itself that their back office functions efficiently; the bank will only deal when properly instructed, and will settle promptly, without adding confusion and delay to the inherent risk.

A London stockbroker may want to do forward exchange business with the bank. This may be sound business if he is dealing in New York and is exposed to exchange risk by the different settlement periods in the two centres; better still if the bank can tie each exchange deal into a specific self-liquidating transaction, or can check that there are security deals outstanding. On the other hand, the bank would be rightly reluctant to do speculative exchange business with a small stockbroker.

These are among the less complicated products. To understand the credit implications of swaps, options, futures, puts and calls, to mention only a few, and their relevance to each client's business is a full-time job. Throw in mortgage lenders, credit card companies and the various securitisation vehicles, and the job becomes very demanding.

Understanding the risk, and monitoring it are both easier if the traders and sales people understand your needs and help to meet them. One argument for special arrangements for treasury credit is just that: the traders see you as on their side in a way they do not always see credit officers or bankers. They are more likely to tell you promptly if they see anything going wrong.

This is critical, because the best, and first warning of this type of counterparty running into trouble often comes from salesperson or traders. It may be evidence that a bank or broker is taking heavy losing positions; that an investment manager's back office is slipping; that banks are turning down a counterparty's name, or that somebody's bonds or commercial paper are having to offer an above market yield; or any one or more of a range of comparable items. Sometimes several apply. Whatever the precise detail, the market sees them first; banks can lose money through the failure of this information to reach those who make credit judgements. One critical aspect of any system for managing treasury credit, therefore, is the flow of information from the market to the credit people.

Following the Product

An alternative approach is to have one or more groups approve the credit in all treasury products, regardless of the client. This at first sounds good, since somebody whose job is to understand their credit implications looks at each treasury transaction.

However, in practice this is not so sensible. In dealing with corporates, who use treasury products only to a limited extent, the features of a particular product are rarely the major factor in the credit decision. The strength of the counterparty is usually more important, and in most cases will override the credit aspects of the products. But the treasury credit officer will not know the client's strength, and will need to have that portion of the decision cleared with someone who does. This can cause friction.

Each as Appropriate?

Despite the above, in some cases the credit aspects of the product are critical to the credit decision. This may be because the corporate is marginal, so that the credit risk inherent in the product can tip the balance: a bank would not make a five-year loan to this company, so would it do a five-year swap? Only if there is something about the swap which means it is less risky than a loan. This is not usually so, but can be.

Sometimes judicious use of hedging transactions can reduce the credit risk of existing loans, as when the bank has a floating rate term loan to a company. If rates are currently low an interest swap, fixing the rate at today's level reduces the company's exposure to increases, and improves the quality of the loan credit. The same is true of currency swaps and exposure, and of many types of hedging product. In the right circumstances, agreeing to them can reduce, rather than increase, the total credit risk. This will never show just by looking at the product, however, since the same product can as easily be used for damaging speculation. To know which applies, bankers need to know the characteristics of both instrument and counterparty.

Each as appropriate will often mean therefore 'both when appropriate'. The difficulty is to know in advance when it is appropriate, or decide reliably in each case. This in turn means laying down rules which become a matter of sometimes disputed interpretation. Or, rather better, relying on common sense to follow a general rule to 'consult when you need to'.

Both Together?

A better solution may be to have both together. This can take one of two forms. Either a 'product credit officer' is responsible for understanding and advising on the credit aspects of his product in each case, or you have a 'credit sponsor' for those products where there is not an account officer. In either case, they work with the credit decision-maker.

Product credit officer

The product credit officer covers one or a group of products, such as swaps, and perhaps related products such as caps and collars. This involves understanding not only the straightforward credit implications of the product, but the way in which complex variations can change the credit impact. In particular, he should look out for hidden credit risks which arise because of the use of a specific product in a specific situation. These occur more often and are harder to spot, as the market develops combinations to meet unusual needs.

The product credit officer does not need to have sole approval authority. He may have a veto, or merely be required to advise on the risk of the product before someone else approves it. Whatever the precise requirement, his existence excludes any excuse for anyone to take a decision without understanding the implications.

Although he may not take initial decisions, the product credit officer may well have 'excession authority', approving excessions over existing lines, within set limits; and perhaps approving the use of the lines for related products when satisfied that the credit implications are the same. This type of excession authority can be crucial when a European office requires to settle a transaction with a Japanese client at three a.m. Tokyo-time.

Credit sponsor

A variant on this approach is the credit sponsor. This concept applies to the orphan problem in particular, but links back to the need for sponsorship discussed in earlier chapters. Where there is no natural account officer, with credit training and attitudes, to sponsor a client, banks still need a sponsor. This should be the person who wants to do the business, or perhaps the head of their business unit. Sponsorship in this sense recognises that the sponsor has no qualifications to judge the credit. The sponsorship role then covers several aspects. The sponsor certifies that he knows the client's management and business, and that both aspects make them a proper client for the bank (sometimes referred to as the smell test), as well as knowing that what they do makes sense and is within the scope of their business competence, and that it makes good business sense from the bank's point of view. Finally, he recognises that if these facts ever change in a way that threatens the client's creditworthiness, the sponsor is most likely to be the first to see the warning signs; he accepts the responsibility to pass any such warnings on to whoever is responsible for the credit.

Unfortunately, experience suggests that not all traders or sales people are willing to accept even this degree of responsibility.

SOME OTHER FEATURES

There are several areas, some touched on earlier in the chapter, which are important whatever the precise structure. They include research, setting limits and communicating about problems.

Research

There are two aspects of research. One, mentioned earlier, deals with loan equivalents. It aims first to establish general criteria, and then to apply them to the specific facts of each case, to calculate a loan equivalent for each product. Given the proliferation of products, this alone can be a full-time job. But there is more to it than that. The calculation then has to be built into the operating systems, so that it can be recorded. Where the product is suitable for a line, the loan equivalent covers change in outstandings as each item comes on or runs off, or the loan equivalent changes as it approaches maturity. Without this, there is no way of knowing whether the line is fully used or not. This is hardest where the transaction is longer term. A line for swaps must adjust not only to new transactions, but to the changes in the market which affect the exposure of existing swaps, and to the impact as payments are made and time expires.

This means first setting the parameters for the research. Looking at settlement risk means examining the settlement mechanism, deciding whether it is DVP; if it is, assessing the period between committing to buy or sell and learning of failure to settle, and the volatility of the instrument in the period discovered. These facts then allow the bank to calculate a percentage of face value as the loan equivalent.

With swaps, it is more complex. The loan equivalent varies widely with the nature of the swap, volatility of the interest rate, currency or commodity being swapped, maturity and the assumptions made. It is possible simply to ignore this, and pick a blanket loan equivalent – x per cent of face value for each remaining year of life, for instance. But this, while simple, is accurate only by accident. A more complex approach makes assumptions about future movements, based on historical or expected volatility. This will give a series of exposure figures as the resulting curve and the reduced remaining life (and, with interest swaps, amounts due) first offset each other and then reinforce each other. This research can involve mathematics well above a credit officer's head. Equally, however, it can involve making assumptions based on pure mathematics that have little or no relationship to risk in real life. It is therefore important that decision-makers understand at least the general concepts behind these calculations, and apply appropriate scepticism in assessing the risk. They, not the researchers, are responsible for the credit judgement.

The second broad area for research is enhancement or mitigation. The risk in some products can be reduced, or occasionally almost eliminated, in various ways. Netting of swap and related exposures is one example; marking them to market, another; various forms of charge over assets being settled can reduce settlement risk, and so on. In each case, research needs to estimate the size of the reduction, the legal aspects, and the practicality of the various steps required to achieve the enhancement, and their cost.

Netting, for instance, can apply in liquidation only, or on a continuing payment basis. The former, if it works, reduces the loss if the counterparty fails; the latter, if there are opposing flows, reduces the amounts transferred and at risk.

The legal possibility of netting in liquidation varies from country to country, and has been tested in few. In some, including the United States, bankruptcy laws have been changed to make netting easier in some or all cases. The conditions that have to be met in each country to give the best chance of success may also vary. Or there may be limitations on who can do swaps, let alone net them. The ruling in the Hammersmith and Fulham swap case in the United Kingdom is a particularly painful example of this.

The rules on collateral in settlement also vary by country. In some, it is easily obtainable; in others it is available only if the broker or other counterparty owns the securities, rather than acting as agent for a third party; in others, banks can get around these points if they can show that the funds borrowed paid for the specific shares, and so on.

In these and other cases, banks need to research the law in each country. They may then have to operate in a particular way to preserve their legal rights, perhaps to check that the securities in each case are the broker's own property, or to identify which securities were purchased with the borrowed money. This can be burdensome operationally, and in extreme cases can add so much to the costs that the business becomes uneconomic.

All this may seem excessive. How often, after all, do banks lose money on settlement or swaps? Do all the losses add up to the amount spent on controlling them?

The answer is that it is easy to overdo the concern and run up too much cost. It is, however, just as easy to go too far the other way. There have not been many Herrstats (a German bank which collapsed in the middle of the day, so that counterparties who had paid Deutchemarks in settlement of exchange contracts failed to receive their dollars), but most bankers think that one is enough. Volumes of traditional transactions are multiplying and new types of transaction, with new credit risks, are exploding in number and volume. If banks do not spend time and effort researching both the nature of the risk, and the best method of reducing it, the long-run impact is bound to be painful. Moreover, while settlement has been around a long time, swaps are relatively recent and some of the other products more recent still. The argument about not losing money therefore needs one vital qualifying word – 'yet'.

Setting Limits

Once the bank has identified the risk and quantified it, it then has to control the level of risk it takes. This in most cases falls into two parts. One is the operating side: deciding the loan equivalents and programming the computers so that they can record the usage under lines accurately. This is relatively simple for products which all have the same loan equivalent – a line for UK government bonds traded on the London Stock Exchange, for instance. It is much harder for swaps and other products where not only can each swap have a different loan equivalent (as a percentage of notional), but the loan equivalent changes over time. Nevertheless, unless a bank can record usage accurately, it has no way of setting or keeping to lines and no serious idea as to what its actual exposure is.

Setting limits is an established part of traditional credit control, and few banks have any problem with setting them for, say, overdrafts. When the credit risk arises on a product which is not thought of by its exponents as credit, control becomes more difficult. People working in global custody or marketing swaps rarely understand or care about credit risk. Persuading them that they cannot deliver shares to a broker unless there is a line in place can be difficult. It will be doubly difficult if the person in the bank who can approve is on the other side of the world, does not understand the problem and is slow in responding to requests for a line.

It can also be difficult sometimes to decide what the line should be. If a client normally needs a line for $10 million but occasionally does a single transaction of $50 million, where do you set the line? If at $10 million you need a system to approve a large deal, without disrupting the client's business. If, on the other hand, you set the line at $50 million, you tie up an unnecessarily large amount of the company's credit and may prevent yourself doing other profitable business with the client.

These problems arise whatever the form of approval, but some of them are easier to deal with if you have a dedicated credit function for treasury products or clients.

Communicating about Problems

As discussed earlier in the chapter, traders or salespeople are often the first to see the warning signs of trouble for many treasury products and clients. It is vital, whatever the precise form of credit approval used, that they be trained to recognise and to communicate these signs.

The first is not difficult. Traders have a nose for risk; they can usually sniff credit risk out, even if they do not always know that is what they are doing. Credit people often find that their forex or bond dealers stopped dealing with a name months ago because they did not like something about it. Or traders in bonds or commercial paper may have noticed that an issuer was having to pay above the market. The best dealers take this as a warning sign, but less experienced dealers just see the extra profit. The system must require them to ask for a bigger line, if the warning is to come through.

A bank which can ensure that even an inexperienced dealer is promptly on the telephone to the relevant credit officer will, over the years, save itself millions. It is not an easy communication channel to establish, but it is worth its weight in gold.

Part II

Monitoring

7 Monitoring Each Loan

INTRODUCTORY COMMENT

The importance of monitoring cannot be overstated, but can easily be over-looked. It is at best unglamorous, since the best proof of success is that nothing untoward happens, making it hard to reward and to motivate people. 'The losses we did not make' is not an inspiring basis for a claim for higher salary or recognition, which is a pity because it often describes a major achievement.

Banks make such a small return on lending that they cannot afford risky decisions. Apart from occasional madness, few loans lose money solely because the original decision was bad. Even when the risk was higher than the bank thought, the chances of loss should be only a few per cent. And most borrowers, particularly the larger ones, take time to deteriorate, and show warning signs before the terminal stage. With smaller borrowers the whole process happens faster, so that tight monitoring is even more important to give the best chance of retrieving the situation.

This makes monitoring a major management challenge. As with the basic decision, monitoring is most important when it seems least necessary; that is, in good times. A strong economy can generate bad habits in companies, and conceal their impact from the casual eye. When the economy turns down, companies with weaknesses which good monitoring should spot suffer most and first. Monitoring has many arguments in favour, but the greatest is to ensure that problems do not come like a bolt from the blue.

THE STRUCTURE OF MONITORING

Some of the questions tie in closely with the similar questions in the first section. Some of the answers will be the same, but they need not be. It is possible to have one structure for approval and another for monitoring, though it is unusual.

91

Who Monitors?

The responsibility for monitoring should usually lie with the person closest
to the client. Where there is an account officer with lending authority, the
answer is easy: that is the person responsible for monitoring. Equally, when
the bank treats credit as a product, the product banker will be responsible.
Where the analyst or other credit specialist analyses and recommends, then
usually he will monitor too.

Responsibility does not mean doing all the work. Some aspects of monitoring are routine, and can be done by clerks or computers. The responsibility is then first to establish the requirement for routine monitoring,
and see that it is carried out; secondly, to review the results of the work,
and react to any questions.

However, not all monitoring is routine or mechanical. The account
officer's frequent contact with the company can provide one of the most
effective forms of monitoring. He can ask questions and assess the
answers; the officer wants to be seen as a solver of problems and trusted
adviser, which should encourage the company to talk openly; and almost
everything a company says has some credit significance, if listened to in
the right frame of mind.

A marketing banker may not listen with credit in mind. It is management's task to ensure that he does so, and reports back any items of interest
that are heard. One way of doing this is to require a memo on each sub-
stantive discussion. This should be put in a central credit file, electronic if
available, where other people interested in assessing the credit can see it.
This may provide an *aide-mémoire* for bankers themselves, or information
to others who can use it only if they know about it. Where the account
officer is pure marketer, with product specialists having much of the
contact with the client, they too should think of the credit aspects of the
information they gain, and record it.

The routine elements of monitoring – obtaining and setting up interim
and annual figures, checking compliance with the terms of any agreement,
valuing and replacing collateral, to give some examples – probably are
better done by a support function. Computers should be used to reduce the
drudgery and cost of this type of monitoring whenever possible. A bank
with many small clients may find it essential.

Management must provide systems and resources to carry out this
routine. The bank must ensure that the client knows and agrees what he
should provide, and that the bank's own support people know what to
require and how to handle it in each case. They must also understand
enough to move promptly when the monitoring shows something wrong.

This again is a key area for management, which will be discussed in more detail in Part IV. There is a tendency to ignore or play down the early warnings. Client managements may take any suggestion of problems as criticism, and marketing bankers may be reluctant to face them with the unpalatable facts. Moreover, the early warning signs shown by monitoring may be false alarms, or management may be able to explain them or may be aware of, and coping with them. It requires determination linked with tact to make the early move which is the chief benefit of monitoring. As discussed in Chapter 12, this move can be supportive, rather than panicky. Indeed, if the relationship and the bank's avowed intention to monitor are properly presented to the borrower, he may welcome the understanding shown by the bank and use it to help solve his problem.

But this will only happen if the banker is trained to see it this way; even then, he will often require senior or specialist help. This is particularly true where the banker is less credit-oriented and perhaps does not have lending authority.

In the traditional arrangement, this help would be more likely to come from a senior colleague than from a credit specialist. In all other arrangements it should come mainly from the specialist, but with full senior backing. Management must see that the credit culture encourages bankers to seek advice as soon as they have any doubts; and that the seniors or specialists also keep an independent eye out for trouble.

Specialist analysts also have a key role in monitoring. Its exact level depends on their numbers and the overall scope of their involvement. Where they rate all names on the book, they should update those ratings at least annually. To be cost-effective and credible, the scope of these reviews should vary widely. For a name rated A or better (using the terminology practised by Standard & Poors, the leading rating agency), with no sign of deterioration or major change, a one-line comment may be enough. Even such names may require a more detailed review every three or four years, but it is probably excessive to do it every year. Less well-rated names and those with signs of deterioration should be reviewed in more depth. Where there are fewer analysts, with less universal involvement, a more selective approach may concentrate on larger exposures to weaker names.

The criteria should set minimum requirements. The analyst should always be required to take an independent look at anything which arouses concern. Equally, if either the banker or credit specialist becomes concerned, he should be able to ask the analyst to look at it without any argument. And any analyst who for any reason is temporarily underworked should be encouraged to look at any borderline names or any which nobody has looked at recently.

In brief, the monitoring should clearly be the responsibility of a named function. Where possible this should be the account officer or 'credit as a product' officer, who should in any case gather information. The bank should provide support to handle the routine aspects, and analytical support as appropriate, which should also move independently.

What Should They Monitor?

There are broadly three aspects that banks should monitor: the company itself and its progress; the transaction; and for asset-based lending, the quality of the assets and of the company's control. A fourth, security, should be monitored only as a means of monitoring one of the others, but unfortunately is often the sole aspect monitored.

It is always true that if the borrower/counterparty survives in good health it will be able to meet its obligations. Conversely if it fails, banks face trouble; even if they recover all the exposure in the end, the cost in management time may be great.

Therefore it is always right to monitor the company. For manufacturing and commercial companies, this is fairly straightforward. It may well be all that the bank needs to monitor, apart from routine items, such as payment of interest on time.

For asset-based companies it is harder to be specific. The viability of the company remains important, but it may depend so much on the quality of the assets that the best way to monitor the company is to monitor the assets. This is clearly true of some property companies, for instance. But others, such as leasing companies depend on two main factors: the quality of assets, and the matching financing. Thus a leasing company with good asset controls can still fail if it mismatches the interest rates, and sometimes currencies, on its borrowing and assets. And a surprising number of companies in countries with less sophisticated financial systems fail to hedge.

Or it may be best to monitor the transaction or flow of transactions. This may be as well as monitoring the company, or may be the main way of doing so.

A five-year term loan with ratio covenants and amortisation may need monitoring in several ways. First, obviously, the amortisation payments; secondly, compliance with the ratios. If the ratios are well designed, however, they suggest more than mere compliance or non-compliance. Gradual erosion of a large initial safety margin on a ratio covenant gives the chance to talk to the company before there is an event of default. The bank may find that the company is alert and dealing with the problem credibly, which makes the decision as to how to react if the event occurs easier. Or the company may not be taking the risk of an event of default seriously, in which case the bank can try to change its mind while there is still time. Or, in the worst case, the bank may be better placed to act swiftly when the event of default occurs.

The other possibility is that the agreement may include a recapture clause, under which the borrower has to amortise faster if it performs better than forecast. This is most common in rescue situations, but also works when lending to cyclical companies, especially if the cycle is erratic and hard to predict in detail. Manufacturers dependent on the weather are good examples. Here the monitoring is almost automatic, but useful none the less.

Other types of transaction include commodity lending. If the bank finances shipments of cocoa from Ghana to UK chocolate-makers, for instance, it may be able to track the progress of each shipment, and ensure that the proceeds come first to pay the loan which made the whole transaction possible.

Then there are the treasury transactions discussed in the last chapter. The transaction may be the key item to monitor, but the monitoring may require the involvement of the trader or salesperson who understands it better than any credit specialist can. There may be some difficulty in persuading traders to cooperate; on the other hand, they will be monitoring the market aspects of the transaction anyway, so there is little extra burden. This comes back to the culture: if traders have been taught to be even mildly credit conscious, and to feel part of the bank not just of their unit, it becomes much easier. If they feel credit is a support not a barrier, better still. This is partly a management role, partly for the credit specialists themselves.

Finally, there is security. Often, in monitoring one of the other factors, particularly assets, the bank monitors aspects of the security. In other cases the reverse is true. In monitoring the quality of receivables or the value of plant and machinery, over which it has a charge, the bank partly monitors the company, since these are essential to its operations. The same is true when the bank monitors the value of commodities or securities over which it has a charge, but which are also a good indicator of the company's success.

Banks must also monitor purely mechanical aspects of security, such as the renewal of insurance and that ships, for instance, have their Lloyds inspection on time.

The danger of monitoring the security is to rely too much on the mechanical aspects, or even the narrow value, without focusing on their implications for the health of the company.

How to Monitor?

When we know who should monitor, and what they should monitor, we have some pointers on how to do it, but not the whole answer.

There are at least five areas where banks can monitor corporate borrowers, though not all apply in all cases.

1. The flow of business through the bank's account is particularly useful for smaller companies with a single operating account, but may have value elsewhere. The bank can see to whom the company makes payments; can notice if all its cheque start to be in round amounts (few bills are in round amounts); to whom and from whom it is receiving payments – particularly useful if the company is heavily dependent on a few large customers; what foreign exchange it is buying and selling; whether it is hedging exchange or interest rate risks, and so on. The bank can also see whether the usage of an overdraft ties in with the reasons given for needing it, and fluctuates as expected.

2. Local information. This is most important when lending to small, single location borrowers. If senior bank staff are part of local society, they will hear rumbles of something wrong sooner than more distant competitors. People laid off will be their customers, as will strikers; dissatisfied customers or suppliers not paid on time will be in the same business or social clubs, even when they are not themselves customers. And if a local company gets into trouble it will be natural for the bank to check what business it does with the bank's own clients, and how far they could be dragged down in its wake.

   An alert management will encourage its people to garner all these types of information wherever they can, and see that they reach the right parts of the bank.

3. Industry knowledge. Any industry analyst should keep the banker informed of developments which might affect the standing of each client. A large bank needs a formal mechanism for this.

   Where the bank has no industry specialist, then the account officer must become familiar with industry conditions. He should be able to find government statistics on the industry; locate specialist magazines; perhaps find a trade association; from these and other sources be aware, when appropriate, of what contracts are available and which his client is getting or missing. In other words generally understand the basic facts of the industry and the way in which they are developing and how that might help or hurt the client.

4. The company and its business. Some of this will come with the industry knowledge, but some needs to be more specific. What is the product line? What are its selling points? Is it gaining or losing market share and why in either case? What is the competition doing, and how successfully is it reacting? How important is innovation/new product introduction and how well is it doing that? How strong is management? How deep? What is the succession? And finally what is the impact of all this and other points particular to the company on the financial results.

5. The financial results and condition. This is an area where banks and many companies are often lax, and where probably most chances to catch a problem early are missed. It is vital to banks that their borrowers have good financial reporting systems and controls; for smaller companies, cash management is most critical although it is important for all. Equally, they need good budgets and projections as far forward as makes sense. This should be checked in making the early decision, because it also is a key point for monitoring. Banks should expect to get, routinely, interim management figures from borrowing clients. Depending on the size and strength of the borrower, interim can mean as frequently as monthly, or as infrequently as semi-annually. They can be in almost any form that the company uses in managing its business; they should however be compatible with the budgets or projections, so that the bank, and the borrower's management, can see how closely actual results compare with expectations. In some cases, these figures may need to be supplemented with short-term cash projections, a breakdown of inventory or receivables or other items of special interest.

Unfortunately, banks rarely ask for this type of information, and even more rarely insist if the borrower objects. One reason borrowers often object is that they do not have the information, and do not want to undertake the work of preparing it. Some may prepare it in a different form to that in which the bank wants it. If so, the bank should satisfy itself the borrower uses the information to manage the business effectively, and accept it. If the bank cannot satisfy itself, or if the borrower does not prepare figures in the first place, the bank should not lend. If, mistakenly, it lends without ensuring that the borrower prepares such information, the borrower is more likely to run into trouble, because it has no financial map. Neither the borrower nor the bank will quickly be able to tell how serious the difficulty is or how best to get out of it.

The need for a financial map should be obvious to all competent companies. All banks should recognise its vital nature and refuse to operate without one. Unfortunately that is not the case. The major domestic banks in each country should set the standard, which other banks could then follow, or perhaps improve on. In practice, this happens only in the United States, which makes it much harder for banks in other countries to insist. Nevertheless, the failure to insist on decent financial information, based on solid financial and cash controls, is a major contribution to the wave of bankruptcies and bad debts seen in many countries in the 1989–93 recessions.

Where the focus of monitoring is not the company, it becomes more a matter of the specifics of each case, and it is harder to lay down general guidelines. Nevertheless, there are some examples which make the more general point.

With self-liquidating loans to finance commodity movements, for instance, the bank will need to look at the mechanics of each transaction – the date and conditions of shipment, the correctness of bills of lading, etc. Most banks have well-experienced departments which can take care of this. Not all pay attention to the quality of the buyers, which is critical to the self-liquidating nature of the transaction. If the original buyer is unable to pay, the borrower may have to sell the commodity in the market. As one reason for the original buyer's failure may well be a market decline, this can cause a loss. Worse still, if the commodities have been released before payment, the whole value may be lost.

With shipping and property loans, the bank needs to review and monitor the charterers and tenants, since they are the source of the cash flow which makes the asset valuable.

With non-lending risks such as swaps, foreign exchange, bond underwriting, the bank will need to monitor the underlying market, to assess the prospective loss if the counterparty fails; where appropriate this may provide a trigger for enhancement such as mark to market or security.

FITTING IN WITH OTHER RESPONSIBILITIES

Monitoring is rarely given high priority, in part because people responsible often have other, more immediate if no more important, responsibilities. Also, monitoring is visibly important only when it is largely too late – i.e., when the borrower is already in difficulty. Most of the time, a borrower appears sound and the bank's main concentration is on marketing products, including but not limited to credit products. This is likely to be particularly true of the account officer.

These tendencies are often strengthened by a management attitude which gives the message: 'Your job is to market; your reward depends on revenue; we may say we expect you to monitor, but we will give no marks for it in assessing your performance.' It is then not surprising that monitoring gets little attention. Experience with bad debt write-offs in the recession suggests that many bank managements gave this message. And yet probably few if any of them realised that they were giving it; most would have been horrified if they had realised.

Management needs, therefore, to be clear in its own mind that monitoring is important, and then needs to give the message. This must be more than a statement. It must be backed up in other ways.

First, resources: analytical and other. The analytical needs no further discussion. The other resources consist of computer time and programs to help in the monitoring; and people. The people may be clerical or trainee analysts or some combination. They should, for instance, pursue the interim statements if they are late; spread them, probably with the help of a computer, when received; check them against any ratio covenants, and advise of default or warning of imminent default. Where matters of security or asset value are involved, there may be experts who can help. Treasury people who understand the development of risks in their product should also be willing and able to discuss the meaning of market developments for the risk.

Secondly, remuneration. Management should make it clear to those with primary responsibility for monitoring that the quality of their work in this area will affect their remuneration and promotion prospects. A vague statement to this effect is not enough. There must be criteria. The state of the credit files and the quality of call memoranda might be examples. Or the appraisal process might include, and be seen to take seriously, comments from relevant credit specialists who have to rely on the quality of monitoring material to help them do their job.

Thirdly, time and priorities. A work-load which precludes spending much time on monitoring, or where people get pulled off monitoring tasks all the time, does not add to the credibility.

Fourthly, training. Account officers in particular, but all marketing and product officers who have regular contact with the client, must be trained to look for and record relevant credit information. This means among other things recognising that credit and marketing are linked.

Credit, Monitoring, Marketing

One reason why credit tends to receive low priority is that many bankers see it as conflicting with marketing, when the reverse is true. Marketing gives the best source of credit information, at the original decision and thereafter. Equally, good understanding of the company's business and credit risk is a prime marketing tool, while many individual items of credit information are valuable marketing leads, and much marketing information is also useful in monitoring the credit.

Take the overall argument first. A banker who shows an informed interest in the company's business, the challenges it faces and the measures it proposes to meet them, flatters management. A bank which uses that knowledge to support clients when they are in trouble develops the most reassuring possible reputation. Standing by a client in difficulty, or lending when other banks will not, cements a relationship more than any other single action. And while many companies think they have little to learn from their bankers, the better ones recognise the value of a well-informed banker.

Conversely, a client who values the bank's advice for other reasons will, in seeking that advice, tell the bank much which is relevant to its credit judgement. Moreover, if he values the bank's advice, he will be more likely to listen to it. This can be crucial if the information leads the bank to believe the company faces threats which management has not recognised; or has underestimated.

A particular subset of the perception of credit as opposed to marketing arises in a situation mentioned earlier in the chapter. The monitoring shows a potential problem, but the bank is not at first clear how serious it is. The temptation is therefore to do nothing; the fear of damaging the relationship is greater than the fear of unnecessary loss. Management must be aware of this temptation and inculcate the reverse view. The bank must establish a relationship where the borrower expects and welcomes its probes, and regards them as a safety net. The client who says 'I love Bank X: every time I see them they have questions I had never thought of' is rare, but does exist. Bankers who can persuade most of their clients to take a similar, if less enthusiastic stance, are worth their weight in gold. The credit specialist who can persuade other bankers that now, not later, is the time to probe the problem is also valuable. And the bank management which encourages both approaches successfully will keep its bad debt record better than average.

There are also numerous products where credit and marketing reinforce each other, if allowed to. To give only a few examples:

- In advising on an acquisition, the bank must ensure a capital structure which leaves the company creditworthy. Often the purchaser needs to borrow some or all of the acquisition cost.

- Other types of advisory business may be more directly related to credit information. A debt capacity study, or advice on approaching the rating agencies for a public rating, requires the bank to have sound credit skills, but also the company to provide it with detailed information on its plans as well as latest finances.

The interreaction between swaps and marketing is only one of the examples we will discuss in Chapter 16.

The aim here is to illustrate the point, not give a catalogue. Part of the point is that it is always worthwhile to improve the quality of your credit; to be paid for doing so is best of all.

JUSTIFYING THE COST

There are in any situation two requirements for justifying cost, both of which must be met. One is to show that the cost is as low as it can reasonably be and still achieve the objective; the other is to show that the gains, whether in revenue or avoidance of other costs/losses/risks leave a worthwhile net gain.

The cost of monitoring can be kept low in several ways. One is the combination of marketing and monitoring discussed above. If information gained in marketing contacts is used for credit monitoring, the extra cost of obtaining it is almost nil. For other types, the cost can best be reduced by a systematic approach, which ensures that each task is performed at the lowest level capable of doing it. There are standard systems for following up the requirement for interim figures. Administrative assistants can operate them, calling on the banker for help if the client does not cooperate; if the banker has sold the requirement effectively, however, this should rarely be a problem. Again, a standard approach to spreading the figures as received, preferably computerised to calculate the ratios easily, saves time and requires relatively low-level operators, as does compliance checking of ratio covenants in loan agreements. Moreover, if the volume is great enough to have one person or a small team doing nothing else, they can develop a level of skill that an experienced banker would be hard put to match. But all this requires management to recognise the need for a standardised approach and to allocate the resource, and the training, to make it work.

The main benefit is lower bad debts. It is impossible to put a figure on this, at least without detailed research into actual bad debts and those which might have gone bad but did not. We can, however, illustrate the order of magnitude. The British clearing banks have written off nearly £10 billion in the last few years; American banks have written off even more; both can expect further write-offs in 1993 and 1994; bad debts at the Japanese banks are large and probably underestimated; European banks face heavy losses in 1993–95 – French and Italian banks in particular. If better monitoring could have avoided even 10 per cent of these losses, the saving would be several billion dollars, far more than any conceivable cost. Even if we only attribute 10 per cent of the difference between the best and worst banks to monitoring, the cost looks minuscule.

This is before you allow for the more modest gains from using monitoring to back up your marketing.

8 Monitoring the Portfolio

THE OVERALL APPROACH

The complexity of monitoring the portfolio varies widely with the nature of the bank. For a small private bank, with one office and all the decisions taken by the board, it is simple; for a major international bank with widespread domestic retail operations, and hundreds of overseas branches, it requires formal procedures and bureaucracy. But as with the decision and individual monitoring, it also requires a credit culture which takes the whole subject seriously, and fits it within the bank's overall strategy.

Whatever the precise format, there are at least four different aspects all banks need to monitor. They are listed below.

- The overall quality of the portfolio, and the direction of any changes in it.

- Concentration of risk, whether by company, industry, country, region, dependency on a particular product or any other feature – this includes the setting of country limits.

- The monitoring of identified and potential problems. Much of this comes under damage limitation and will be discussed there. Apart from individual problems, however, management should always be monitoring the level and intensity of total problems in the portfolio.

- The quality of the bank's overall decision-making and monitoring, and the same in each branch. To monitor the portfolio, a bank must also monitor itself.

THE OVERALL QUALITY OF THE PORTFOLIO

Unless a bank monitors the overall quality of its portfolio, it cannot know whether its procedures are working; more importantly, it cannot foresee and avoid a catastrophe as the portfolio deteriorates. The first decision a bank needs to make is whether to monitor centrally, or whether to have regional, local or even branch monitoring, and if the latter, how the centre will be sure the monitoring is adequate.

103

Again, the best way of doing this depends on the nature of the bank. A small bank, with a central credit committee needs very little formal procedure. The committee makes all the decisions, renews all facilities as they fall due, and in effect monitors the portfolio all the time. A purely domestic bank, with only a few branches, can do the same; if it delegates any significant authority to the branches it may need to use some of the techniques discussed below, but the problem is relatively simple. A domestic bank with several hundred or even thousand branches, many of which do a mainly retail business, but all of which have some corporate business, and some of which handle mainly corporate clients, is more complex. Throw in an international branch network, and you have a major challenge. To meet this challenge requires some uniformity in the assessment of credit standards.

Internal Rating Systems

A standard approach to rating companies provides a key tool for monitoring. It has other uses, such as pricing, but we are concerned with its use in monitoring here. If a bank decides to use internal ratings, there are several questions as to how best to do it.

Establishing consistent standards

To have full value, ratings should be consistent. This is relatively simple in a small domestic operation, but becomes harder the more branches there are, and with an international operation. In a small country, the best company will seem AAA, and the rest scale down from there. Put that same AAA company in a larger country, and it may struggle to be A. Thus banks cannot allow analysts to say 'Company X is AA by Country Y standards', with no valid comparison between Country Y standards and other countries.

One way to overcome this is to have all ratings provided by one body, which is trained to the same standard. This also has the advantage of independence, and is discussed below under the subheading 'Who sets the ratings?'

Another is to have a standard format. The rating can assume, for instance, that the bank is making a seven-year unsecured term loan to the borrower being rated. There is no (or stated) amortisation; no (or stated minimal) covenants and nothing else unusual about the facility. This is probably a crucial assumption to any rating of the company, but is not enough on its own. See further under 'What to rate'.

A third is to have clear definitions for each rating, making it clear the standards are absolute, not relative.

A fourth is to use a group of ratios to indicate rating levels. This requires care. First, companies and capital structures, as well as countries, vary widely. They thus need different combinations to give the best guide to financial strength. Blindly following one set for all types of company can lead to distorted views. Secondly, one still needs judgement to offset different strengths and weaknesses even in similar companies. Company A, with strong cash flow cover but high leverage may be stronger or weaker than Company B with lower leverage but poorer cash flow cover. Thirdly, ratios are never the only basis for judging a credit rating, and only rarely the best. Having said which, a standard set at least makes the rate setter justify any divergence from the rating it suggests.

Some banks, wrongly, use the quality of the collateral as a factor in rating. Some have a detailed score based on the handling of all accounts.

What to rate

The bank needs a clear view as to what it is rating. Is it a company rating, regardless of the particular facility? Or is it a rating of the particular facility? Or both, and if so how do you distinguish between the two?

Again, should banks rate subsidiaries and state-owned companies on a stand-alone basis, or in light of the ownership and any support?

The arguments in favour of a company rating are that banks lend to companies, not to facilities. The risk of lending short term, or secured, to a company may be less than lending long-term unsecured to the same company. But the risk of lending to B rated companies is greater than any exposure to AAA rated companies. Moreover, any facility rating is affected by the company rating. In effect, it is a company rating adjusted to take account of the facility.

This is one reason for suggesting that both be used. It also allows different people to express a view from different angles. Take the standard suggested above (seven-year unsecured bullet, with no unusual covenants). It is a fair standard for most manufacturing and commercial companies. However, many borrow for shorter periods or secured or for a self-liquidating transaction, or in some other way less risky than the standard. It is therefore reasonable to say 'The company rating is BBB, but the facility rating for this seasonal overdraft is A.' Or, less likely but quite possible 'Company rating BBB, facility rating for this 10-year bullet BB.'

In neither case can you give a facility rating without knowing the company rating.

There are also borrowers who do not fit the company rating template. Banks rarely lend to shipping or property companies unsecured, for instance; or to stock or commodity brokers medium term. Either type would get a low rating if the bank used only one template, and no facility ratings. To use different templates for different types of borrower undermines consistency. It is sensible to say, however, that shipping company A has a company rating of B, or even CCC, but the seven-year amortising facility secured by ship mortgages warrants a facility rating of BBB. Similarly that broker Z has a company rating of B, but a facility rating for DVP settlements of A.

This approach also fits well in rating subsidiaries. The company rating should stand alone, with any support, implicit or explicit reflected only in the facility rating. A company rating B, with a facility rating BBB, makes it clear how much the bank needs the parent support, and what it expects from it. If, for instance, the BBB facility rating is the parent's own rating, but the bank has only a vague statement that the parent is interested in the subsidiary's well-being, the rating is probably too high. The same facility and company rating, and a parent rated A and giving a strong written keepwell is more easily justified. A simple BBB company rating 'taking into account ownership' does not highlight the differences.

Who should rate?

Where there is an independent analytical function, its members should set the company rating. There should, of course, be some supervision from senior analysts, and some discussion with the account officer, in case the analyst has missed any critical points. It must be clear, however, that the banker can correct facts, and can even suggest a different interpretation. He cannot dispute the rating given after the discussion or, most important of all, pressure the analyst to change the rating. To do so should risk a severe downgrading in salary and promotion prospects, and if repeated, be grounds for dismissal. This may sound excessive; it is not. The independence of analysts generally, and of the rating process in particular, is crucial to the quality of a loan portfolio. Its existence does not guarantee success, but its absence virtually guarantees failure. The treatment of an analyst who gives in to pressure should be almost as severe.

Given the above, bankers can sensibly set facility ratings. The time and place to do this is probably when approving or renewing the facility. Where more than one banker signs, they should all give a facility rating. There should be some procedure for reconciling more than the normal variations in professional judgement.

Where there is no specialist analytical function, or where it cannot rate everything, there are two alternatives. One is to allow the officers approving, or renewing, the facility to set the rating. If there is any discrepancy, banks will need a way of choosing between the ratings. There are broadly three approaches: to use the lowest rating given; to give priority to the rating of the senior, or perhaps of the credit specialist. Or there can be a mechanism for settling disputes. These can be combined: for example, the senior sets the rating unless the rating is more than one notch apart from others in which case the settlement mechanism applies.

The second is to have a rating committee. This can be central or regional, or can apply within each branch; in which case the bank may need a review mechanism to ensure uniform standards. The membership depends on the organisation of the bank or branch. It should include the senior analyst, and the senior credit specialist; probably the senior manager in a branch or region, and the Chairman of the Credit Policy Committee in Head Office. Otherwise it should represent a combination of knowledge and interest, at a senior level, to take a balanced rather than purely departmental view. Membership of such a committee should be recognised internally so as to encourage people to want to serve; and partisanship should be a reason for removal from the committee.

What ratings to use?

The format for ratings depends on the type of portfolio. One can follow the Standard & Poors (AAA down to B) type of rating, for a wholesale bank with a large company clientele, although perhaps with one modification. Banks need to add CCC to C to the S&P ratings to allow them to cover various levels of troubled borrower. Then B is the rating for the lowest level of still acceptable credit, CCC the least serious of troubled credits, and C a write-off.

For banks with a wider ranging portfolio, these standards may be too tight, S&P and Moody's (the other leading rating agency) rate only companies which can raise debt on the security markets; access to these markets implies a size which many bank borrowers lack. To squeeze all bank borrowers into this small range loses some of the value of the rating system. An extension to DDD or even EEE as the troubled level is one solution. Another is to use numbers, perhaps from one to twenty. A third is to use some combination of numbers and letters to indicate different aspects. A to F might relate purely to ratio measurements, and one to nine to size. Thus A1 would be a billion-dollar company with strong ratios, D1 a similar sized company with weaker ratios, D4 a weak $50 million company, and so on. Or there could be a third category, for more subjective matters, such as management, market leadership, innovation, etc. The range might then be from A1A through D5C to F9F.

The exact format is not critical, provided it fits the portfolio, and everybody in the bank understands it.

Using ratings to monitor the portfolio

With a computer record, it becomes easy to keep track of the average rating of the portfolio; of the percentage of each level in the total, and of trends in these and other cases. This can be looked at in isolation, or in relation to various policies. In either case, a deterioration in the average rating or an increase in the weaker levels requires investigation and perhaps action.

Central, regional and local managements can also use the ratings to review given parts of the portfolio. The branch manager in France may want to monitor his portfolio; or the European credit controller may wish to review each branch and the whole region, while Head Office may wish to be sure that there is no one branch or region doing substantially worse than the rest.

Other Ways of Monitoring the Overall Portfolio

Lacking reliable ratings, it is hard to avoid some loss of overall control. The various parts of the portfolio cannot be accurately compared with each other, or with the past. Monitoring then has to concentrate on achieving minimum standards in various units, which follow the procedures in spirit as well as in letter. But since the best procedures rely on the judgement of those following them, this type of monitoring is more subjective.

There are various ways of monitoring the portfolio, many of them variants of the same theme. It could be called 'loan audit' or 'inspection' or some other name. But all involve sending people in from outside the unit concerned to review a selection of borrowers. The timing of this varies, but usually will be more frequent with weaker units. The auditors or inspectors may be permanent, or may be experienced bankers rotating through the role, to gain a different viewpoint and to ensure that they apply commercial criteria to the review.

Whether supplemented by outside examiners (auditors or regulators) or not, such monitoring has a genuine but limited value. It tends to focus on procedures rather than underlying quality, and on existing problems rather than potential ones. Certainly it helps to catch the gross failures before they become even grosser; but it will rarely highlight the apparently minor weakness before it becomes critical.

The only way to catch those is with an alert and involved credit specialist or group of them, either in the branch or in a regional headquarters. They are involved in the day-to-day decision-taking; they see whether the procedures are being followed at all, and if so whether by rote or with conviction; they know who takes credit seriously, who regards it as an obstacle to be surmounted and who simply does not understand it. Unfortunately, they are on the firing line. If they do a good job, this includes monitoring successfully; it may also involve inter-office politics, and good credit judgement does not guarantee political skill. So even the best monitors need to be monitored.

DIFFERENT FORMS OF CONCENTRATION

The various forms of concentration all carry the same basic risk, that a statistically small probability of loss is turned into a large actual loss, because it affects a high volume of loans. Banks need systems to make sure that such conglomerations never undermine their standing; and to recognise when an acceptable concentration becomes less so because the probability of loss has increased.

Individual Borrowers

This should include all groups of related companies. If a bank lends to Company AAA, it needs also to know its exposure to all its subsidiaries, before it knows whether AAA's failure would break the bank. If it would, the bank should probably cut back, however unlikely AAA may be to fail.

But some companies are more likely to fail; some which seemed unlikely may become more so. Concentration is a serious risk at a lower level for weak than for strong names. Banks need systems to track exposures, and to highlight large exposures on request. In an ideal world, computer lights would flash as exposure passed varying levels, with the light flashing earlier for smaller and weaker companies. In the real world, banks can use the computer to answer questions, but not yet to ask them. Nevertheless, all banks above a minimal size should have computer systems to track total exposure, and ability to call up information on large exposures which start to look vulnerable.

Some of this can be done by a 'large exposure review', where at least annually an officer with the highest lending authority reviews all names *with exposure above, say,* $100 million (less for any except the largest banks).

Other ways may include a rolling review, perhaps quarterly, of all names in the portfolio with exposure below $100 million, but which are not caught in the reviews of weaker names. This should highlight names where there are any signs of weakness, even if far from the crisis level, or where exposure is rising sharply. There need be nothing wrong in the latter case. It may be merely a sign of good marketing, but the higher exposure may change the nature of the risk and needs to be kept under review.

Whatever the precise mechanism, there should be clear rules as to the maximum exposure the bank can take on any one group in any circumstances; and this maximum reduces as the credit rating moves down the scale. In some countries the first part may be imposed by law (legal limits in the United States) or by the regulators (Bank of England 10/25 per cent rules). These limits, which correctly relate to the bank's capital, are rarely either precise or tight enough. They do not distinguish between the limit to a strong credit and that to a weak credit (except possibly by allowing higher limits to certain political entities which may be good credits, but need not be). Banks should therefore usually take the legal or regulatory limits as the extreme and aim at something less.

Industry Concentration

Banks can also concentrate too much risk in one industry. If a bank has exposure to several companies in the same industry, then the combined exposure may hurt it, even though the exposure to any one company may not be enough to do so. Some companies will survive the worst industry conditions. However, the risk of two, three, ten or twenty companies failing for the same reason, owing the bank cumulatively crippling amounts, is one no bank should run. The losses taken by numerous banks in many countries on property loans make the point, as do earlier losses on shipping, computer leasing, bowling alleys and other fads.

There are two broad ways to monitor industry risk. Banks can identify industries known to be high risk and volatile, and control the total exposure. Again, property is an obvious example. As well as criteria on the type of property loan a bank will make, the nature and level of security, banks need to set a limit on total exposure to property. This must be controlled centrally – although some part of the limit may be allocated to a region and suballocated within that region.

The central point can then compare the various proposals, and make sure that within its limit the bank takes the better proposals – better credits, or better earners, preferably both.

However, the obviously risky industries are not the only ones which can cause concentrated loss. Two other types can, and the second approach to monitoring industry limits has to deal with these.

One is the industry which grows very fast, and looks as if it will keep growing indefinitely. Banks often lend too much money to weak companies; the growth in supply eventually outstrips demand, pushing weaker companies to the wall. If demand actually falls, even some stronger companies may fail. If demand continues to grow some survive and even flourish, once the excess supply has been shaken out. Banks which pile in too fast may lend to the weak companies, or may lose because even the better companies do not all survive.

Apart from being generally wary of fashionable – and thus fickle – industries, banks should monitor exposure to each industry and take notice if it starts to rise rapidly in any case. There may be a sound explanation for the high exposure, but unless the bank is very sure that the industry is low risk, it should limit exposure to this industry just as it does to the known high-risk industry.

Then there are the 'mature' industries that start to decline. Often these are fairly concentrated, so that the bank has a few, individually quite large exposures. Perhaps one loss on its own would be bearable, if painful, but two? Three? Automotive manufacture, and its leading component industries such as tyres and batteries, are topical examples. Here the bank needs to recognise its over-exposure early and cut back wherever it can. This may be hard, since it is likely that the borrowers are large, and formerly top quality credits. Sheer inertia may mean that they and the bank's marketers still think they are top quality. Moreover, cars, tyres and batteries will be around for some time, and it is very hard to tell which of these companies will survive. All banks can know is that some of them will not. If a bank has large exposure to all, does it cut back a little from each, or try to escape from the losers altogether?

A chapter on monitoring cannot answer these questions, if indeed they are answerable. However, without monitoring, the bank will never ask the questions, let alone answer them.

To monitor industry concentration, for any but the smallest bank, requires a computer system which records the industry of each borrower.

Some countries have Standard Industrial Codes (SIC) which makes it easier; failing that, the bank will need to develop its own categories.

Monitoring Types of Loan

Some types of loan carry specific risks. They are not always greater than others, though some are, but the concentration is dangerous if they do go wrong.

The most obvious recent example is the leveraged buy-out (LBO) and its variations, generically known as highly leveraged transactions (HLT). Some banks recognised the inherent risks early, and set and monitored a limit. Some even required specialist approval in view of their risk and complexity. These banks sometimes looked a little sleepy when LBOs were all the rage. But although they took some losses when the LBOs turned sour they were not overwhelmed. Project lending is the other main example.

Monitoring Country Risk

The special risks of lending in a country are described in Chapter 3 of my book, *Lending in International Commercial Banking*, Second edition (Macmillan, 1988). Exposure defined as 'X country risk' need not depend wholly or mainly on the credit of the country; indeed the extent to which it does varies quite widely. It is always clear, however, that a British borrower incurs a mixture of economic, currency, political, governmental and legal risks which is different to the mix of risks for any other nationality of borrower. Banks need to take account of this, but also to monitor the type of lending in relation to the risks. The risk of lending to British companies under the Labour Government of the 1970s related much more to government failure or interference; under the early Thatcher government, and again in the early Major years, the risk was that companies would fail because of the recession. Both risks were serious, but the type of borrower they most affected, and the protective measures a bank could take, were different.

Banks therefore need to set country limits, and have a method of recording them. They also need to define what the limit should cover. If a borrower is British, but its parent is French, is that British or French country risk? Does it change depending on whether there is a guarantee? A keep-well? Security? And so on.

Banks should monitor different types of country exposure, too. Trade-related short-term exposure may be less risky than ten-year term loans. Marketable exposure, whether bonds quoted on a stock exchange or the

Eurobond market; swaps or options where there is an active, if less well-organised, market may be less risky than bank loans, though even these are developing a market. Often lending to the government or a government agency is less risky than to the private sector, though the opposite may be true if the private sector has offshore earning assets. Finally, with a branch in the country, local currency lending avoids some of the risks of lending foreign currency.

Each bank must decide which of these aspects it wants to monitor, and this view may change over time as its business with a country develops, or the country does.

MONITORING THE LEVEL OF PROBLEM LOANS

Banks monitor individual problem loans, as described earlier, and in more detail in the later section on damage limitation. But they also should monitor the overall level of actual and developing problems. Again the smallest banks probably do not need formal procedures. If management is alert, it will not need them; if not, they probably will not help.

Watch List

For banks with widespread lending authority or business, however, a formal system and regular review are essential. These should probably start with what may be called the Watch List, but may have its own name within each bank. This should cover all names which have deteriorated to a level where there is concern, even if not yet to the critical stage. It should be simple to put the name on the list – a brief memo from almost any level involved – but harder to take it off. It is important that putting a name on this list be seen as a sign of prudence and foresight, not an admission of bad lending.

Some banks may wish to enforce special procedures for such names – no new exposure without special authority, or a quarterly review of all uncommitted facilities, perhaps. If the bank is confident in its overall procedures this should not be necessary; the fact of putting the name on the list shows the banker is aware of the need for caution, after all. This is one reason for allowing juniors to put names on the list, indeed encouraging them do so, rather than a senior putting it on without consultation.

Where possible, it is best to have one list, controlled from the centre. With large banks with numerous branches, and particularly many small company borrowers, this may not be practical. In this case, branch or regional lists may be necessary for smaller borrowers, with only larger amounts on the central list. The branch or region should then review the detailed names for any signs of concentration of risk, or for similarities which give warning of a failure in control which could lead to further losses. The same should apply centrally.

Charge-off Report

Each bank should also have a regular process for provisioning names. The process depends on several features which are specific to different countries, and will be discussed under Damage Limitation. Whatever the process, it is often done as infrequently as annually, but should be done, for a large bank with many branches, quarterly.

The charge-off process consists first of picking those names for review. This need not be all the names on the Watch List, but the list certainly makes a good starting point. Some names where the situation is static may not need such frequent review, but should perhaps be considered semiannually or even annually. Not every name reviewed should need a provision; indeed, part of the purpose is to give senior management a view of the size and severity of cases which do not yet require a specific provision, but may do so in the future.

The central Charge-Off Committee should, where possible, review all names. Where the size of the bank makes this impractical, then it should review the larger names, and a branch or regional committee review the smaller ones. The lower level committees should report in some detail on the outcome of their main decisions.

Even where the final review is central, local committees should review and recommend. It is vital to involve the branches in the process and make sure they understand what the provisioning means, why the committee has decided on it, or against it, and what the unit should be doing about it.

9 Monitoring Treasury Products

DEFINITION

Treasury products in this chapter include all products sold to the client by traders or salespeople, rather than bankers. They thus exclude normal bank lending and related products, and products such as M&A, debt underwriting, debt capacity studies, which are advisory.

They include trading in debt and other securities, as well as foreign exchange; all settlement exposures; swaps, caps, collars and all derivatives, as well as other hedging products, such as options, futures, forward rate agreements (FRAs), and new products derived from, or which compete with, any of these. They include overdrafts or other traditional exposures which arise solely in connection with these products. Finally, they include exposure a bank takes initially on behalf of the client, but where the exposure may come back to the bank if it has been negligent in any way, or if its client fails.

ESTABLISHING A BASIS FOR COMPARISON

The Concept of Exposure vs Risk

To compare the exposure on a swap or security settlement with that on a loan requires a clear view of the underlying concept.

In traditional lending, exposure is the asset that appears on the balance sheet — or would if facilities were fully used, since the borrower can draw on unused facilities at his option, creating an asset at a moment's notice.

Exposure is thus the amount at risk if the borrower fails. It is rare to lose the whole of a loan even to a bankrupt borrower, but the eventual loss is likely to be a percentage of the exposure.

Exposure then is objective and non-judgemental; it defines the quantity, but says nothing about the quality of the asset, or of the risk; a $10 million loan is $10 million exposure, whether the borrower is rated AAA or CCC. The AAA risk is very low, the CCC one quite high. But both the rating and the chance of loss are matters of judgement, not fact; the size of the loan is a matter of fact.

This simple approach does not work for most treasury products. Take an interest rate swap as an example: a bank agrees to receive fixed rate interest at 10 per cent per annum for five years and in return pay six month LIBOR (London Interbank Offered Rate). If LIBOR goes to five per cent and stays there, the bank, on this swap in isolation, makes a five per cent per annum profit, as long as the counterparty makes the fixed payments on time. If it fails to pay, the profit the bank foregoes measures its credit loss. Or, more often, the cost of replacing that contract is the loss, but in turn reflects the profit expectation.

From Exposure to Loan Equivalents

When a bank enters a swap it does not know what interest rates will be if the counterparty fails, or, therefore, the cost of replacing it. Indeed if LIBOR had risen above 10 per cent instead of falling below it, the bank would theoretically gain from the counterparty's failure. There is therefore no exact equivalent of exposure in the sense described above. And yet, banks and others need a way of comparing the exposure, not just the risk, on these products. This has led to the development of what this book will call loan equivalents; some regulators call them risk equivalents.

Continuing the example, there are several ways to reach a loan equivalent. The simplest, but arbitrary and unlikely to be accurate, is to allocate a percentage of notional value for each year of its life. If this were five per cent, the initial loan equivalent would be 25 per cent of notional value, declining over the life of the swap.

Other ways revolve around the likely pattern of interest rates over the life of the swap. This can be a simplistic assumption – rates double or halve in the first three years, then flatten out, for example – or a more complex pattern, based on a study of historical movements or mathematical assumptions. Whatever the exact pattern, there is likely to be a bell-shaped curve. On Day 1, there will be no theoretical exposure, since rates will not have moved, so that the contract can be replaced at no cost. As time passes, three things happen: the rates can move further from the original levels; the remaining time to run reduces; and payments of interest reduce the remaining amount due. At some stage, the factors pushing the possible mark to market up become weaker than the ones pushing it down, giving a maximum loan equivalent. But this is only the maximum on the assumptions used and no assumption can be guaranteed correct. In many cases the maximum theoretical rate movement is infinity. The assumption should therefore provide the highest sensible probability, without going to ridiculous extremes. A 95% probability sounds good to many traders.

This highlights one of the problems with this whole approach, necessary though it is. A 95% probability sounds high, but allows a 5% chance that the loss is greater. To a credit specialist, a 5% probability of loss is very high. A 5% probability of very high loss indeed is totally unacceptable. Which brings us back to the comments earlier about the importance of the counterparty's health. The 5% does not refer to the risk of the counterparty's failure, but rather to the risk that the counterparty will fail when the cost will be greater than the loan equivalent suggests. In this context, the risk is not 5%, but 5% of the risk that the counterparty may fail, say 5% of 2% or 0.1%. Or at least, so a trader might argue.

A credit specialist would answer this in two ways. One is Murphy's law, backed up by experience. Companies do not go bust for one reason only, even though one may predominate. They fail because of a whole series of disasters; this may be bad luck or bad management or both, but it is consistent. If a company has other problems, a reduction in interest rates might allow it to survive. If it loses the benefit of that reduction because it has swapped into fixed rate, that may break the camel's back. Or it may indicate wider misjudgments about the economy which together ensure disaster. So that although the risk of exceptional loss is not as high as 5%, it is good deal higher than the 0.1% suggested above. And the limited experience of swap defaults suggests that they mostly occur when the mark to market loss is above the theoretical peak loan equivalent.

The other answer is that it is dangerous to say the loan equivalent is $10 million if, however much against the odds it may be, some people are going to lose $15 million, $20 million or even more.

This is not to argue against loan equivalents, but more to warn that they are not perfect. While the concept of exposure is of a known worst outcome – the loss of the whole loan – a loan equivalent can never be that. And while traders and mathematicians may get carried away by portfolio theory or mathematical elegance, credit specialists know that risk strikes in individual cases, and is never elegant. We must use the concept of loan equivalent, but never allow ourselves to forget its imperfections.

The imperfections are probably worst in swaps because they can be more complex and longer term than most treasury products. The same caveats apply to the loan equivalents on, say, settlement risk, but the variation is less. The risk on settling Eurobonds DVP is that between the time the bank deals and the time it realises that its counterparty is not going to complete the deal, the price of the bond moves. It therefore has to buy at a higher price, or sell at a lower one, and loses the amount of movement. It is possible, given knowledge of the settlement process, and historical data on the price movements, to calculate in each case the maximum movement in price that it is reasonable to expect; for a liquid bond and a short settlement period as little as one or two per cent. If the bond is less liquid, or the settlement period longer, it may rise to perhaps five per cent; for corporate bonds or equities it may go even higher. Given DVP, settlement risk is always likely to be a small percentage of the face value. Even here the risk remains that a bond price which has never moved more than 2% in three days suddenly moves 5% in one day; and that the factors which cause it to do so also cause other losses to government bond dealers who then fail to take delivery.

Where settlement is not DVP, the loan equivalent may be more than the face value of the bond. The loss of DVP means that it is possible to pay for the bond and not receive it or deliver if and not be paid. This costs the whole value of the bond, or payment. In addition, the bank may have to buy a replacement bond, with the risk that the price has risen. The exposure in this respect is the same in any non-DVP settlement. The risk of actual loss will vary quite widely depending on the exact settlement procedure, and the time between delivering securities or payment, and the receipt of the other side of the deal.

There are many examples of loan equivalents. For instance, a Forward Rate Agreement (FRA) requires the parties to agree a rate for the future, say that three-month LIBOR two months from now will be 10%. If the actual rate differs, one party pays the other on the strike date. The exact amount depends on three factors: the notional principal, the period and the strike rate. In this case the period is three months, the strike rate 10%; notional principal £100 million. Then if the actual rate two months from now is 12% the cost to the loser is:

$$£100,000,000 \times 0.002 \times 0.25 = £50,000.$$

If the bank is the winner and the counterparty fails, the bank has a credit loss of £50,000.

Again the bank does not know initially that rates will move 2% in its favour. To calculate a loan equivalent it needs historical data about the volatility of three-month interest rates over a two-month period; or a basis for assumptions about the future which is more reliable or more conservative than historical data. However it reaches the conclusions, if the maximum movement expected (with 95% certainty?) is 2%, the exposure is £50,000. This would change if the time to the strike date changed, or the interest period.

This book is not written by a trader or rocket scientist. The more mathematical aspects of calculating loan equivalents for the wide variety of possible products is therefore beyond its scope. The need to understand the way in which the risk arises, and the kind of event that can turn risk into loss is, however, critical. It is important to understand both the exposure, and the risk; both what can happen and how likely it is to do so and why. This applies not only to the products mentioned, but to all; derivatives, options, futures and others. In each case, the credit specialist can trace the transaction and determine where credit risk arises.

All of this is important in making the original decision, and was touched on in earlier chapters for that reason. It is particularly important in monitoring, partly because in so many treasury products, the individual risk is small, but counterparties do a continuous stream of transactions, so that there is a conglomeration of risks.

SETTING LIMITS AND KEEPING WITHIN THEM

The Mechanics

Without loan equivalents banks cannot set limits that have any real meaning; or at least not an overall limit which they can trust or allocate between the various products without breaching the total.

Moreover, there must be a way the trader can know before trading whether he is within the line. This means either having a whole series of separate lines, in effect, one for each trader, or combining the usage of different products under the same line. The former will tend to balloon the exposure, since each trader will want a line for his maximum likely usage, used only occasionally. The latter, while ideal, is difficult to manage in a multibranch bank. Perhaps we will reach the stage where all products can be fed into one line and the results accessed worldwide; every trader in every product will be able to tell what the line is, the usage, how much the proposed deal will add to usage, and whether he can deal. The credit specialist responsible will also know exactly how the usage is moving, and the profile of future run-offs if no further deals are done. If necessary, he can cut the line down to the outstandings, and keep cutting as they run off, so that no dealer has any excuse for dealing with the client if the bank wishes to eliminate its exposure.

There is some doubt as to whether that is achievable or desirable. Given that risk is only one part of the risk reward relationship, all prod-

ucts are not equally entitled to use the available credit exposure. The
bank may allocate a larger part of the total to products with a high
return on equity.

A system which allowed each product or group of similar products to
have one line worldwide, would give maximum control. Dealers could
check outstandings and input deals in real time. Failing that, lines
which cover the largest number of dealers and products within a branch
or region provide some control without ballooning the exposure too
much.

The People

Even with computerised line control, the dealers must still respect the
limits. This is easier said than done, but where the recording is inadequate,
dealers have a built-in excuse for exceeding lines.

To persuade dealers to pay close attention to lines, requires both stick
and carrot. The carrot takes two main forms: they must be able to tell easily
what the line is, and how much room there is; and they must be confident
that if they wish to exceed the line, they will get a fair hearing and quick
response. These are also prerequisites for the stick, which must be a severe
rap over the knuckles for any breach, and a genuine fear of dismissal for
repeated breaches.

A single breach is rarely serious. Lines often have to cover a wide range
of products and are rarely all used at once. A single breach need not mean
that the bank has become overexposed to the counterparty; where it has,
most trades run off quite quickly. Few dealers will pass up a profitable
opportunity in these circumstances. Rather they will convince themselves
the deal would be easily approved if they could get to the right person. This
will be easier if the information they have on usage of the line is unreliable,
and leaves a real chance that they would not exceed it.

For similar reasons, managers who would react ferociously if their traders breached trading limits, may not take a breach of a credit line seriously.
And the suggestion that a dealer should lose his job for exceeding a line
often seems ridiculous.

And yet, it is true that the occasional profitable excession, where the
dealer could indeed get approval easily, will rarely cost the bank anything.
But if he can get approval so easily why is it not sought? More importantly,
if line excessions become a regular occurrence, then the risk of loss multi-
plies. Equally, once dealers get into the habit of exceeding lines, they may
not confine it to cases where they could indeed get approval. And then the
risk of loss is substantial.

To some extent, it is a matter of culture. If dealers share a culture that takes credit seriously, they will rarely exceed lines; if they do not, they often do so. But the culture requires credit to take their needs seriously too. This brings us back to the carrots. If dealers can find out, swiftly and reliably, whether they have room under the line, they are more likely to check, and react appropriately. If the information is slow to come and unreliable when it comes they will trade anyway. Equally, when the line is full, they need to know how to apply for an increase and receive a quick, sympathetic and commercial response. This does not mean automatically positive, but when it is negative the credit specialist must explain why credibly, and explore other ways of doing the business. A trader can accept a 'no' from someone he believes wants to do business, and often says 'yes'; but not from someone he feels never takes the trouble to understand the risks, or the profit opportunities.

Much the same applies to other parts of the bank. Global custody, for instance, may have a number of areas of credit exposure, some on behalf of a client, some where the bank is directly at risk. Many of these will not be obvious credit risks to salespeople and operating people intent on generating the maximum volume and profit; in some cases the bank will have been taking these risks on a smaller scale for years and the custody people will not understand the sudden fuss. (The answer is volume, as much as anything. When banks had only local custody business, done with well-known local clients, the volume and risk involved in settlement was small. Multiply the volumes hundreds of times and do business with clients from all over the world and the risk changes.)

Then there are the risks of trusteeship and paying agencies. Under the latter, the bank may normally need to pay out interest and sometimes principal before the money comes in. This is common in Europe, with dollar payments. So the credit risk must be assessed and monitored. First the bank must decide whether it wants to take that risk, then it must check each time a payment is due that the risk has not changed. This requires the people making the payments to diarise to ask for approval, and the credit specialist to respond promptly when asked.

There are many other examples, but they are not really the point. This is that whatever the product, the bank needs to do several things:

● establish a loan equivalent, and from it program the system to police a limit;

● establish limits and give the traders and other users access to up-to-date details, and ensure that they pay attention to them;

- ensure that there is a clear process for deciding on increases in the limits when needed;

- ensure good excession reporting, so that when the system fails, as it inevitably will sometimes, the fact will be noted, the reasons investigated, and someone will clear the excession promptly;

- instil credit consciousness, and awareness of the bank's procedures in all staff who create or police exposure. The best procedures will fail unless the people operating them believe in them.

STATISTICAL, TRADER'S APPROACH, OR REALISTIC?

One frequent problem is the difference between a trader's approach and a credit approach. Traders handle many deals, few of which individually can cause major problems, and where profit or loss depends on the balance between successes and losses. Nobody expects a trader to have a 99% or better success record; in some products, 55–60% ensures high profitability. The size of a trading loss is roughly equal to that of a trading profit, while for loans the cost of a loss eats up the profits from up to one hundred sound loans of comparable size. A portfolio approach is less applicable where you need a 99+% success ratio.

Moreover, the people best equipped to research the loan equivalents are not bankers but mathematicians – rocket scientists. They can calculate the statistical odds, but they cannot judge the factors that might invalidate the statistics in a particular case; nor do they recognise the harm that might be done if two different types of statistics coincided: the 5% chance of abnormal trading loss happened at the same time as a company went bankrupt.

In trading, the portfolio effect often means that the positions are so opposed to each other that you cannot lose on all simultaneously. This does not apply to lending. It may not even benefit from the secondary factor of diversity making the threatening factors less likely to occur at the same time. This depends at least in part on how well the bank monitors concentration.

Of course there is a portfolio effect in all aspects of credit, including lending. But it works rather differently, and it takes a combination of market and credit knowledge to understand the difference.

For instance, the portfolio effect applies to some extent to the swap portfolio. Most banks have a wide range of swaps and a hedged trading portfolio. The theory may then say that if á swap counterparty fails, it is just as likely to be in the money as out of the money, so the bank loses only half the time. Or to fail when the loss is average rather than peak. Credit experience suggests the contrary. Companies fail when a combination of factors works against them; one of these is often misjudgment of market movements, and therefore the wrong hedging strategy. Even where the lone swap with the bank is too small to have much impact on the credit, it may be a symptom of a wider misjudgment.

The idea that banks gain if a counterparty fails when in the money is only true if the agreement prevents the liquidator enforcing the contract. Or the company may not be liquidated, but rescued by a bank restructuring; a feature of this is likely to be that swap banks continue as if the company were solvent.

There can also be a portfolio effect with an individual counterparty, most often in dealings between banks. Any pair of major international banks will deal with each other in many locations, many combinations of currencies, interest rates, etc. Many of the deals will largely offset each other. Taking the exposure represented by each transaction in isolation, and adding all the figures up, gives a much higher total than the expected net loss even on pessimistic assumptions. If banks could net the gains and losses down to the net present value, the risk would be even less. But again, in the absence of special agreements, the liquidator may be able to enforce those contracts which favour him and repudiate those which do not – known as cherry picking.

The same opportunities may arise on a smaller scale with corporates. This may be with major companies with an active treasury behaving like a miniature bank; or because the client unwinds a hedge with the bank that did that original deal. More often, however, a client will hedge a flow of payments or worry about its exposure in other areas; its deals will all take similar rather than offsetting positions.

There are agreements – the ISDA Master Agreement, the BBA Master and some foreign exchange netting agreements, for instance – which try to lock in the portfolio effect, and give the benefits of netting. They will be discussed in more detail in Chapter 11. As far as the author knows, they have not been tested in court in any country. Lawyers in many countries have given opinions of varying confidence that they probably would stand up. The United States has even passed legislation supporting the ability to net in bankruptcy under such agreements. Unfortunately the legislation only covers banks and near banks.

Banks should monitor the volume of transactions with a counterparty; the type of agreement with it; its probable legal status in the counterparty's home country; and any legislation or court decisions that change that status.

GETTING MARKET KNOWLEDGE TO THE CREDIT SPECIALIST

All banks need a means of getting market knowledge where it will do most good. This is partly organisational/functional, partly cultural.

The organisational part has been touched on in earlier chapters. The provisions of a treasury credit function, credit sponsorship and similar arrangements helps among other things to set up the right channels of communication. Some such arrangements may also put the credit people closer to the trading floor or even on it so that they have a better chance of seeing developments themselves. This is even better than relying on the traders to tell the credit people, although no bank can ever avoid that need altogether. Credit specialists on the trading floor offer many advantages other than monitoring, but increase both the chance that they will be present and hear the warning sign; and that the trader will remember to tell them. There is nothing like seeing Tom to remind you that 'Oh, I meant to tell Tom about . . .'

There is not much new to say about the cultural aspects. A trader who has been taught to think about credit risk, even if peripherally, is more likely to remember to bring the sort of point discussed earlier to a credit specialist's attention. This is even more likely if the trader knows and trusts the credit specialist.

Part III

Structure and Documentation

10 The Structure of the Facility

INTRODUCTORY COMMENT

The structuring of facilities is critical to credit control. Too many banks settle for the easy facility, such as an overdraft or bullet term loan.

Banks should offer facilities which reflect both the reason for borrowing and the source of repayment. In particular, short-term facilities should be for genuine short-term needs; medium-term facilities should tie in with the reason for borrowing; and all facilities should have terms which fit their expected use and repayment. This is easy to overlook when lending in a boom, but failure is especially damaging when the loan comes due for repayment in a downturn.

KEY FEATURES OF A FACILITY

Maturity

There are three levels of maturity, short (under one year), medium (two to ten years) and long. Banks mainly lend in the first two, but occasionally in the third.

Too many bankers look at the nature of the facility, rather than its use and source of repayment. 'An overdraft is payable on demand' they say, 'so we can get our money back whenever we ask for it', or 'Lend for five years maximum, we can see that far ahead.' Both ignore the possibility that the borrower will be unable to pay because, while solvent, he has financed a longer term project which has not come to fruition.

The critical points in deciding whether to lend short or medium term, and in what form, are the reason borrowers need the money, and how they expect to repay it. When a bank lends short for a medium-term purpose it fools itself that it can recall the loan when it really cannot. It also often accepts a lower interest margin than the risk justifies.

Genuine short-term uses fall into several categories. Almost all companies have short-term fluctuations in cash flow although the extent varies

127

quite widely. A short-term facility is entirely appropriate, provided the bank checks that it fluctuates as expected.

Many companies have marked fluctuations for specific reasons; seasonal, as with toy companies, fertiliser producers, or canners of fruit and vegetables; or tied to the cycle of the business – large contracts which require heavy investment which is repaid when the contract is complete, for example. Or a basic uncertainty as to when various payments will be received or, less often, need to be made.

These cases share one point, repayment from the realisation of assets in the normal course of business, i.e. in a way that does not impair the ability to continue in business. This may be the collection of receivables, or the rundown of inventory in a seasonal business, or the payment for the completed contract. The detail does not matter, but the underlying fact does. Only where this is true do we have a genuinely short-term facility.

The other main short-term facilities, for financing self-liquidating transactions, share this feature. To finance cocoa from Ghana to a British chocolate maker is a classic self-liquidating transaction, with the bank financing the purchase and being repaid when the British company pays on receipt; again the realisation of an asset in the normal course of business.

Short-term lending is thus asset-based rather than cash-flow-based, although not all asset-based lending is short term. We can distinguish between asset-based companies where the assets generate cash – shipping, property and leasing are obvious examples – and which require medium- or long-term finance; and those where the asset value directly provides funds to pay the debt, whether or not it generates an overall positive cash flow.

Medium-term loans are almost always repaid from cash flow. Even where the immediate source is another loan or bond or equity issue, they in turn look to cash flow for payment. The apparent exceptions are mostly either not genuinely medium term – a bridge loan, perhaps – or rely on cash flow as a back-up; a loan which is to be repaid from the sale of surplus assets whose value depends on cash flow, or on that of the remaining assets if the sale does not go through.

Cash flow repays debt over time. It is vital to recognise this in the maturity – and other terms – of the loan. To make a short-term loan knowing it cannot be repaid in the time-scale is to ask for trouble. Even worse is to lend without bothering to discover how it will be repaid.

How long is medium term partly depends on the amortisation pattern, discussed in the next subsection; partly on what is acceptable to the bank. Banks sometimes have a policy of limiting lending to say five years. It is then foolish, but common, to lend money for five years which cannot be paid for seven or ten years, since to recognise this undermines the policy. This appears to mean 'we will not lend money unless we believe it can be repaid in five years', but in fact does not.

It is therefore positively dangerous. A bank that recognises that a loan can only be repaid over ten years can refuse, or take proper precautions. A bank that says 'No more than five years' but still makes loans which cannot be repaid in that time has no such protection.

The Form of the Facility

Short- and medium-term facilities come in various forms. The correct use of each is important in credit terms, although there may be other important factors. The choice between an overdraft and a line for six-month advances may depend on whether the loan actually needs to be outstanding for six months. If it does, an overdraft is less than ideal, although a clear-cut source of repayment at the end of six months makes it acceptable. The main advantage may be the ability to set the rate for six months, or use the overdraft to avoid locking the client in, when rates are changing.

The same point applies to the use of letters of credit or acceptance facilities compared with an overdraft. There are credit advantages in tying the advance of funds directly to the underlying transaction, which banks do not get with an overdraft; the direct connection may be essential to ensure a valid lien. But again, there are advantages for the client, and for the bank through the ability to sell the acceptance, that may outweigh the credit aspects.

Similarly, there are credit reasons for preferring different types of medium-term facility in each situation, but the choice may reasonably be made on other grounds where they do not conflict with credit factors.

The arguments between fixed or floating rate term loans relate mainly to the interest rate risk. Of course, avoiding excessive interest rate risk is important for credit reasons, but this will not be the deciding factor.

The difference between a term loan and a revolver may relate more to the use of the money, and often to the source of repayment. Even here credit will rarely be the only factor, and often not the deciding one; but sometimes it should decide. A term loan implies a specific need, of a known amount and timing which should be financed accordingly. It might be the purchase of major equipment, expected to generate cash flow at a rate and for a period which bank and borrower can estimate confidently. It would be unsound to finance this with a revolving commitment, with no specific drawdown or amortisation, and with a maturity tailored to the bank's convenience rather than the ability to repay.

Such a revolver may, however, be the best solution when the timing of the need is unknown, or when the need is not certain at all, but the company is prudently insuring against it. Or to meet fluctuating needs, temporary but longer term than it would be prudent to finance with an overdraft. Examples are disputed payments such as taxes; immediate funding for an acquisition, which can then be refinanced at leisure; the risk that a switch from customers buying to leasing can cut cash flow sharply initially, although in the medium term the situation reverses itself; and so on.

Where a company builds a factory or other major installation, it may need elements of both. Before it commits to the contract it must have the funds available; to borrow them all on day 1, however, would be expensive and distort the balance sheet. The timing of the need may not be certain, as contractors often miss deadlines and the contract may require, say, an engineer's certificate before payment. A revolving facility for the first two or three years, which converts into a term loan with maturity suited to the nature of the project may be the answer.

There are often other reasons why tailoring is good marketing as well as good credit. But the best way of ensuring a loan will be repaid on time and without difficulty is to tailor it to the use of the money and the source of repayment.

Amortisation

Amortisation is a vital part of credit control, but poorly understood and enforced by banks and clients.

No company is sure it can repay a debt several times its annual cash flow on one day. It may prove able to do so by reborrowing, issuing securities, selling assets or some other means. But no banker or finance director should assume so five or more years in advance. To make or take a loan on that assumption is ill-judged.

Whether the source of repayment is the cash flow from the project financed or the general cash flow of the company or a mixture of both, it is sensible to time repayments in line with it. The whole of the cash flow need not be used to repay debt; indeed, setting an appropriate amortisation schedule involves assessing the residual left by competing claims on cash flow. If the residual cannot service the debt in the time-scale proposed, with a margin for safety, the loan is unsound. It may be only slightly unsound – the maturity should be a year or two longer – or it may be fundamentally unsound, with a need for equity, or perhaps for a twenty-year bond issue. Whatever the answer, to lend for five years when the borrower clearly cannot repay in less than ten is nearly always a nonsense; it is slightly less nonsense to require some amortisation, leaving a balloon of 50% after five years than it is to lend a five-year bullet, but only slightly.

The exceptions to this statement do not change its essential correctness. For instance, it is one thing to insist on a five-year life when it is clear the borrower cannot repay; another when it is possible but not certain that he can pay. Or it may be that the borrower expects to refinance the loan in one of the ways outlined earlier, but does not wish to be tied down to a short-term timetable which might force him to do so in unfavourable conditions.

One answer is the recapture clause, with perhaps also a voluntary right of prepayment in modest round amounts. A recapture involves setting the amortisation and maturity at levels which the borrower can meet on any reasonable downside case; then establishing a benchmark, preferably taken from the borrower's own projections, which shows when he does better than the downside case. Depending on how much better, he must then repay an additional amount, related to the benchmark, in each year that it is bettered. The borrower may thus pay off the loan in the shorter period, but the bank has not fooled itself into an artificial crisis if he fails. Recapture is particularly suitable for cyclical companies: banks can be sure there will be ups and downs, but not when they will come; and for recovery situations, when banks want to get the maximum back each year without putting an overwhelming burden on the company. They can, however, be used wherever there is doubt as to how fast the borrower can pay, and the bank is reluctant to extend longer credit than it has to.

Where the borrower expects to refinance, it may be right to set a shorter maturity, if the bank would be prepared to lend for longer. It should then set an amortisation pattern which matches the longer maturity. Then, if the refinancing fails, it is faced at formal maturity of the loan with an amount which it would have been prepared to have outstanding anyway.

We do not aim to explore all the various possibilities. Rather, to establish basic principles:

1. Where cash flow is the source of repayment, it is rarely able to pay off all the debt in one year; therefore a loan which requires that ignores underlying realities.
2. To know what is reasonable as an amortisation schedule requires analysis of the cash flow, and tailoring to the results of that analysis.
3. There may be reasons for varying the pattern from what the analysis suggests is ideal; or the analysis may indicate that the best pattern is unsure. These are reasons for building in flexibility, not for abandoning the principle.

4. Lack of amortisation means that at maturity, the borrower will probably need to refinance all or most of the loan. This may not be difficult, but sometimes it will be; and it is most likely to be when other factors make it hardest to deal with. The borrower may be struggling; or market conditions unfavourable, so that the bank has to extend the loan, often when it is least happy to do so.

There are other purely credit factors, which do not qualify as basic principles, but are important in reducing bad debts. One is the importance of average life versus maturity. The second is the advantage of keeping each payment as small as practicable.

To illustrate them, take a loan of £100 million analysed as a BBB risk; and where the borrower should start to generate surplus cash flow in the third year, and on reasonable assumptions be able to pay off the loan over the next four years. This suggests a seven-year loan, with amortisation starting in year 3, in equal annual or more frequent instalments, to give a five-year average life. Now compare this with a five-year bullet to the same borrower for the same purpose.

If all goes well, the seven-year amortising loan is superior. At the end of five years, half of it has been repaid, and the borrower is clearly on track to repay the balance. If other borrowing needs occur, he is well placed to fund them, probably from the same bank. With a five-year loan, the question of refinancing arises. The bank may be willing to extend the loan (perhaps with another five-year bullet?), but this takes it beyond the period in which the borrower could have repaid it from cash flow; it also makes a mockery of the original argument that the bank was not prepared to lend beyond five years. Of course the loan may be refinanced elsewhere; indeed if all goes well it probably will be and the disadvantages of the five-year bullet may not appear to matter.

However, the borrower may do less well for several reasons, some more serious than others.

1. It may begin to fail within the first three years and never generate cash to repay the debt. In this case, neither loan has any advantage (with one possible exception discussed below); the best that can be said is that the need to analyse cash flow to establish the amortisation pattern slightly improves the chance of seeing this in advance. However, if the original analysis of the borrower was so wrong, or conditions have changed so sharply, this is unlikely to be much help.
2. The difficulty could come a little later. Conditions start to deteriorate late in the third year and the company is on the verge of collapse by

the end of the fifth. It can just make the year-end amortisation, but not the bullet. The difference here is critical: the amortising bank has recovered half of its loan, the bullet bank nothing; the remaining amortisation payments are easier to handle and less likely to need rescheduling than the bullet; if this is the only loan, or all loans have been handled similarly, the borrower has about half the total debt with the amortising loan that it does with the bullet loan.

3. The borrower does well, and pays high dividends, for the first five years, but persuades the bank to renew it for another five years – amortising or bullet. However, in the sixth and seventh year, the borrower goes downhill rapidly. It just manages to make the sixth and perhaps the final payment on the original seven-year loan, but enters a restructuring shortly thereafter. The amortising loan is wholly repaid, or nearly so, while the original five-year loan is still between 60% and 100% outstanding, depending on the terms on which it was refinanced.

4. The company declines less than in the earlier examples, but never generates the cash flow initially forecast. It is always short of cash and struggling to meet all its obligations. With the amortising loans, payments are smaller, and earlier, so that it makes the effort to meet them. Nobody ever expected it to pay the five-year bullet on maturity anyway and by the time it comes due, the company will have been underperforming for several years. The chance of its refinancing the debt elsewhere is small. A refinancing with the same bank is likely to require a long maturity with slow amortisation. If the bank refuses, this will almost certainly push the borrower into restructuring, administration or outright insolvency, leaving the bank a choice of evils.

It is easier for a company to make a series of small payments than one large one. Even if in the end it cannot pay the whole amount, it is more likely to try to pay each instalment as it comes due, and succeed in at least the first few.

This is an argument for amortisation, but also for keeping payments as small and frequent as practicable within the overall pattern. Thus quarterly or semi-annual payments for the same annual total are better than annual. Indeed, in the first example above, if quarterly payments had begun in the first quarter of Year 3, instead of annual payments beginning at the end of Year 3, the borrower might make one or two payments before it failed; in the fourth example, the chance that it will make all the payments increases modestly.

The cost of not making an amortisation payment is the same whatever its size: the bank has an event of default, with all the rights that gives it. The cost to the borrower of making the payment, and avoiding the damage, is less each time with smaller payments. This makes it more likely that the company will choose to allocate its scarce funds for that purpose; and less likely that it will simply not have the funds to allocate.

The pattern should be tailored to the ability to pay, even if this is not straight line. A seven-year loan can have annual amortisation, set at 0, 0, 10, 10, 20, 30, 30 per cent if that fits the cash flow. There is no reason why the first two (small) payments should not be annual, and the subsequent ones semi-annual. Equally, to fit in with uneven cash availability: 0, 0, 10, 20, 20, 10, 40 is quite feasible. Where cash flow is lower, or less certain in later years, a pattern of 30, 20, 20, 10, 10, 10, is sensible. A ship with a three-year charter and fair prospects for rechartering, but no certainty, might meet that pattern.

Credit control includes two major aims: to ensure that the bank loses money on as few loans as possible; and to ensure that the losses it takes are, individually, as small as possible. Amortisation helps with both, but is more critical in the latter.

PROTECTION WITHIN THE STRUCTURE

Two types of protection can be built into a loan facility. One, covenants, applies mainly to medium-term facilities and falls into two subtypes: ratio and non-ratio. The other, security, comes in many different forms, and can be used in any type of facility.

What follows will examine the aim of covenants and security rather than their individual details; and how banks decide what they want and how to negotiate it with the client. There may be constraints on the freedom to do what is ideal for credit reasons, but with training and flexibility these can be overcome.

Covenants

Covenants have two main aims. One is to prevent the borrower doing any-thing which threatens its credit standing overall, or weakens the bank's standing *vis-à-vis* other parties. The other is to set benchmarks to monitor financial strength, and give rights to the bank if this falls below an agreed level.

While all covenants tend to help both aims, non-ratio covenants do more for the first, ratio covenants for the second. Thus the setting of appropriate ratio covenants, while an important part of structuring the loan, is also a key tool in effective monitoring.

Ratio covenants

For covenant benchmarks to have full value, the covenants, and the process of setting them, need to meet several standards. (Note the word full; failure to meet all these standards does not make covenants worthless, just less effective than they could be.)

Ratio covenants then should ideally be:

- set in the light of forecast results and financial condition;

- set to allow reasonable deviation from forecast without triggering a default, but to trigger it well before the borrower reaches the point of no return;

- designed to highlight areas which are key to the strength of the particular company; there are no ratios which are useful in every case, and to insist on unsuitable ratios is counter-productive;

- ratios which management takes seriously; if they are ratios which it uses in its own financial management so much the better, since this will help reach the final criterion;

- designed not to cause the company too much additional work to track.

To achieve these objectives, and to obtain the maximum benefit from the main aims, banks should negotiate flexibly with borrowers. Because banks have been clumsy in their use of ratio covenants, and for other reasons, many borrowers are reluctant to accept them. Banks must persuade borrowers that well-designed ratios help them as well as the bank; and that their acceptance of the concept, and involvement in the design, makes it more likely that they will achieve good design. To do this, most banks need to improve their own understanding and use of covenants.

The main benefit of ratio covenants comes in showing that a healthy company is weakening. It follows therefore that it is critical to set covenants for healthy companies, rather than, as some banks seem to, when the borrower is already known to be in trouble. (Covenants have a value in that case, but it is different to, and less important than, the role in a healthy company.)

It follows equally that the design of the covenants, to focus on key areas of the particular company, is vital. Also, that their relation to forecasts is important both in their design, and as a check that the original decision to lend or borrow was correct.

Banks should thus not impose the design of covenants on a company, but work with the borrower to agree sensible ratios. The value of ratio covenants increases if the borrower understands and agrees why they are there; that they are sensible and practical; and that the message to the borrower as to when it approaches a danger zone is as important as the rights of the bank if it breaches the covenant. The ideal is if the bank can agree ratios which the borrower anyway uses in managing the business, and set them at levels which the borrower agrees would require prompt action by it. Establishing this also involves a useful dialogue about the forecasts, whether prepared by the company or bank, around which the covenants are designed.

The greatest benefit comes when the borrower uses the ratios as a warning sign, and itself takes measures to avoid a breach by dealing with whatever is causing the decline. Failing this, covenants help the bank to pin-point factors which the company has agreed in advance would be a matter of concern.

This ideal of cooperative negotiation is unfortunately rarely achieved. Too often, borrowers refuse to cooperate: too often a factor in the refusal is mishandling of previous negotiations by banks.

Where the company initially rejects covenants, it may still be forced to accept them; indeed, to accept whatever ratios the bank has chosen. In this case they will often be ill-chosen, and even where well designed, the company will have no belief in them.

Banks whose borrowers will not cooperate should aim as close as possible to the same end-result. They must use their knowledge of the company and its forecasts to decide the areas they wish the covenants to cover. There are always several combinations which can reach the objectives; within a given grouping there are trade-offs between the power of different covenants. As a simple example, a higher coverage ratio makes a higher leverage ratio more acceptable; and vice versa.

The best approach therefore is to explain to the borrower how the bank sees the position, what is wants covenants to achieve and why it thinks those it proposes do so. It is best to suggest more ratios than the bank actually expects to need; not as a preparation to haggle, but because the borrower may have legitimate or emotional arguments against one or more, If the bank has tied itself to too few ratios, they may lead to an impasse; it is better to say 'We think there are four or five ratios which are relevant; we would be happy with any combination of three, please help us choose the best three, or suggest others'. The borrower then need not accept a ratio it regards as anathema; nor can it complain that the bank is forcing unreasonable ratios on it without consultation.

Some companies, more constructively, decide what ratios they think are appropriate and offer them to all their banks. This has many advantages and banks should encourage it, provided those chosen are useful to the banks as well as to the company.

Bank management must control the approach to ratio covenants. The bankers negotiating with the borrower must understand the general arguments in favour of covenants, and those peculiar to the case. Ideally they should discuss and agree the bank's attitude to covenants, as part of its overall credit philosophy, with clients well before any loan request. Unfortunately, this seems to be rare.

The approval process can help or hinder. Frequently, approval is too precise on covenants; worse still, it is often standardised. 'We must have a debt-to-worth ratio for all loans' sounds sensible. However, some borrower's asset values move rapidly without affecting their cash flow or debt-servicing ability; for these companies, a debt-to-worth ratio is a dangerous nonsense, and to insist on it may sour them on the concept of covenants. Rightly so, too; while well-designed covenants help both the bank and the borrower, badly designed ones help banks less, but positively damage the borrower.

The approval process must therefore aim to meet a stated objective, rather than setting covenants in stone before they have even been discussed with the borrower. This requires a high standard of training and trust of both approver and negotiator.

One final point: there are three damaging misapprehensions about the ability to accelerate if there is breach of covenant:

1. Too many bankers think that acceleration is the main point of having a covenant; in fact it is a deterrent to help the bank to gain the main benefits. These, apart from the monitoring effect already referred to, can best be summed up as 'a seat at the table', that is, an ability to join negotiations with other creditors, rather than watching helplessly while they improve their comparative position or are paid in full. Like any deterrent, it has failed in its primary purpose if it is ever used.

2. Because of the first misapprehension, too many bankers feel that in countries where the courts (probably) will not allow acceleration, covenants are not worth fighting for. This is not true, although it does make it even more important to get the management's co-operation.
3. Borrowers often feel that an event of default delivers the company into the bank's hands. Some expect the banks to try to run the company; others arbitrarily to bankrupt it; either way they feel that they are abrogating the board's duties.

Bankers who understand covenants can assuage borrower's fears, although the event of default is somewhat of a blunderbus. There are many cases of breach of covenant that the banks take seriously, but not seriously enough for acceleration to be an attractive, or in some cases even acceptable, option.

It is worth looking for an intermediate step. Unfortunately, there are no standard suggestions, since companies vary so widely. Examples could be deferral of capital expenditure; dividend restriction; prohibition of acquisition; or control of expenditure in specific areas important to the banks.

In summary, ratio covenants are a key tool in credit control of medium-term lending. Borrowers often resist them, usually for misguided reasons. Bankers need to understand the theory and practice of covenants to overcome the resistance and design covenants which achieve the desired end. This is primarily as a monitoring tool, with all the ability to take early and cooperative action discussed under that heading. Poor understanding makes it harder to overcome the borrower's reluctance as well as contributing some of the better-founded reasons for that reluctance. It almost invariably leaves the bank with less effective covenants than it might have obtained, often with none.

The key point remains that ratio covenants are most important when the borrower is healthy. This makes them one of the specific areas where weakness in a boom proves most costly in recession.

Lest we seem to overstate the benefit of covenants, we should make it clear that they are no panacea. As Maureen Hendricks, a Managing Director of J. P. Morgan, comments 'Covenants never repaid a loan'. They are helpful however in three ways:

1. Deciding what covenants the bank needs, helps to focus the analysis on the key factors. It does not guarantee that the bank recognises and avoids all the weaknesses; it improves the chance.

2. The discussion allows management to understand what the bank expects, and to measure whether it is meeting those expectations in time to take remedial action if necessary. The dialogue generated may lead to wider discussions and greater communication between bank and company.
3. The ability to monitor and take early action has already been discussed.

Non-ratio covenants

Non-ratio covenants – negative pledge, dividend restraint, change of ownership, alienation of assets and similar clauses – are generally less contentious than ratio covenants. Most borrowers understand why banks refuse to lend unsecured if other leaders can subsequently secure themselves; and that banks do not like to see shareholders taking money out of a weakening company.

This does not imply that borrowers always agree with the bank's reasoning; still less that they accept the full restriction the bank proposes. Nevertheless, negotiations start at a different level, and are more often about the specific wording of a clause than about whether it should exist.

Banks still need to understand the borrower's business and the impact or variations in each clause, to ensure that they get the form they need and which the borrower will accept.

For instance, an unsecured medium-term lender should always have negative pledge. Its complete absence should be a reason for withdrawing from medium-term credit even to AAA borrowers. There are, however, many forms of negative pledge, most of which exempt certain types of secured borrowing from their scope. Few companies sign an absolute negative pledge with no exemptions. Deciding which exemptions to accept for each borrower is an important part of structuring a medium-term loan.

Except that more companies avoid them altogether, similar comments apply to dividend restraints, changes of ownership clauses, alienation of assets, etc. The bank must decide whether it needs the clause at all, and if so, in which form.

Occasionally a borrower will resist a standard clause for no apparent reason. Some major companies refuses to sign a negative pledge, usually on the grounds that they would never grant security, but want to be able to, if they change their minds. The impression given is usually that there is no reason other than corporate machismo.

Banks need a clear view as to whether, and when, they will concede key clauses, or how far they will insist on the particular form they want. To concede too easily undermines the basis of the credit; to insist may lose the loan and perhaps damage a valuable relationship. Banks must be prepared to run that risk for key clauses, but also maximise their ability to persuade the borrower. A reputation for taking credit seriously is itself helpful in persuading borrowers.

Other clauses

There are a few clauses in loan agreements which are critical to credit standards, but are not covenants. Here again, management must educate the bankers and decision-makers in the arguments and how far the bank's policy allows flexibility. Where it does, who should decide how far to go in a particular case?

Event of default and related issues

All medium-loan term agreements have some version of an event of default, but it varies enormously, although there is a fairly standard approach used in many agreements. Variations can recognise that the borrower's business is in some way unusual, or that the borrower's credit strength gives it negotiating power, or can be unreasonable. A bank's failure to ensure a consistent approach to this aspect can lead to a weakening in its position in most agreements. Although a weak event of default is rarely critical in any one case, the cumulative impact if the clause is generally weak in all agreements is serious.

Cross-default

This clause too is one no lender should be without. (The arguments are somewhat different in swaps, see below.) Borrowers sometimes think that they are too strong to have to give it. This is, of course, nonsense; the stronger they are, the less they need to worry about giving it, but the more catastrophic the change will have been if it ever becomes relevant.

There are, however, many forms the clause can take; some give the bank the right to call a cross-default if there is a potential event of default in another agreement, an actual event or only if the party to the agreement in default calls it. Some apply only to the borrower, others cover all its subsidiaries, or its parent and fellow subsidiaries; or possibly a guarantor. Or they can relate only to default on given types of agreement (more common in swap agreements); or to minimum amounts.

A too rigid stance on these items can lose the bank good business. If it can be shown to be unrealistic, the bank may end up accepting a weaker clause than if it had negotiated more sensibly to begin with.

Material adverse change clause (MAC)

This clause is deceptive, in that it appears to give banks an easy way out of the loan without bothering with ratio covenants and perhaps even some of the other clauses.

Nothing could be further from the truth. There are specific cases where MAC is valuable, but to use it to avoid the detailed analysis and protection covenants is a major error.

MAC can be useful where the borrower deteriorates before it has drawn down the loan; and to protect against catastrophic deterioration which ratios cannot catch, such as product liability. Where the loan is fully drawn, a continuing representation and warranty, perhaps tied to an interest rate setting, has value. It may cause the directors, often on legal advice as to personal liability, to disclose an event of which banks were ignorant; or to act to avoid a change which the banks would consider adverse.

Apart from these special situations, MAC has little value and can even be dangerous. It is rarely possible to pin-point what constitutes such a change beyond doubt; if the situation is so bad that the MAC is unanswerable, there should be other events of default which are clearer. If, however, the default is one which would have breached, say, a leverage covenant, proving that it meets the precise wording of the MAC may be difficult, compared with proving it had breached the covenant. To demand repayment of the loan on this subjective basis, where the borrower disputes it, is highly dangerous. It cannot avoid becoming public, and the damage to confidence makes it likely the borrower will enter an insolvency procedure. It the courts then refuse the demand, and decide that the deterioration did not match the MAC terms, the bank may be liable not only for its own losses, but a large claim for damages as well, from the borrower and other creditors who lose money. No bank is likely to risk this, and the MAC in these circumstances lacks credibility.

Security

The details of security are massive, highly technical and vary from country to country. Once the bank has decided to take security, it must take legal advice to ensure that the security works. Most banks are quite good at this in their domestic market. Not all are as good internationally. Common mistakes include:

1. Assuming that because the agreement is written under English (or New York) law, the bank can ignore the impact of Spanish law on a Spanish borrower or assets in Spain; this overlooks the fact that in bankruptcy, the bankruptcy law of the country of origin normally decides, particularly if the asset is in Spain.
2. Assuming that because an aspect of law looks superficially similar in two countries, therefore it works in identical ways.
3. Worse still, assuming that other countries' laws are similar to, or will in some mysterious way conform to, your own. American bankers and lawyers are particularly prone to do this.
4. Failing to recognise the difference in philosophy between common law and civil law; and in particular the different attitude to the enforcement of contracts.
5. Failing to keep in touch with changes in critical areas; the impact of the Charge Card case on the validity of cash collateral is an example.

However, although there are pitfalls in this area, and the general need to manage security well is important, the greatest area of loss lies in the decision whether and how to rely on security.

The great mistake is to assume that security reduces or eliminates the need for analysis, covenants and other protection. It never justifies less analysis; sometimes requires more; at best, changes its nature.

There are broadly four types of security for the purpose of this discussion.

1. Security over the direct source of repayment

This falls into two subcategories which coincide with whether the lending is short or medium term. For both, security is merely a way of ensuring that the expected source of repayment is used as intended.

First, pure self-liquidating security such as the cocoa from Ghana referred to in the previous chapter. Since it is always intended that this should be the source of repayment, the basic analysis is the same whether or not the bank takes a pledge. Some additional analysis may be needed as to the validity of the pledge, but never less for secured than for unsecured.

The second case is self-liquidating only in the longer term, either from cash flow generated by the asset pledged, or by sale proceeds, which in turn usually reflect actual or potential cash flow. Shipping loans and loans against fully let properties are two examples. In both cases the bank must analyse the asset, the source of cash flow, the management required to maintain it and the risks which might harm it. If the results are positive, the pledge ensures that the cash flow or sale proceeds are not diverted to other purposes. Where the results of the analysis are negative, it is clear that a pledge is an inadequate basis for lending.

2. Security over assets outside the company

This is unaffected by events within the company. It may arise when a parent pledges assets to support, or in lieu of, a guarantee. Here the bank analyses the guarantor, the security or both, to ensure that they justify the loan. It still, however, should analyse the borrower for several reasons:

First, banks are rightly reluctant to make such a loan if they expect to call the guarantee or security. If there is no chance of the borrower repaying, then lending to it is a farce, and the loan would be better made direct to the guarantor, or the security sold to realise the funding.

Secondly, the reluctance to lend reflects the fear that, however clear the legal right and moral obligation, guarantors often take offence if a guarantee is called; this in turn makes the bank reluctant to call the guarantee.

Thirdly, the borrower's failure may threaten the guarantor's standing; or the value of the security may fall at the same time, if for different reasons, as the borrower runs into difficulties.

3. Security over the main working assets of the company

These usually are fixed assets, inventory and receivables, but may include brand names, patent rights, mailing lists or other intangible assets. The cash from these assets is the prime source of repayment. Unlike self-liquidating assets, however, the bank cannot reimburse itself from the assets, as opposed to the cash flow they generate, without seriously damaging the borrower's ability to continue in business. It needs to analyse the cash flow in the same way whether or not it takes security. If the analysis suggests that the cash flow is marginal, then it throws doubt on the value of the assets. Almost all assets lose value in liquidation, and in the conditions which precede it; not all do so to the same extent. The bank needs to analyse the assets to see how likely they are to provide a second way out if cash flow fails.

4. Assets surplus and for sale

The bank must analyse them and their market, as well as, perhaps, their ability to service the loan until they are sold, or if they prove unsaleable; or that of the company if the failure to sell throws the onus back onto it.

The danger of any type of security, but particularly the latter two types, is that banks relax, thinking secured loans are safe. A strong borrower does not need to give security; so secured loans start off by being, in almost all cases, weaker than unsecured. Only if the security can be shown to add real value to the basically weak loan is it justified. Too many banks, however unconsciously, look to the security alone and fail to analyse either it or the borrower.

This whole question of security is thus a prime cause of loss. A vital aspect of credit control is ensuring that everybody concerned recognises that the need for security is a sign of a weak credit. The security may alleviate the weakness, and make the whole package acceptable. Banks can only be sure that it does so if they analyse the borrower, the security and the way in which the security compensates for weaknesses in the borrower.

One last point relates back to the title of the book. The price of most pledged assets is higher in a boom, and highest just before the boom breaks. Many attempts to realise security occur during a recession, often near the bottom, when prices are at their lowest and buyers hardest to find. Unless analysis takes account of this, it will give more value to the security than is justified, and the result will be a loss.

Special Factors for Swaps and Other Products

The underlying credit factors are the same for a five-year swap as for a five-year loan. However, features peculiar to swaps and other products cause problems in applying the same structure as to a loan. There is an important balancing act between applying standard, but inappropriate credit criteria, and giving up credit criteria altogether.

The most important factor is the mutual credit risk. Because the interest rate or currency can move in either direction, the counterparty has broadly the same credit risk on the bank as the bank has on the counterparty. When almost all banks were undoubted credits, this might not have mattered, but when many banks are weaker than the strongest corporates, the latter are reluctant to concede a one-sided credit structure; and of course banks do far more swaps with other banks than with individual corporates. Thus banks asking for a negative pledge or cross-default may need to give the same clauses in return. And if they want the clause to cover, say, the counterparty's subsidiaries, it may have to cover their own as well.

The second factor arises from the need for netting for multiple transactions. The clause deals with what happens to all swaps, and other products such as caps, floors and collars, which may be covered by the same master agreement. If a defaulter could be owed money on a net basis, this might encourage default, so the bank has to decide whether to allow the defaulter to receive payment, or only the non-defaulting party. Then there are factors, such as imposition of withholding tax or other government acts, which may render the agreement uneconomic, with neither side to blame.

Banks also consider the question of events of default, ratio covenants, etc., in the mutual case. To insist on covenants if the bank has to give similar ones is hard enough; where dealing with a corporate, different covenants may apply to it than to the bank; and sometimes arguments against covenants look rather stronger when the bank is asked to give them.

Where the bank does a single swap, or swaps in a single direction, with a counterparty there is some doubt as to the value of covenants if all they do is trigger an event of default. If this comes some years into the swap, the amount due may equal the original peak exposure, and the borrower may have difficulty in paying it, even though it had met all the payments due so far, and was continuing to make payments as they fell due. If the swap was for ten years or longer, this could be five years or so after the strike date and more from maturity. Where the peak is high, to allow the swap to continue means that the bank receives more payments. This may reduce the cost of replacement, dramatically if rates move, but if rates move the other way, the bank may find its exposure growing rapidly. Or the default may happen when the swap is out of money; if so, the bank may be unwilling to call it. To do so could bring down, for no gain, a company where the bank itself or other banks had large loan exposure.

One solution requires the swap to be marked to market periodically; at agreed times the bank and counterparty check rates and the out-of-the-money party pays cash, or supplies collateral to the other.

This has drawbacks, but is increasingly common in various forms. It does not eliminate the risk, but reduces it. If the mark to market is for say six months, the risk reduces to the amount by which rates can move it in six months, instead of five years or more. Even though that risk stays in place for the whole life of the loan, a fifteen-year exposure for, say, $5 million may be acceptable where it would not for $50 or $100 million.

Some of the other clauses will be discussed in the next chapter. The point here is that the structure changes for reasons related to the nature of the swap, and this the bank must understand and adjust for, if it is not to leave out or insert items which do not fit with its overall credit culture.

11 Documentation

FOR LENDING

General Principles

Documentation is critical for medium-term lending. Short-term facilities are mostly either on demand or for a specific period or purpose. Banks therefore need not spell out the rights and obligations of each party, or build in complex protection. If the bank does not like the way things are going, it can withdraw.

However, most countries' laws take a dim view if banks abuse the right to withdraw. Banks must therefore avoid giving hostages to fortune by appearing to commit where no commitment is intended, or by suggesting the facility is available for longer than the bank intends.

Where banks, despite the arguments of the previous chapter, have lent short term for a medium-term purpose, they are unlikely to recognise their mistake formally by documenting a short-term facility.

A medium-term facility needs documentation for reasons which influence the form the document should take.

First, bank and borrower are committed for several years. They must therefore be clear as to details of the commitment, and any breach of contract which would allow the other party to withdraw.

The terms are often complex, and must be drafted carefully to avoid doubt as to what is intended. This is as important with non-credit terms (interest, multicurrency, use by more than one member of the group, size of each drawing), as for the credit terms.

Those who negotiated the facility rarely operate it, and often move on or retire before it matures. The document should therefore allow clerks to understand clearly what they are expected to do.

The document is legally binding and may need to be reviewed by a judge in court, for several main reasons:

- the meaning of the document is so unclear that the parties need a judge to tell them what to do;

- one party, usually the borrower, fails to fulfil the obligations and the other seeks the court's aid;

- a combination of the first two; the conditions are clear, but it is not clear whether the facts breach them. The MAC clause discussed in the previous chapter is a prime example.

To go to court for any reason is undesirable, but to do so because of poor drafting is unacceptable.

Against this background, there are several points that banks need to inculcate in their negotiators.

First, although lawyers draft agreements, they do so on the bank's instructions. Bankers must have some grasp of the legalities, and a clear view as to the commercial priorities. If lawyers dictate what goes into the agreement, it will at best annoy the client unnecessarily, at worst be an unworkable monstrosity. The relationship between bankers and lawyers needs to be clear: the lawyer puts into legal form what the bank has agreed with the borrower. He does not renegotiate a better deal than the bank has agreed. And where details have not been covered in the outline agreement, the lawyer advises the bank as to the merits of various courses; whether a proposal is normal market practice; perhaps on the bank's standard policy on various clauses. It is the bank's money, and relationship, that is at stake. No lawyer, even a full-time bank employee, is qualified to decide what risks the bank will accept to either of these. The worst possible answer to a complaint from the client – or a superior – is 'my lawyer made me.'

This applies equally to the borrower. Banks should be wary of clients who allow lawyers, particularly in-house lawyers, to negotiate agreements on their behalf. In addition to the weaknesses common to all lawyers, these often have two others. They may be unfamiliar with market practice, or even the latest legal developments, in this specialised field. And they may seek to make a name for themselves by 'improving' the deal the finance department has negotiated.

Secondly, with a few honourable exceptions, lawyers believe that agreements should be written in a special language. It uses English words, though always too many, and always the longest and most Latinate form. (Lawyers probably add a page to a fifty-page agreement by phrases such as 'in the event that' instead of 'if', and another by words such as 'facilitate' for 'help' or 'utilise' for 'use'.) But they rarely use English sentence structure or grammar, and never English punctuation. Their excuse is that the judge must have no option but to interpret the document as intended. It is not clear why, or even whether, a judge finds it easier to understand a sentence of twenty to fifty lines with no punctuation and the most labyrinthine construction than the same concept in plain English. Unfortunately, non-lawyers find it hard to prove that he does not.

Most agreements do not end up in court, but they all have to be operated. Unless the people charged with operating them can understand them, they cannot operate them correctly. Bankers should therefore insist that the agreement is written in language that they themselves can understand, and that it is clear to the people who must operate the agreement.

Thirdly, quite apart from language, it is easy to write an agreement which cannot be operated; or which is unnecessarily difficult and expensive to operate. Banks should certainly involve their operating people in the early stages of drafting an agreement, to make sure they understand how to work it, but more importantly to ensure that, as written, it will work.

Fourthly, all the mistakes which banks can make on security documentation, as discussed in Chapter 10, apply with even greater force to documentation generally.

SPECIFIC ITEMS

Apart from the general points made above, banks need to review several areas in the agreement closely. Some are routine, others appear so, but may slip from sight under marketing and other pressures. This section will not discuss all exhaustively, but highlight those which are most easily overlooked.

Preamble, to Establish the Basis of the Loan

The preamble sets out who the parties are; the nature of the transaction; the powers of the borrower, and where appropriate, guarantors, to enter into the transaction; and who should sign the agreement and various documents, such as drawdown notices, arising under it.

This appears routine, and mostly is. It is useful to ensure that the borrower understands and takes seriously what he is saying. Occasionally this acts as a reminder that he does not have the powers, or needs to take some extra steps to exercise them. This more often saves embarrassment than avoids a credit risk, but sometimes does both.

The purpose clause tends to get overlooked, with sometimes damaging credit implications. Where this would be 'general corporate use' or some similar phrase, its omission may not be too important. Where there is a more specific purpose, the clause can be critical to ensure that the funds are used as intended, and repaid when the original purpose ceases to be valid.

Mechanics of the Loan

Most of the mechanics make sure the loan operates as intended. Some have credit implications and should be closely watched.

Agreements must clearly describe interest and commitment and other fees, with the timing and method of payment. This usually affects earnings – delays in collection are costly. But a delay in, or dispute about, payment can give a troubled company an excuse for witholding it; if troubles then overwhelm it, the money may be permanently lost.

Equally, events of default should be quite clear; in a syndicated loan the authority of the agent to call an event, of one or more banks to require it to do so, and the voting mechanism must all be beyond argument. In deciding what percentage of the borrowers they need to pass various items, the argument is between retaining the ability to block something the bank dislikes, and giving to others the ability to prevent the majority doing what it believes is best to recover the loan.

The mechanics of any multicurrency clause should be carefully reviewed, particularly where a new or unusual facility is involved. The standard clauses work most of the time but they are complicated and may not work so well if even minor adjustments are needed. The bank must also decide how far it is prepared to allow increases in total exposure in its accounting currency, because of changes in exchange rates against the borrowed currency.

Tying in Third Parties

Many agreements call for a guarantor, allow more than one member of a group to borrow, or require cross-guarantees between fellow subsidiaries. They may also require affiliates to pledge collateral, and may include subsidiaries or parents in a cross-default, or involve third parties in other ways.

These require two types of care. First, the bank must be clear why it requires the particular involvement (which may have been considered under Chapter 10); only then can it check that the wording of the agreement does what it wants.

Secondly, the lawyers must ensure that the proposal actually works legally. An international group may have subsidiaries in several different countries. The requirements for guarantees vary and may be onerous in some countries where a subsidiary guarantees either a parent or fellow subsidiary. The normal requirement to show that the guarantor gets some value from the guarantee takes extreme forms in some countries; it may be almost impossible in some; in others it requires cooperation from interested third parties such as the unions. In a complicated loan, particularly but not only a restructuring, banks cannot always put all this package in place before the funds are needed. But to leave it until afterwards runs the risk that it may never prove possible; or that it comes so late that when the borrower fails, the pledge has not 'hardened' and can be disregarded by the bankruptcy courts. This raises the additional need to understand the rules for hardening in each country. ('Hardening' means ensuring that the security has been in place long enough, and meets all other conditions, to remove the judge's power to overthrow the pledge in bankruptcy.)

Representations and Warranties

These need adjustments to meet the requirements of each borrower, but are fairly standard. The contentious point is whether they are repeated, and if so when. If not repeated at all, they merely help to establish the position when the bank lends. Some may naturally relate to that time and not need repeating. Others may need to be adjusted slightly in repetition, but banks need to be careful not to give away part of the value of repetition by these modifications.

The decision then is whether to repeat them at set intervals, probably annually, or at each rollover or other convenient date, or whether to require that they be valid at all times. The answer depends partly on the nature of the facility – a fixed rate loan, for instance, has no rollovers; partly on the nature of the representations – a MAC whether general or covering a specific event such as litigation or product liability should be clearly repeated continuously, and any breach reported as soon as known; partly on the strength of the borrower's ability to minimise repetitions.

There are few clear points of principle in representations and warranties. Nevertheless, bankers need a sound understanding of what they offer, and their impact in each case. As with many other items in the agreement, a weakness is rarely significant in any one case. Spread the weakness across the portfolio, however, and it will catch the bank out somewhere.

Bankers also need to understand how representations and warranties fit in with the rest of the agreement. It may be a mistake to fight too hard for one representation which is covered elsewhere in the agreement, if this means conceding another that provides the only protection against a particular risk.

Covenants

Covenants play a more positive role than representations and warranties, which are largely defensive. Their structural role was discussed in the last chapter. In documenting them there are three main points to control.

First, the drafting should be as simple and straightforward as possible. The concept of a covenant is usually simple, the details not so simple. Lawyers, partly for the reasons discussed earlier, partly where they do not fully understand each covenant, can turn complicated details into a nightmare. In particular, they sometimes turn the approach inside out, giving a clause which seems correct, but when examined closely proves to have a wrinkle in it which changes the effect.

Secondly, the covenant as drafted must tie in with the information requirements. It is easy to have a well-designed clause, with one major failing: the borrower need not provide the information to check whether the clause has been breached. As a safety measure, insist on 'such other information as the bank may reasonably require' wording in the information clauses. A judge, at least in the UK, will probably agree that it is reasonable for a bank to ask for information needed to check a covenant.

Thirdly, make sure the covenant applies when you want it to. A leverage covenant should normally apply at all times, not just at year end; however, there may be seasonal peaks which the bank agrees to accommodate temporarily but not at year end. Then it has the choice between requiring compliance only at year end, or allowing different levels throughout the year. Either may be sound in given conditions, but it requires judgement to choose.

Event Risk Protection

Event risk in origin is acts of God and other rare happenings. These change a company abruptly in ways nobody could protect against in advance. During the surge in leveraged takeovers and buyouts (LBOs) in the middle and late 1980s, event risk was associated with those which 'trashed the balance sheet' of an otherwise healthy borrower. Many companies were downgraded from AA or A to B by the leading rating agencies following such an event.

Lenders hoped that covenants in their agreements would protect them, but this did not always work. They therefore developed various clauses intended to catch the specific event, and make it an event of default in itself. This entitled them to demand repayment of their loan before the new debt was actually loaded onto the balance sheet.

With the ending of the LBO boom, this particular version of event risk has fallen out of fashion. Nevertheless, the chance that LBOs will return in the next boom remains; even in a more restrained form they still pose a threat. Banks should always consider event risk protection in this sense; but will not always receive what they want. They need a clear view as to how much event risk they will accept, and the level of protection they require.

Nor should banks ignore other types of event risk. It is impossible to specify what these should be in all cases, but litigation, product liability, flooding, terrorist action are examples which might be appropriate in individual cases.

An event risk which banks should take more seriously than ever before is liability for land pollution. CERCLA and Superfund liability in the United States and the move towards similar requirements in other countries make this a growing risk. It is doubly dangerous because it often applies to ownership of polluted land, whether or not the owner caused the pollution; and because at least some of the laws are retroactive, so that a change in law may bring liability for an act which was legal when performed. Or the value of land may be decimated because there is a potential liability attached to it. Worst of all, a bank which lends against the security of the land can become directly liable for clean-up costs which may be as much as or more than the loan. Even without being secured, a bank which is considered to have interfered in management, perhaps as part of an attempt to rescue the company, may become liable.

Indeed pollution laws, and the political impetus behind them, need to be taken increasingly seriously by banks. Those who lend secured stand to suffer most, but even an unsecured lender can suffer severely, if less directly.

Events of Default and Acceleration

In one sense, these are boilerplate: there is an event of default for failure to pay principal or interest when due; for breach of any covenant or understanding; for any act which suggests that the borrower is bankrupt or on the verge of it. While the specific acts may differ slightly from country to country, the underlying bases are the same.

It is surprising how often something happens which at first glance seems a clear default, but this is thrown into doubt before the bank can call it. The lawyers argue as to whether the event precisely meets the definition. To call an event of default in the light of their doubt is too great a risk for most banks. The claim for damages if a bank brought the company down and then the court ruled against it, could be enormous.

Agreements require the borrower to advise the bank(s) of any actual or potential event of which it becomes aware. This removes some, though not all, of the risk. Either the borrower agrees that it is an event of default, or as he raised the question it is harder to argue that the bank is being unreasonable in calling a default on the same facts. Of course this makes some borrowers less inclined to report the default; but directors take a personal risk if they conceal something which they are obliged by the agreement to disclose. The exact rules on this vary from country to country, but most lawyers will advise the board to be cautious.

Apart from the various events, the other key item in such clauses is the grace period, if any. Grace periods for some types of default are perfectly reasonable, provided they reflect the nature of the event and merely allow the borrower to correct the default. Grace periods on payment are another matter, which originally banks refused to allow. Then as payments became more complicated, a grace period was accepted for specific reasons; initially at least only for interest, but later for principal as well. Later the original application to administrative error was lost; then the period began to extend to cater for assumed error, without any control to ensure that the failure to pay was in fact due to error.

Grace periods on payment of principal, and only slightly less so on interest, are pernicious and banks should resist them; where they have to concede they should keep the period as short as possible, and attach conditions to ensure that it covers only the events for which it was designed.

Unfortunately, banks have mostly failed to do this. It is hard for an individual bank to resist, when market practice is too generous to the borrower. Nevertheless, banks should be looking to restrict grace periods, and push the market to shortening or eliminating them.

Banks should control the start of the grace period. Many agreements start it from the date the bank advises the borrower of non-payment. The argument, reasonable where it applies, is that if the borrower's instructions to pay are not carried out, the borrower cannot know this until the lender tells him. However, if the borrower knowingly fails to make the payment, the grace period should start immediately. Banks should start grace periods from the moment the borrower is aware of non-payment. Where the reason is indeed third-party error, this would be when the lender advised non-receipt. But where the fault was with the borrower, then the grace period starts independently of action by the lender.

Law and Jurisdiction

Usually governing law is not contentious. England and New York provide the two main laws of the Euromarkets. Domestic loans, even for international banks, normally use domestic law.

Sometimes a borrower will insist on domestic law in an international agreement. This is most dangerous when the borrower is sovereign, or supported by the sovereign. There are several risks here; some more political than strictly legal.

First, a borrower may expect court decisions in its favour. This may be quasi-corrupt, or may just be built into judges' psychology.

Secondly, even where the system is fair, it may be different. English and New York law have the same origins, and the same common-law way of approaching a range of subjects. Civil law in general, or its particular versions in leading countries, are no better or worse than common law. Nevertheless, their view of a contract gives more discretion to the judge to decide whether it is reasonable; common-law judges ensure that it was freely entered into, and does not conflict with public policy. Covenants are thus more easily enforced in common law; civil-law judges, to degrees varying by country, tend to treat covenants as technical and refuse to enforce them. In Spain, for instance, judges refuse acceleration for any reason other than non-payment.

Common-law judges rarely decide on the commercial merit of a covenant, but only whether it is clear, and freely entered into by both parties. A banker used to this approach can get a nasty shock if he or she tries to enforce covenants in a civil-law country. Equally, a common-law legal opinion which says the agreement is enforceable usually means that it will be enforced; in civil law it means only that the judge can enforce it if he sees fit but may choose not to. (This is not a law text. These statements should be taken as indications of tendencies, rather than hard and fast facts.)

Thirdly, even in countries with fair legal systems the courts may not understand the complexities of international finance, and this may make a sound case much harder to win.

Finally, some countries have legal systems that are wholly unacceptable for a variety of reasons.

The law of the agreement will not always apply, or overrule the law of the borrower's home country. An English law agreement cannot give a French company powers that it lacks under French law, even if an English company would have them. Nor can an English law agreement overrule German bankruptcy rules if a German company runs into difficulty.

One way around some of these problems is the jurisdiction clause. An English law agreement between an English bank and American borrower may give jurisdiction to US as well as English courts. The US courts may not accept jurisdiction, and if they do will need advice on the relevant English law. But where local procedures are better for the particular case, or where the local courts have greater knowledge of business practices, a move of jurisdiction may be helpful.

Nevertheless, an appeal to law in any jurisdiction is chancy. It is better to write the agreement in plain language and to work with the borrower to avoid reference to the courts.

Security Where Appropriate

The arguments for and against security were discussed in the previous chapter. Once the bank has decided to take security, documenting it correctly is largely a matter for lawyers. Banks must understand the general background to the different types of pledge, the rules on registering security, the hardening period and any features (such as lending new money) which will make it less onerous. In particular they need to understand the different types of security (equitable versus legal charge under English law, for instance) and the impact this may have on their position.

In taking security, banks must avoid unexpected liability. This is not a purely documentary point; some liability is inherent – although perhaps only triggering when the bank tries to realise the security – regardless of the documentation. In other cases, however, the wording of the agreement can help to trigger or avoid liability.

Examples of liability include the pollution liability discussed above; the liability on an arrested ship to return the crew to the point of origin, pay port and lay-up charges; the risk of product liability in a pharmaceutical company. While in theory, lawyers should protect the bank from these risks, the bank should not rely on this. Lawyers must protect the bank against a variety of risks; often protection against one can only come by reducing protection against another. The bank, not the lawyers, must make the commercial decision as to which risk to avoid.

DOCUMENTATION FOR SWAPS AND OTHER INSTRUMENTS

Similarities

Of all capital markets instruments, swaps are in some ways most like loans. Documentation therefore includes many of the same points as a loan agreement would: preamble, representations and warranties, events of default and perhaps covenants.

Dissimilarities

There are several ways in which swaps differ from loans and require different forms of documentation. They are broadly similar to those already discussed under 'Structure' in Chapter 10, and require amendments to documentation.

The impact of two-way credit

The main impact is the need to allow for the clauses to bite in both directions. With covenants, each side has to undertake to meet the agreed levels and each creates an event of default if it fails. The event of default then spells out what happens in even-handed terms.

Setting the loss in the event of default

Because an event of default can go either way, and because the defaulter may be in profit, the decision as to how to deal with it depends on which of three circumstances prevails: defaulter in profit, defaulter in loss, no defaulter but a 'termination event' due to government or third-party action. The result must not encourage the counterparty to default when it has a loss on the transaction which default would wipe out, or a profit which it could take.

Netting and master agreements

A major difference between loans and swaps is the possibility of netting. A loan can only go one way, and the more loans a bank makes the more it loses in bankruptcy. Swaps, however, can have profits on some offset by losses on others, but in bankruptcy liquidators may choose to adopt or reject each contract ('cherrypick'). To achieve netting therefore banks need a master agreement, which covers all the swaps done between two parties, perhaps including their subsidiaries and affiliates. This gives just one contract, with a separate deal sheet giving the details of each swap, but relating back to the agreement, known as a master. This should ensure that a liquidator must adopt or reject the whole contract; if he rejects it, the bank then claims as an unsecured creditor for the net amount due on all the contracts.

There is no certainty in most countries that the courts will accept this, but banks word the agreement to give them the best chance. There are some semi-standard agreements which have been worked out by expert groups and perhaps supported by central banks. The best known of these is the ISDA (International Swap Dealers Association) Master, used by most international banks in the London and New York markets. Unfortunately, while legally excellent, it is written in unpunctuated, jargon-ridden non-English. Very few non-lawyers can understand it in less than four or five readings; the author doubts whether any judge without active experience in the market would have the faintest idea of what much of it means; and nobody whose native language is not English can be criticised for refusing even to try to understand it. The idea of a civil-law judge, who does not speak English and is not familiar with swap markets, trying to enforce the ISDA Master, frankly, makes the mind boggle.

Regrettably, many corporates refuse to use the ISDA Master. Even international banks may reject it in their home market. A number of other masters are therefore also in use. They are perhaps more likely to work in their domestic market because they are designed for it in a way ISDA cannot be; but they are less likely to work in other markets.

Banks active in the swap markets therefore need to understand the implications of using non-standard masters, and only do so if they have satisfied themselves that the one used works as well as possible in the market in which it is used.

Banks should check legal power in swaps and other hedging products. The power to borrow is usually clear, though the bank may need to ensure that each borrowing falls within the power. Swaps and other products are so new that they are rarely covered in legislation on bodies such as local authorities, insurance companies, savings banks, etc. As banks dealing with local authorities found in the UK, the lack of power can prove expensive. The particular facts are peculiar to English law, and to governmental bodies. The broader question is universal, and the answer often complicated. For instance, building societies in the UK can do swaps if the building society and the swap meet certain criteria. Some criteria are objective, but some relate to the purpose of the swap, where the bank must take the counterparty's word. The French Government in late 1992 promulgated similar rules as to French local government bodies' power to swap.

The bank must review the nature of the counterparty and the rules which apply. It may be essential to include wording in the master to ensure that the bank deals within the permitted areas; or at least come as close to that aim as possible.

With the development of related products, such as caps, floors collars, Forward Rate Agreements and options, the scope of the ISDA Master has been extended to cover most of these. Banks using other masters should check how well they cover non-swap products.

THIRD-PARTY DOCUMENTATION

Lawyers should routinely examine any other loan agreements, debentures, etc., which the borrower has signed. They will look for incompatibilities with the bank's agreement, as well as for specific information. For instance, if a negative pledge excludes existing pledges the lawyers will need to know what these are so that the exclusion can be properly worded.

The banker should also be aware of all of this, and check that the existing pledges are as he had understood in agreeing to the exclusion. A bank taking security will want to avoid causing a breach of a negative pledge in any other agreement.

The bank will check cross-defaults in other agreements, and covenants and representations and warranties. It must ensure that other lenders cannot move before it if trouble looms, since any strengthening of one creditor's position at that stage usually weakens the others'.

The most careful examination should be of debt which purports to be subordinated. There are three points here.

First, the concept of subordination is American in origin, and is not specifically catered for in many countries' laws. While still enforceable, in each country the approach is different.

Secondly, subordination terms vary widely, and much subordinated debt gives senior lenders less protection than the word implies. Too many lenders accept the word without delving into exactly what it means.

Thirdly, subordinated lenders can use events of default to negotiate a better deal than the documentation strictly allows. A trustee for bond-holders, or liquidator for a failing parent, has no reason to refrain from using that negotiating strength.

Many of the same points apply to quasi-equity or other hybrid instruments, such as convertible or preference shares. Their exact nature can be critical to the recovery a bank makes in an insolvency, and sometimes to its ability to negotiate a rescue which protects its interests.

Part IV

Damage Limitation

12 Managing the Internal Process

RECOGNISING THE PROBLEM

The first aspect of damage limitation is early recognition. This comes, or fails to, largely from monitoring. But monitoring gives the facts, which alone are not enough. The bank needs to judge the extent of the problem; whether management is aware of it, and if so, can cope; what the bank can do to alert management if needed, or to help it deal with the problem; how the bank can protect its own position.

All this requires a culture to be in place well before the problem appears. The person who gains the knowledge must have judgement or it must reach someone who does. The best answer combines an alert account officer with a more experienced banker to make the final judgement. Account officers with judgement and access to experience is a long first step in damage limitation.

More often it will not be as simple as this. The account officer's job, to gain management's confidence, is a two-way process. It is hard to switch from working with management to criticising it, particularly while there is a real chance that the criticism is unjustified.

If the relationship has developed in the constructive way described earlier, the borrower will act on the early warning. This should always be the aim, but it is hard to reach, and damage limitation must allow for its failure. There is a built-in reluctance among account officers to recognise a developing problem; this increases with the emphasis on marketing. Thus the bank needs to use the information they provide, often the first pointer to a developing problem, without putting too much weight on their ability to spot a crisis.

One tool is the watch list, discussed later in the chapter. A second is the interrelationship between the credit people and the bankers discussed in earlier chapters. A third is the cultural factor, which management must inculcate. Bankers at all levels and specialities must be taught to believe that identifying a loan as a problem is a sign of alertness and forward thinking, rather than of failure. To raise the prospect of a problem should be seen as an important aspect of a policy of no surprises. This policy says that some loans inevitably go sour. In any individual case this is neither a sign of poor banking nor that a lender has made a mistake. To fail to notice the deterioration, or worse still to notice it and not do anything, is the serious error. In brief, problem loans are no problem, unless they come as a surprise to senior management.

DECIDING WHO SHOULD FOLLOW PROBLEMS

There are arguments for and against a number of different methods of following troubled loans.

The Original or Current Account Officer

There used to be a strong feeling that the account officer should retain the main responsibility, on three grounds. First, 'He got us into this, he should get us out.' Secondly, experience of problem loans is one of the best tutors of credit judgement there is. (These two together avoid the punitive connotations of the first on its own, which conflicts with the no surprises approach outlined above.) Thirdly, the account officer knew the business and its management, and could handle the problem as well as or better than any other. Of course, handling problem loans is time-consuming and takes experience to do well, but the basic skills are only an extension of normal credit skills, and can be learnt under supervision.

This view may still be valid for banks with straightforward lending to smaller companies from smaller branches which cannot easily justify a credit or restructuring specialist. Even here the complications of working with a company, the risk of shadow directorship or related problems, and the sheer time it diverts from other clients, make this method less attractive. Additional factors such as pollution risk may argue against allowing inexperienced people, even under supervision, to run the rescue.

They should not be excluded altogether, however, as discussed below in the section on 'Timing the Change'.

A Credit, Workout or Structured Specialist

The difference between the three is detailed below.

Credit specialists cover all aspects of credit, but particularly decision-making and monitoring. To an extent, therefore, they need to manage workouts only when they fail to prevent them.

Workout specialists do nothing but handle problems; they therefore get involved only when the company has passed a certain point; often the chance of recovery is small.

Structured specialists handle all loans which need complex structuring, often including security. During recessions, most of these may be problems, but even then a large bank will be making some new structured loans. In better times, the specialist may work mostly on new loans, with only an occasional restructuring.

The workout specialist knows the problems, is trained to be tough, and has no clients demanding his attention. He recognises that the need to recover money, however and wherever possible, overrides everything. It certainly overrides any concern about relationships, because he does not expect there to be one.

In a situation beyond hope, where the only question is whether the banks will recover more by working it out themselves than in an insolvency procedure, the workout specialist is usually the best bet.

However, alert monitoring should catch the company before it is hopeless, or while the strategy is to allow management hope, as without it they have no incentive to run the company; and without incentives, even a hopeless case may lose more than it needs to do. In these situations even the best workout specialist tends to be a little too rigid and harsh on management; less good ones can push for action which turns a problem into a disaster.

The structured or credit specialist, or both working together, may be more effective in these cases. They have the knowledge and the toughness, but they often also have more flexibility and a greater willingness to see hope, and the other side of the case.

Thus the question is whether to allow the account officer to run with the ball, or whether to pass it to a specialist, and if so, which one. The answer depends partly on how the bank is organised and its people, and partly on the situation. If the bankers are competent to handle at least the early part, and can be adequately supervised and assisted, this may be the best solution in many cases. Where cases deteriorate beyond a certain point, this may cease to be effective, and a specialist may need to take over.

Specialist or Hospital?

Some banks need to decide whether to have specialists in each location, or at least region, or whether to have one central unit, often referred to as the 'hospital'.

An international bank will find it impractical to have one hospital covering all its businesses. A bank with enough branches in one country might have a small hospital in that country; and if it has many branches in different countries, it should certainly have a central group of specialists to provide advice and help in negotiations. But the banking systems, bankruptcy and other laws, client expectation from banks, back-up resources, as well as language, are very different. Nobody can transfer expertise completely from one country to another.

Conversely a small bank with few branches probably only needs one or two specialists at most, and may not always have enough problems to keep even that number fully occupied. So the need for a hospital arises mainly in large or multibranched domestic banks.

The arguments in favour are cross-fertilisation of ideas and experience; greater flexibility in allocating resources when one case can require several people full-time for weeks, and then drop right away, only to return to prominence a few months later; and a cadre of experienced people with a uniform approach.

The arguments against are loss of local knowledge; the uniform approach may be damaging in cases which need more imagination; a spread of experience through the branches may help to deal with new cases earlier than remote expertise; remoteness may mean that sending a client to the hospital is seen as a failure; or that the hospital's staff may be seen as in some way antagonistic.

Ultimately the decision may depend on volume. With too many problem loans, a hospital may be the only solution which works.

Time to Change

Whatever the exact method a bank chooses to handle problems, it needs to time the change correctly. It does not want to overreact at the first sign of trouble, and perhaps damage a good relationship; or earn a reputation for panicking which costs it business elsewhere. Nor does it want to lose money through complacency.

What guidelines should a bank have, and how rigid should they be? A secondary question is whether to have one single and final change, or a more gradual and flexible one, perhaps with several stages.

The answer depends on the bank's structure and the type of banker it has. A bank with account officers strong on credit can take a more flexible attitude than one with pure marketers; then the bank will need procedures in place to support the banker much sooner than with a credit conscious banker.

There can be no firm rules, until a borrower declares a moratorium, or calls a meeting of all its banks or something equally specific. The purpose of damage limitation is where possible to avoid moratoria, or at least reduce exposure before they happen. To start damage limitation when they happen is too late. Moreover, moratoria and bank meetings are the tools of larger companies; smaller companies often have only one bank, and the interest may be added to the overdraft until it exceeds the line. With poor monitoring, this may be the first time the bank becomes aware there is any serious risk; again, too late to start damage limitation.

If the bank has a watch list (see later section), it may include procedures for following the troubled borrower in those triggered by entrance to the list. Equally, if the bank has an internal rating system (see Chapter 18), downgrading the name below B might trigger a review of who should handle the name. Where neither of these exist, there can be rules which trigger a review in different cases, but none which cover all adequately.

In lending on seasonal or other fluctuating overdraft, the bank might set an internal rule as to the average useage it expects over a normal year, or the period during a year for which it expects the facility to be unused, or used below a certain level. Failure to meet these requirements might call for a review, as might breach of a ratio or other covenant. For a secured loan where the security has a market or other definable value, a fall below a certain value might be the trigger.

Each of these items, and any others the bank might use, may suggest that the borrower needs special treatment, but will not be definitive. The bank needs to look at them as part of its overall monitoring, and to have some general guidelines as to when to make the change. The actual decision must be based on the facts of each case. Getting the decision right is a matter of important judgement.

The guidelines will need to relate to the nature of the banker as well as the facts of the case. They may need to go by stages. For instance, the bank might require a credit specialist to work with the banker for a minimum period after any of the warning events. The specialist should assess all the information to decide if there was genuine cause for concern or merely a hiccup; meet management; offer specialist advice if required; and assess whether this name required special attention and if so at what level – within the parameters of the bank's resources.

This assessment should focus on the borrower's possible need for additional borrowing. New money is one of the most difficult decisions for a bank to make. It is best to have an experienced specialist involved in the discussions and familiar with all aspects of the case. To have a relatively junior banker reporting to a credit committee or senior lender who is naturally sceptical is risky. The scepticism may feed on itself by making the junior reluctant to recommend the new money strongly, even when he believes it is the best solution. These decisions are hard partly because providing new money is sometimes the best hope of recovering old, but adds to the risk.

After banker and specialist have worked together, the bank may want to review whether the specialist should take complete control, or take charge, with the banker continuing on the account under his orders. This meets some of the traditional views mentioned above. It preserves continuity and the trust the banker may have built up with the management; it also makes clear to everybody that the main consideration now is credit, and that the client's main concern should be with debt reduction.

A main factor in the decision is the borrower's prospects. The more able it seems to deal with the problem, the less the need for the specialist's skills, and the greater the unnecessary damage to the relationship. Conversely the worse the prospects, the greater the need for both special skills and the harder nosed attitude of the specialist. Moreover, the worse the prospects, the more time the case will take up, and the greater the diversion of the banker's time from his other commitments, and thus the greater the cost to the bank of his involvement.

At a later stage, the same may be true of the choice between a credit or structured specialist and a workout specialist. The more complex, and hopeful, cases need a more flexible approach than what is often referred to as 'Workout 101'. They give scope for imagination, and constructive negotiation, rather than unadulterated toughness, important though that can be.

A further point is the size of the borrower, and of the bank's exposure; also the bank's position among lenders in a multi-bank case. A small exposure to a small borrower justifies less senior time, or experience. Large exposure to a large borrower will justify and require more expertise. In a multi-bank situation, it will depend whether the bank is a leader or follower. To be Chairman of the Steering Committee, or an active member, needs more experience; and more weight with the other banks. This requires at least a senior specialist; in a large case, the Chairman may have to put anywhere from two or three to eight or ten people on the case for prolonged periods; even membership of the Steering Committee requires a minimum of two or three people to provide continuity.

Where the bank is content to let a Chairman or Steering Committee make the running, it will need less people on the case. There is an argument, however, that they should be more senior. Those on the Steering Committee will see at first hand the negotiations and development of a position which they believe gives the best chance of recovery. They should therefore be fully convinced of that case and able to obtain whatever internal approvals they need. Banks not on the Committee lack that close involvement. Moreover, committees – and borrowers – present the arguments for the solution with varying degrees of conviction. If the bank's representative is junior he may lack the experience to recognise the strength – or weakness – of the case. This will reduce his ability to present a well thought-out argument to the credit committee; in some banks the credibility of certain offices is so poor that they are a stumbling block to most restructurings in which they are involved.

Indeed, most banks should rethink their approval process in problem cases. Because they are both complex and important decisions, the normal procedures, especially a distant credit committee, are often inadequate. The normal process forces a junior to present a voluntary decision to the committee, which is aware of the marketing and other reasons for making the loan; at worst, it will exercise a free choice the wrong way. With a problem loan, the bank rarely has a free choice. It is faced with a decision it must make, which will affect, for better or worse, its chances of recovery. It is usually asked whether it will approve a specific proposal; since the proposal is usually unattractive, it is tempting to say 'no'. But this may be the wrong answer to the wrong question. The question should often be 'We have two options, to approve the restructuring (or the amendment or waiver), or to see the company go into a formal insolvency procedure. Which is better for the bank?' Or, at an earlier stage in the negotiation while the details are still open to adjustment, 'We have two (or more) choices. Which do we think gives the best chance of recovery? (And if the other banks vote against us, is it important enough to bring the whole effort to nothing?)' Or the committee may be asked to approve a series of items, including waivers but also items like the sale of assets, or the release of a charge over assets being sold; or technical questions like changes in the security package to allow a tax reorganisation. These are not susceptible to sensible discussion in committee, nor do they stand up well to the ladder process. Moreover, they take up far more senior time than their importance usually justifies, and delays in getting approval often make life unnecessarily difficult for the borrower, and thus jeopardise the prospects of recovery.

Banks should recognise the need for more flexible approval processes, designed to speed up decisions, and, critically, to give authority to people best placed to decide. This means, first, giving authority to approve technical amendments and waivers which do not justify senior consideration. Secondly, ensuring that a senior and experienced lender follows the case closely, and can take informed decisions on more important matters when they arise. Where the bank uses individual lending authority, and decentralises it, this is fairly simple. In other cases it may mean an apparent breach of the bank's lending procedures. It may therefore be better for it to be informal rather than formal. Banks must recognise, however, that the present practice many follow, of assigning a junior to the case, allowing other banks to do the work, and then being more or less obstructive about the results works against their own best interests.

POLICY OF NO SURPRISES

All lending banks suffer some bad debts. Banks which take particular types of risk, including lending to small companies, may on average suffer higher bad debts than others, but should be paid accordingly. Finally, all banks suffer in adverse economic conditions.

But their inevitability means they should not be a surprise. And yet many banks are surprised by individual losses, and by the overall size of their bad debts.

A policy of no surprises cannot prevent bad debts, though it may help to reduce them by making it more likely that each problem loan is identified early, thus giving the best chance of minimising loss. It can also allow the bank to make provisions early where necessary; this reduces the risk of enormous provisions at one time, which makes it seem (often rightly) that the bank has lost control of its portfolio. This risk may affect the bank's own credit.

There are various tools the bank can use to implement a policy of no surprises. We discuss the main ones below. But the major factor is cultural, and it is worth repeating earlier comments. If the culture punishes bad debts as such, the banker will be less inclined to recognise them. If it punishes failure to recognise and report them, but rewards recognition, the number of bad debts recognised too late will fall. The banker, who is best placed to recognise a problem, must be encouraged to do so, and rewarded if he does; if he is discouraged the cost to the bank may be great.

The bank's culture should also be supportive where the borrower recognises its difficulty and is striving to deal with it. This makes it easier for the banker to report his concerns, since the bank will not immediately cut and run, devastating their relationship. A supportive reputation also makes it easier for the borrower to disclose the problem early, and work with the bank to solve it. Where the borrower fails to recognise the difficulty, it is more likely to discuss information which enables a supportive bank to do so; and more likely to react positively when the bank raises the question.

The Watch List

Each bank should have a watch list, although the form and name will differ. It should identify early those names which begin to cause concern and perhaps warrant special action. Early means before the situation is beyond repair and often means before it is sure that there is a problem. If half the names that go on the watch list end up as a problem, and a third of those cause a loss, the proportion is about right. The watch list provides a focus for bankers who are, or ought to be, worried about a particular credit; a way in which seniors can emphasise their concern to juniors and vice versa; and a pointer to senior management of the potential problems it faces. In some cases it may be a warning of a concentration of risk; while probably too late to avoid some excessive loss, a prompt reaction may reduce it.

Usually the account officer or his senior, or any involved credit specialist, can put a name on the watch list. It should require minimal formality; the aim is to encourage people to put names on rather than to make it so hard that they shy away. (Taking a name off, however, should require full justification.) If the system works well, the account officer will put the name on, and seniors and credit specialists must encourage account officers to do so. Where this fails, however, they should do so themselves.

Where the size of the bank allows, there should be one watch list for the whole bank. Where this is impractical, there should still be one list for all exposures above a certain size. In addition each branch should report regularly the total size of its watch list (except names appearing on the central list); the number of additions or deletions; the industry mix and any concentration; any trends; most importantly any deterioration of trend. The largest banks, with thousands of branches, may need a two-tier process, whereby the branches report to a region, which in turn reports to the centre. Whatever the precise process, two points are critical; head office must have a reliable picture of the position bankwide; and local management must be alerted to the individual problems and prepared to deal with them.

A watch list for an industry or other category of borrower is also sound practice for banks with a wide international network, and perhaps others. This would highlight industries where the bank had excessive exposure or where industry conditions were depressed. Apart from obvious industries such as property and shipping these could include categories such as LBOs. Bankers would be on notice not to accept new exposures to the industry lightly. The bank might freeze all new exposure or establish an overall list, which would need to be centrally allocated.

Each bank must decide what special procedures it needs for names on the watch list. There may be no need for procedures relating directly to the borrower, on two grounds: first, the fact that the name is on the list shows that somebody is alert to the risk; secondly, no set of procedures will be equally valid for all types of borrower. However, it may be sensible to control new exposure to the name, by requiring a higher level of authority to approve it; or to have a more frequent, and more formal, review of watch list names than of normal names.

Provisions and Non-performing Loans

Although closely linked and probably dealt with in the same procedure, these are slightly different concepts.

Provisions

Provisions are damage recognition rather than limitation, but they can help in damage limitation too. The exact form of provision varies by country and tax rules sometimes discourage sensible provisioning. For this discussion, we will use the American approach, of a reserve charged against earnings, and charge-offs/recoveries applied to the reserve. The intent is not to advocate a particular approach, but to show how banks can use the process to help control loss and avoid surprises. (Provisions, in this chapter, include the whole process and any part of it regardless of the precise form used in each country.)

The bank will need a regular procedure for setting provisions – a Charge Off Committee or COC. As with the watch list, some banks will have one central COC, others will deal with smaller amounts at regional or branch level. There should be clear guidelines as to how the process works. Membership of the COC should include some who have no lending or marketing responsibilities; perhaps the Controller or Resident Counsel, or both. The procedure should be formal, and should take place at least semi-annually. For a large bank, quarterly COC meetings are best. A large bank may also want to have outside auditors and – at least in the United States – legal advisers present.

Not every name needs to be reviewed by the COC every quarter. A typical pattern would be for head office, or region, to list names it wants each branch to review; the branch should also suggest names. The head office list might include names recently put on the watch list; a semi-annual or annual review of names which were stable at a low level; any name where the bank had already taken a provision; and other names changing fast, or in a critical position. Many, perhaps most, of these names will be presented with a recommendation for no (further) action, and this is entirely appropriate. The COC needs to take a view as to the names at risk in deciding the size of the overall reserve, and to be able to comment on the handling of important loans.

The bank may also highlight other serious problems by allocating part of the general reserve against named loans. This does not affect the total size of the reserve, nor does it express the near certainty of loss implied by a charge off. It acts as a form of provision, recognising that loss is not certain, but is more than usually possible; or to put it the other way, recovery is doubtful. It is, of course, possible to have part of a loan charged off and part allocated, where the bank is convinced it will lose something, but is not sure how much.

This approach also allows the bank to review the reserve. Part of it is to provide for loans known to be in difficulty, but where loss is not yet certain; part against the inevitable bad loans that have not yet been identified. The balance between these two parts should probably be roughly even. If the allocated part is too large it suggests that the reserve is not large enough; if it is too small, either the reserve is too big, or the bank is lax in its allocations.

Where tax or regulation prevent this approach, the underlying principle, to identify problems early, and highlight probable losses before they become certain, remains valid. Banks should design their procedures, within the constraints imposed on them, to achieve these objectives.

Non-performing loans

Provisions largely deal with capital values. Non-performing status looks more to income, though in some cases the treatment of income affects reported capital values.

The simplest non-performing loan is either not paying full interest, or there is doubt it will continue to do so. This usually implies doubt as to whether the bank will recover full principal. The question is then whether it is correct to take this 'income' into earnings; or even income received when the principal will not be.

There are two ways of handling this, depending on the seriousness of each case. One converts interest accounting from accrual to cash, taking interest into income only as it is received. The bank continues to expense the cost of funding, earnings reduce, and in due course so do net worth and dividend-paying capacity. If the interest is paid partly or erratically or just too late, it is included in earnings when paid. This type of non-performing treatment is most appropriate to loans which are still paying interest and expected to be recovered, but perhaps after a delay, and some extra effort.

The other, more severe, form applies monies received from any source to principal. Only when the book balance has been reduced to zero does the bank take payments into income. If the borrower recovers and pays full principal and interest, the amounts taken into income are the same either way. The only difference is the timing of tax payments. But where the bank is right to be concerned and loses some part of the loan, or interest, the application avoids paying tax and then recovering it.

Where any part of the loan has been charged off, banks should probably apply interest to principal automatically. They should also do so even without a charge-off when the doubt as to final payment justifies it. This will reduce the book value of the loan and the need for future charge-offs.

Non-accrual usually applies when interest is late. Regulators often set a maximum period, such as 90 days, after which it becomes obligatory. Banks may choose a shorter period, but with more discretion, where payment is expected with a known reason for the delay.

The bank may also want to recognise other types of non-performing loan, of which the most common is 'renegotiated'. Here a bank has agreed to change the terms because the borrower cannot meet the original ones. The change is driven by the borrower's weakness, and is usually sub-commercial, which distinguishes it from normal commercially negotiated terms.

The most extreme form of renegotiation is forgiveness, or conversion into equity, of part of the principal. Other forms are a lower than commercial rate of interest; a longer maturity and slower amortisation; senior debt becoming subordinated, perhaps to new debt; and loss or weakening of a security package. These can of course be combined in various ways. For instance, senior debt due in two or three years can be converted to fifteen-year subordinated debentures with a 4% coupon for the first five years, rising to a market rate in stages thereafter.

The key difference between these and non-performing loans is that these perform on the new terms, but not on the old. Thus 'renegotiated' means the borrower has failed to meet the original terms. Only if he then fails to meet the renegotiated terms is it non-performing in the full sense.

There is no magic to any of these concepts, and banks with different regulatory or tax climates will, quite rightly, use different approaches. The underlying point, however, is twofold. First, whatever the precise format, banks need a mechanism to identify the various types of loan early in their development. This gives a better chance of limiting the damage they cause, and allows the bank to provide early and smoothly for the losses it will inevitably take. Banks which do not provide early and often may find themselves making massive provisions which suggests to the market a weakness in their credit control. This can damage the bank's own standing, and in extreme cases can even threaten its survival.

A mechanism alone, while vital, is not enough. There must be a culture which encourages bankers at all levels to bring forward names for consideration early. Without this, the mechanism will lack sensitivity and pick up only names which have deteriorated substantially. This is better than nothing, but will still mean that most names hit the system when it is too late to improve the recovery by much.

The final point relates to all provisions and non-performing loans, except some renegotiated loans. Provisions and non-accrual are internal to the bank, and are, in essence, valuation points. In making a provision the bank is saying, to itself but emphatically not to the borrower: 'The legal claim is for X, but we do not believe it will be paid in full. Therefore a more accurate value for this claim is 3/4 X.' Too often banks which have provided against a loan slacken their attempt to recover the loan. They may give in too easily on negotiations, or sell the loan for less than it is worth, or relax in a less specific but equally damaging way. Conversely, where banks have not provided, they may resist a solution which requires them to do so even though it is clearly the best available.

Valuation of loans is a matter of opinion, not fact, particularly the early provisions. The attitude ought to be 'This is only worth 3/4 X, but I am doing my damnedest to prove that value too low.' Secondly, banks should be conservative in their reserving. If the bank has charged off 50% of a loan, it ought to be confident it will recover the other 50%, and hope to do better. Otherwise it should provide more. Thirdly, the valuation assumes the bank will pursue recovery with full vigour. Failure to do this means the valuation is probably still too high.

In brief, whether or not the bank has provided for a loan, or how much, should be of no concern to the bankers working to salvage it. If they allow it to become a factor, the bank may well lose more than it need.

13 Dealing with the Borrower or Counterparty

INTRODUCTION

A positive relationship makes it easier to deal with a troubled borrower, but not easy. The problems are complex and varied. Here we highlight the major points.

MANAGING THE MANAGEMENT

Making Management Face the Problem

Few managements willingly face up to the depth of their problem and take the actions required. Some refuse to admit that they face a problem; others believe it is only a temporary hiccup. Even those that recognise there is more at stake are often reluctant to take drastic action. They will control cash tightly, but not manage for cash (see later). They fear to upset customers, although a slow-pay customer, never worth much, is positively damaging in a crisis; or insist on capital expenditure to meet expected demand three years ahead, though they may not survive until then. In brief, they are slow to recognise the change from 'What is best in the long term?' to 'What will ensure a long term?' While strategic thinking remains important in a crisis, there is no more important strategic objective than survival.

However, severe measures would be damaging in a less serious situation than the bank supposed. Companies are right not to irritate clients unnecessarily; the definition of what is necessary changes with the status of the company. The best monitoring picks up problems before they are critical, when the need for drastic action may not be proven.

A good relationship and sound monitoring help the bank to persuade the management to start less drastic action early. If it proves sufficient, the crisis never develops; if not, there is a better chance that management itself will see that more drastic measures are necessary.

Where the bank's monitoring has failed until a crisis is imminent, it cannot expect to convert management overnight. The need is for steady,

174

reasoned pressure, rather than panic. If only panic measures will work, the borrower is probably beyond hope anyway.

This ties back to the bank's internal handling, and the timing of any change. While the bank lets the account officer play the main role, it is probably right to keep the pressure fairly low key. The bank can suggest conventional measures, or longer term ones such as sale of non-core assets. As the concern grows, and a specialist begins to take over, the pressure for urgent measures should grow. Management should review its definition of core subsidiaries and recognise which it retains for non-economic reasons. It should prune capital expenditure with a long pay-back carefully and overheads ruthlessly, recognising that it is harsher to go into liquidation in six months than to lay off staff now, and so on. When survival is threatened there are no sacred cows. Convincing management of this is one of the hardest things a banker can do.

The banker will not convince unless he is sure of his own analysis and is able to explain it. He must show not just that there is urgent need for action, but that action helps management as well as the bank. To do this, he needs a clear view of whether the company is viable in the long term, and what is needed to make it so. The banker must also listen to the counter-arguments with an open mind.

Assessing Long-Term Viability

Ideally, before mounting a rescue, the bank satisfies itself that the borrower is viable. In a crisis, the main focus is inevitably on the short term, and often on buying time. It is right that this should be so, since if the borrower does not survive the short term, there will not be a long term. Nevertheless, short-term remedies do not ensure that the company has a long-term future; at best they keep the possibility alive. And bought time is only of value if it can be put to good use. The bank needs to assess how strong the possibility is, and whether the borrower can bear the cost (not just financial) of achieving it.

Pulling a company back from the brink involves a wide range of costs. Some are financial – fees to bankers, lawyers, accountants and others, redundancy costs, losses selling assets to raise critical cash. Some are emotional and morale costs. For a paternal company, laying off people can be so traumatic that the reaction tips a borderline case over the edge. Some are customer and reputation related. It may be right to annoy the customer by insisting he pay his bills on time, but annoying customers in other ways can be damaging. In some areas, however, it is unavoidable; in others the management and the banks can help to mitigate the damage, if both parties understand and balance the risks against the benefits. It is thus vital that the bank can explain to the borrower why it needs to take certain actions, and understands the risks they impose and seeks to mitigate them.

A good relationship allows discussion in a favourable atmosphere. Many banks discount management's fears about customer or supplier damage. Often that is justified, but not automatically; customers or suppliers can become uneasy in rescues. The cost may range from tighter terms which put pressure on liquidity to loss of important business. And while all companies complain in similar terms, the validity of the complaint is not the same in all cases. Banks which dismiss the complaint without examining its validity make almost as bad a mistake as banks which accept it uncritically.

Can Management Handle the Problem?

If the company is potentially viable, and can absorb the costs, it still requires sound management to survive. The bank must ask, the borrower *can* survive, but *will* it with this management? Often the answer is not clear, so the question may remain under review for a later answer.

In reaching even a tentative answer, the bank will look at several factors. One is why the company is in difficulty: continuing bad management; a single ill-considered decision; excessive borrowing, for unsound reasons; deteriorating demand for the product; increases in competition; a damaging change in government policy. Or a combination of these and lesser factors.

In looking at which of these apply, and how management reacted, the bank can find pointers to management's ability to cope. In some cases, management changes shortly before the crisis breaks, suggesting the board was alert to the problem. To that extent it is a good sign. If the new management is known to the bank, it may be even better. Otherwise, the bank has to wait to obtain a clear view of its competence.

Where the old management is in place, the bank can assess its competence in normal conditions. But normally competent managements are not always good in a crisis; nor always adjust to the reasons for the crisis. Particularly where the problem arises abruptly, some managers may be shell-shocked, and take too long to recover.

There may be one aspect rather than the whole team that is weak. The two most evident to banks are the chief executive, and the finance director, but marketing, production, in some companies servicing, are just as possible, as are divisional or product management. Wherever the weakness is other than the chief executive (CEO), it raises a doubt about his ability to ensure that other managers are up to scratch. However, the management structure or board may inhibit the CEO's freedom of action, and the bank may need to focus on these aspects.

Changing the Management

If the bank considers present management weak, it can withdraw support from the borrower, which will force some form of insolvency process; or it can insist on a change in management. In practice the latter is hard to do, and the bank's negotiating position often weak. To attempt to change management, the bank must be convinced of several things: that change is essential to justify support; that there is a better replacement available; and that it can in fact push the change through. To attempt to change management, fail and continue to work with the old one is almost impossible.

The decision to change, in turn, depends on three things: on how bad management is; on how confident the bank is that new management can make the difference; and on how damaging a formal insolvency process would be.

The cost-effectiveness of insolvency, and the ability to choose between different forms, varies widely from country to country. Within any one country it varies depending on the nature of the business. In service/people businesses, insolvency often means almost 100% loss, because their value depends so heavily on the ability to generate cash flow. Tangible assets are negligible, and in liquidation there is naturally no cash flow. Even with an effective intermediate insolvency process the chances of retaining value depend almost entirely on finding a buyer quickly. One specialist believes the opportunity lasts no more than two weeks; after that, too many of the people are gone. At the other extreme, an asset-based company may give 90% or more pay-out in liquidation, so the bank has less incentive to keep it alive, and to do so with inadequate management may run up losses greater than the cost of liquidation.

The decision as to whether new management is desirable or essential is therefore a complex one. The balance between the various factors is rarely clear-cut, and changes as the situation develops. Finally, the board of directors alone can dismiss management or hire a new one. 'Changing management' must be understood in this context. And the decision must always take into account the practicalities and the bank's negotiating strength or weakness.

It is easiest when the bank concludes early that the problem is with the chief executive, or with one other named manager, such as the finance director. It can make agreement to a restructuring conditional on a change.

Once the restructuring is signed, forcing a change becomes harder, until the concerns are justified by the need for further restructuring. If there is no such need, the concern abates.

Outside these periods, banks have little direct ability to initiate changes. If the board is dissatisfied, or if the CEO is doubtful about a particular manager, the bank's views may tip the balance. If banks feel the need to replace a manager with whom the board is well satisfied, it suggests a more widespread weakness than just the one executive. This may be an argument in favour of liquidation; where that is either impractical or undesirable the bank may have to resign itself to working with the present team. It can hope that if this fails, the board will recognise the weaknesses and take the action the bank wanted it to; better late than never can apply here.

If the bank wants to change either a single manager, or the whole team, one question is: 'who will replace him/it?' Where the weakness is a single manager, the answer will often be simple; the company will have an adequate replacement. In multidivisional companies, for instance, there may be a division head ready to move up to CEO, or a divisional finance director or treasurer to the group position. If the bank knows the people concerned, it may be entirely content; or it may be sceptical but willing to give them the benefit of the doubt. It is more difficult when the bank knows them and believes them to be inadequate. With a good relationship, the board or CEO may well sound out the bank before deciding; the bank can then make its reservations known. It is much harder to do so if the board makes the appointment and then tells the bank. To resist now would risk undermining the new managers without much chance of changing them. A board will rarely dismiss someone it has only just appointed with no chance to prove competence.

Where the whole team is suspect, or where there is no internal replacement, the need for external replacements may mean delaying any change until the replacement has been found; or it may mean operating with a stop gap until one can be found. Probably the most difficult of all is the inadequate one-man band, who may be almost impossible to replace without disrupting the company. The bank may then have to take the process in stages, by introducing a chairman or stronger directors until it becomes possible to do without the strong man who is bringing the company to its knees.

In brief, the assessment of management's ability to cope with the crisis; the availability of an effective insolvency process, and the borrower's susceptibility to it; the ability to cause a change; and the availability of an effective replacement; all affect the decision as to whether, and when, to change management or rely on the bank's ability to improve it.

THE NATURE OF THE PROBLEM

Whatever the decision, the banks depend on management to solve the problem. This, after all, is why it is so important. But the degree of dependence varies with the nature of the problem, which in turn affects whether a rescue is worthwhile, and what form it should take.

Oversimplifying grossly, there are two main types of reason why a company is in trouble. The first reason is an operational one, reflecting a failure of the business. It may be poor product or marketing; unsound strategy including diversification; failed research; weak cost control or labour relations; a general inability to do anything well; failure to match competition; or any combination of these and other weaknesses. Unless these can be turned around, and the company generate cash to service debt, there is nothing the bank can do. Any attempt at rescue will only allow more losses and when the company collapses the bank loses more than it need have.

Where there is hope that the weaknesses can be overcome, the banks may be able to help. The operating weaknesses will often have undermined the company's finances, and the company will need support while it corrects the weaknesses. New money in these situations is one of the hardest decisions for a bank to make. This is one more reason to catch the problem early, while there is still enough cash flow to avoid new money. But even where new money is not needed, there is no point in buying time unless the borrower can use it.

The other problem may be primarily financial. This does not mean there are no operating weaknesses at all; in fact almost always the company is generating less cash than expected when the balance sheet was overloaded. This may be a simple misjudgement as to capacity, perhaps based on extrapolating earnings from a boom period; or there may genuinely have been a weakening in operations, which may or may not be remediable. However, while the operating earnings will not service the existing debt, they will service some; and the current debt is not primarily due to the operating weakness, but to financial misjudgement. The severest examples arise with LBOs, where the banks and investors deliberately load the balance sheet with far more debt than would usually be considered sound. They believe, naturally, that the company can repay the debt from varying combinations of asset sales and (improved) cash generation. Often they are right, and investors and lenders make large profits; that, after all, is why they do it. But profits reflect risk, which often comes home to roost.

Acquisitions financed with too much debt run similar risks, even where the operation purchased is sound. If it is unsound, the banks may have both operational and financial risk. Sometimes, too, banks mistakenly finance major capital expenditure or new product programmes, only to recognise too late the need for more equity.

Whatever the precise reason, the company has more debt than its present operations can service and a low chance of improving the operations enough to service it all in the future.

The position is not always as clear as the above, but usually it is clear enough.

Whatever the cause, banks can solve financial problems. The question though is to what end? To solve financial problems the bank can do one or more – mostly more – of the following:

1. defer or forgive interest, in whole or in part;
2. defer or forgive principal in varying amounts;
3. accept a lower standing for its debt, in whole or in part. This may mean giving up or sharing collateral, or accepting a subordinate position. While this is not quite as extreme as outright forgiveness, it risks having the same end result;
4. advance new money: at best, short term for seasonal or other working capital needs; at worst medium to long term with no clear source of repayment.

Before seriously considering any of these unpalatable options the bank must see a commercial probability that one or more of the following is true:

1. The problem is purely financial and the financial solution proposed will cure it, or the operating problems are curable, and the financial cure will allow the operating cure to happen.
2. The resulting recovery will be at least as great, and probably greater, than with the best available insolvency procedure.
   And
3. Any risk of increasing the loss is outweighed by the prospect of improving the recovery.

Unfortunately, these requirements are more easily stated than met. Full information is rarely available in the early stages, and even a bank which has monitored well relies heavily on hope; with poor monitoring it may be some time before it can have more than the faintest idea. And yet the bank cannot say to the company 'Nothing happens until we know the position.' Or, rather, banks often try to, but it rarely works. Companies and their creditors will not simply stand still; unless the banks do something positive, however qualified, the company will fail before it can provide the information. After all, in most cases a contributing factor, and in a few the main factor, in company failures is lack of adequate financial controls and reporting systems.

Moreover, even where historical information is good, what happens in the future is a matter of judgement, not fact. It will be affected by the management issues already discussed; by the state of the economy, or particular parts of it; by specific aspects such as inflation, labour relations and law; by government actions in areas such as pollution control, or trade; by asset prices and costs of raw materials; by the reaction of competitors, customers, suppliers, staff and investors; and by whether the banks and company restructure the debt efficiently; or whether they run up costs and generate adverse publicity which undermines its chances of recovery. While each is inclined to blame the other for this result, in fact it is an area where both have the same interest and should work together.

A successful rescue is therefore usually at least a two-stage process and often three or more. This can be frustrating to both sides, but usually happens for better reasons than they recognise.

The first stage is often a moratorium, during which no principal is repaid, and sometimes no interest either. This period initially is set at about three months, but often has to be extended. It allows time to prepare information, often for an investigating accountant to produce a report, and for the company and its advisers to design a plan, although often the lead bank, or steering committee, plays a part in preparing it.

Smaller companies may have one, two or perhaps three banks, all secured in similar ways. A moratorium then may be informal; indeed, if no debt is immediately due, a quiet agreement between the banks may suffice. Larger companies may have anywhere from six or seven banks to over 100. They may have a wide range of facilities, from overdrafts to term loans, and ancillaries such as forward exchange, swaps, FRAs, etc. Some may be secured, others have cross-guarantees, others are to subsidiaries with or without parent guarantees. In these cases it is vital to get everyone on side.

Ideally, the plan produced during the moratorium should put the company permanently back on an even keel. In practice, this is rare even when that is the intent. There are several reasons for this.

First, the banks want to take the least pain, and keep the maximum pressure on the company. They therefore do just enough to save the company if its base case projections are accurate, but not if there is any slippage.

Secondly, banks insist on tight and numerous covenants. Even when the basic results are acceptable, it is almost impossible to avoid breaching a covenant somewhere.

Thirdly, some plans require the banks to give up part of their claim altogether or take a junior position. If the plan then fails, they may lose more and other creditors or shareholders less than if the company had collapsed straight away. For this reason, banks may choose to do just enough to keep the company going until they see solid evidence of recovery; only then will they allow the second stage to give the company long-term viability.

All of this can be difficult for a shell-shocked management to stomach, and can cause the negotiations to drag on longer than they should. With a high-profile company, this can cause press speculation which can damage the borrower's business; in a really marginal case it can bring the company down. To avoid this, the banks need to keep management fully informed as to their reasoning. Management must accept their apparent reluctance to agree to a permanent solution; the banks require proof of progress before they commit themselves. Sometimes a public company's advisers worry about a hidden agenda. In one sense they are right to, but sometimes they push the point so far that they cease to work for shareholders' interests, whether they realise it or not.

Looking at the actual process, there are several possible sources of cash. These can be classified as: asset sales; capital injection; short-term cash management; longer term cost savings; new products or markets. Some may actually use cash initially in order to generate longer term savings and debt service; this can be one argument for putting up new money.

Sale of assets

Assets for this purpose include shares in subsidiaries which can be sold without damaging the rest of the business.

Broadly assets in this context fall into four categories:

1. Those which are surplus to needs – a factory or warehouse no longer used may be a good example. They generate no worthwhile cash flow and may be a cash drain. The banks should expect to see real efforts being made to sell these even during the moratorium, and should certainly expect them to go as soon as possible thereafter.
2. Assets – usually subsidiaries, but sometimes assets tied to a particular product – which are either losing money, or at best contributing no cash. There may be a clear plan to turn them round to generate cash quickly; or they may be essential to some other part of the business, in which case, see below. Otherwise, these too should be sold, with speed more important than price.
3. Assets which are cash positive, but peripheral to the main business. These should usually be sold, but here price is more important than speed. Unless the reduction in interest on the debt repaid is greater than

the cash flow lost, there is no reason to hurry; it may be better to wait for a higher price. Of course, there may be factors pushing for a quick sale; the borrower may be able to use the funds to get a better return elsewhere, or the assets may be the only ones saleable quickly, or the cash flow may be vulnerable and thus the current price be the best bet. But inherently, there is less reason to hurry to sell at a weak price.

4. Assets which are losing money or making an inadequate return, and absorbing cash, but which are either core in their own right, or contribute to the profits of a core product range. Here the bank needs to look closely at the analysis which may show one of several situations:

● They are only key to the product in the short run. What they supply could be bought in easily and at lower cost. The plan should be to make the change swiftly, and then sell the assets.

● They are indeed key to another part of the business. Then the question is whether the combined assets are profitable enough or whether both should be sold.

● They are key, but the assets to which they are key are not core; then if a good enough price is available it is right to sell both.

Asset sales, if appropriate, may relieve a cash shortage, or remove a problem area or both. They are thus helpful, but are essentially defensive, and no panacea. However, they often provide a critical breathing space, or a vital first step to recovery. Banks must therefore be sure that the company is serious in its attempts to sell, and willing to be realistic about price. Too often, managements drag their feet; sometimes they do not want to sell; in others they reject a fast sale at a 'low' price and suffer long delays to obtain a lower price at the end. Public companies often get bad advice from merchant bankers or boards who are rightly concerned to protect the shareholders' interest, but fail to recognise that not selling increases the chance of ultimate – or sometimes immediate – collapse, which is far more damaging to shareholders than a weak sale.

Having said which, it is true that banks sometimes force a sale of good assets at silly prices. As in all aspects of debt recovery a balanced view gives the best result.

Capital injection

There is rarely much chance of a capital injection from sources other than the banks in the first stage. Where there is, it can make the difference between the success and failure of a rescue, particularly if it meets the need for new money. It also answers the feeling banks have that the shareholders should contribute to the rescue since they stand to gain or lose the most.

In structuring a rescue, banks should be wary of anything that deters serious capital providers. Even where new capital is not part of the first round, it may be a useful part of a second round. In considering dividend restraint, for instance, banks may distinguish between dividends paid on old capital and new. Even in setting them on old capital they may be sensitive to possible new capital.

However, banks need to be careful how they accept this argument. It is certainly valid in some cases; in many more it is not. Shareholders need to see value before they support a capital raising; if they do not, a dividend is unlikely to change their minds.

Shareholders who contribute nothing to maintaining the value, do not deserve to keep all of it; equally, if the banks take equity risks they should get equity returns. Either way it adds up to banks getting a share of the equity, in one form or another, in companies they rescue with no help from shareholders, and serious risk of loss. This need not be ordinary shares; it can be conversion rights, warrants or options, or even a cash payment geared to the share price.

This argument is obvious when banks make a capital injection, whether in the form of new money or by forgiving debt. In the latter case they are directly creating equity value and should obtain most of it. Even when this is not so, shareholders' function is to take the first level of losses. If they refuse new money they cannot expect to benefit at the cost of those who provide it. Conversely, in claiming equity, banks are making a statement about the state of the company which they should be able to support.

Short-term cash management

Many companies have cash tied up in working capital. A part of this is unavoidable; another part carries real benefits so that in normal times it may be right to allow it. Nevertheless, most companies can reduce working capital without damaging the business.

Most plans should focus on how the company currently manages its cash and working capital, and on how much can be released how quickly. A failure often warns banks of poor financial management, which in turn raises questions about the viability of the rescue. Even where the routine cash management is sound, however, the banks need to see specific evidence of 'managing for cash'.

This differs from normal cash management; instead of managing cash in a balanced way it gives priority to cash over all other aspects. This is not just chasing trade receivables faster, or tightening up on inventory, important though both are. It also means looking at investments, whether in fixed assets, or build-up of inventory and advertising expense for a new launch, in a different light. Unless they can bring in some cash almost immediately, and be cash positive within, say, eighteen months, they probably have to go on the back-burner. If they are genuinely beneficial to the company, any longer term strategy will have to allow them, but only when the company can survive to receive the benefit.

Cost control

Whatever the major difficulty, poor cost control often contributes. Or some costs become redundant, due to loss of volume or other reasons. The banks need to satisfy themselves that any cost-cutting plan has a coherent approach. Saving costs in the medium term may cause a short-term cash drain; redundancy costs in some countries, for instance, are very high, but still worthwhile if the company survives to get the long-term benefits. In these situations the more common error is for management to cut costs too gently, but sometimes they cut them in the wrong place altogether, and do more harm than good. This is rarely obvious, and may be highly debatable, but it is a serious risk if it happens.

Pulling them together

There is, of course, some overlap between these various aspects of getting in cash. For instance, selling off unprofitable assets raises cash and reduces costs at the same time. If people who would otherwise have to be paid off can go with the assets, this is a further saving.

Accentuating the Positive

The measures discussed in the previous section are usually critical, but they are essentially defensive. They buy time, perhaps deal with the immediate short-term position; on their own they do little to ensure the long term.

Banks stress short-term priorities because there is no long term without surviving the short term. However, the point of surviving in the short term is to give time to put a long-term solution in place, which makes it vital to have a coherent strategy, credible in its use of resources and within management's scope.

There is no point in going through the first stage unless one of two outcomes looks probable. The first is a long-term future for the company. The second is a clear prospect for recovering more money by a rescue, even though it may not succeed, than by going straight into insolvency.

Fortunately, the two are often compatible, and banks need not decide at once which is likely. As long as there is a reasonable chance that either is true, they can start the restructuring without having decided which. Equally, many of the measures are the same whether the aim is a rescue or an informal liquidation, so that again the banks do not need to decide which they are aiming for at first.

For instance, short-term cash collection can provide cash to keep the company alive to implement a long-term strategy, or merely while the company finds buyers for the assets. Or it may be right to lay people off, whether the aim is to put the company on a sound footing, or to get parts of it in shape to be sold at the best price. Where, as in many countries, the redundancy costs are preferential debts anyway, insolvency would not avoid them.

But although the bank, and indeed the company, can often take this dual route initially, they must still assess the future. The routes are not the same indefinitely, and sooner or later the banks will have to choose.

There is another point too. To keep the company alive in the short term, and keep alive the possibility of a long-term future, the best salvage operation requires management and commitment at all levels. In many businesses, especially service businesses, this is a major reason for going for a rescue, even if it seems likely to end as an informal liquidation. Few managers are interested in a career as corporate undertakers. Without them, the recovery may be much lower. Thus it positively helps if the bank does not make up its mind too soon. As long as it is still trying to find a way to save the company, it can keep the management in place. The same applies to other types of stakeholder; it may need to keep suppliers, customers, creditors convinced that the company has a future. This can be difficult if the bank is not sincere, and indeed is unwise. Sometimes it may be right to make commitments to management or others which actually make it harder to wind down the company if developments make this the best course.

Information and Covenants

Banks require detailed and frequent information to monitor developments, and covenants to give them power to act if the monitoring shows failure.

Information is vital both to enable the banks to know precisely what is happening, and to ensure that management has the information to manage.

This is true at all times, not just in a rescue, but too many banks allow healthy borrowers to provide too little information. They then over-react and demand reams of information from troubled borrowers. This can overload systems, add to costs which reduces recovery – and provide the banks with masses of detail which add very little to their understanding; sometimes actually inhibit it. In extreme cases, the provision of this information can overburden the financial staff severely, and contribute to the company's collapse; staff are after all likely to be under pressure to begin with.

Thus, while banks need prompt, frequent and reliable information, they also need to be selective about it. They should focus on the key items of information, should wherever possible use information the company produces for its own use and should avoid duplication. Unfortunately, these prescriptions are too often ignored. Particularly in a multi-bank case, the tendency is to ask for everything any bank can think of. This can create a monster of work and expense for the company, with little benefit to the banks. Indeed, the mass of information can prevent the banks focusing on the key items.

Much the same point applies to covenants, the main benefit of which is to tell the bank when a healthy company begins to weaken. In that sense, it is too late for covenants if the debt needs to be restructured. There are covenants which can be helpful in tracking progress on a restructured company, although often the most important guideline is whether the company is paying interest and principal on time. Covenants need to be carefully designed and few in number. They should often tighten over time, since banks know that the company cannot meet normal covenants at first. So initially, banks set the covenants at just below the present level because they are looking for evidence of deterioration, but only slightly because the present level is already too low. If they set it too close, or if they have too many ratios, the company will breach the covenants regularly, but without the situation having changed enough to justify action. So banks keep waiving the breach. With a large syndicate, the work and aggravation involved can add a small but unnecessary factor to the risk of failure.

It is thus essential to be selective in choosing covenants and events of default in a restructuring. Often, however, banks insist on numerous covenants, overloading the company's financial staff checking them and providing calculations, but for little real value.

As the company improves, the banks can expect signs of progress, and can set ratio covenants to monitor this. Sometimes they only become effective after the first or second year, depending on expectations. Or they start at a low level – interest cover of 1.00, for instance – but gradually increase – to 1.25 in the second year, 1.5 in the third, 2.0 thereafter, perhaps.

In summary, a restructuring should reflect the facts of each case; it should use flexible tools such as a recapture and variable covenants to adjust to change and should set demanding but possible standards for a management which is on trial, but which the banks are prepared to trust provisionally.

14 Dealing with Other Banks

The problems of dealing with other banks vary with the number involved and their attitude. In many cases – probably most in number, although not by money at risk – there are two or three banks, perhaps sharing a floating charge or other security, or all unsecured. These raise little in the way of interbank problems.

Often there are groups of banks with different backgrounds and interests and types of facility. The position then is more difficult, particularly if there are several levels of borrowing subsidiary with lenders at each level, some of whom have parent or cross-guarantees and others do not.

Someone then must take a lead. The lead may be a single bank, a steering committee with a chairman doing most of the work, or a more evenly balanced committee. Often this will fall into place naturally. The company may have a lead bank to which it turns, and which the others accept; or there may be a large syndicate whose agent naturally falls into the lead; or several syndicates, whose agents form a natural core to a steering committee. The chairman is often one of the agents.

However chosen, the leaders must work for all the banks, not just for themselves or a particular group, still less for the company. Even when they are a natural choice, therefore, all banks must ratify that choice. Where there is no natural choice, the banks must choose.

DECIDING THE ROLES

Each bank must decide what role to play, and what it expects of those playing other roles. To do this it needs to assess several factors, in relation both to itself and the other banks.

Resources

Any active role in a rescue requires substantial resources. These are greatest for the lead bank, but are also considerable for the committee members. Exactly how great depends on the size and complexity of the borrower; the competence of its management team; the number of banks involved and their state of mind; the concentration or dispersal of the borrower's operations and banking facilities, and other factors.

The lead bank will deal with the borrower at a high level, and must be credible to the banks. It will need analytical and modelling capacity to check the information the company and its advisers provide; or with a less competent borrower to prepare much of the package itself. It will need at least one banker, possibly more, to deal with the queries from the banks and other creditors. It may need syndication and agency skills. And this ignores the possibility of a complex capital structure with senior, subordinated or retail bondholders. Negotiations with these can take weeks of senior time.

In a medium complex deal, with 20–30 reasonably calm banks, the lead bank may require from three to nine or ten people full-time for short periods, and up to four spending 60–80% of their time on it for months. Any bank which is considering the lead position must be sure it can spare these resources; once in the lead, the bank must dedicate to the project whatever is needed to complete it.

Membership of a committee requires less resources than the leader. For continuity, there should be at least two reasonably senior people on the case. They should have, or have access to, substantial authority to take decisions; they will recommend aspects of the plan as it evolves, and they must carry their own banks with them. In some cases the committee will divide the various tasks among it.

Skill and Standing

The requirement is for quality, both actual and perceived, as well as volume of resources. It covers the ability to concentrate on what is important; to deal with recalcitrant borrowers; to craft a deal that works, even if nobody likes parts of it; to sell a difficult deal to banks reacting with shock, anger and disbelief; to give them back-up which they can use to persuade their credit committees – sometimes thousands of miles away with little understanding of local practices. And to do all this under great pressure, with banks asking for information the company does not have, demanding the impossible, while overlooking or failing to understand the critical points. To keep costs under control; to stop banks tying up the lawyers and accountants with trivialities, diverting them from the important factors and running up costs the company can ill afford; and yet recognise which factors may seem trivial but are essential to persuade the banks to agree the deal. And having agreed the basic deal, drive it through the lawyers and then the banks without the deadline slipping too far. (There is no hope that it will not slip at all; but if it slips too far, the deal can die.)

For membership of the Steering Committee, some of the same qualities are desirable, although in lesser degree. A Steering Committee may be a good place to learn the skills needed to lead, and to generate the confidence to take the lead in future cases.

Members and leaders represent the interests of all the banks – and sometimes other creditors – equally. Members can, nevertheless, share attributes with some of the other banks. They may include different nationalities; a Japanese, American, and Continental European bank on the Steering Committee for a British company, for instance. This is not to give one nationality an advantage, but to identify and allow for the special preoccupations of each group in the final plan; ensure that no national tax, regulatory or other quirks undermine a sound plan; and that the plan caters for banking principles which are crucial to each group. A Japanese or German Steering Committee member may be able to explain the contentious points – and there are some in any plan – better to its fellow nationals than any other bank could do. And in appealing the local branch's refusal to its head office, the co-national may have better contacts and credibility. This may be even more important if the local office is supportive but cannot convince its head office.

The Steering Committee must work together as a unit, so that while the banks make the final choice of members, the leaders can influence that choice and should do so, discreetly, to keep disruptive banks off. In the marginal case disruption can make the difference between success and failure; at best it can delay the final solution and add to its cost.

It is almost equally important that the members are prepared to send people with experience and authority to contribute. A passive or fractious committee can be a severe drag on an overstretched chairman.

Amount at Risk

One factor to consider is the amount the Chairman and members have at stake. Some banks feel that a large exposure assures them that the leaders will supply the resources and balanced attitude needed. Small banks with small exposures, however, sometimes fear that the big banks will ride roughshod over their interests, and want at least one smaller bank on the Committee.

In practice, this is often an academic argument. Usually, the banks willing to take on the tasks are bigger lenders, though not always the biggest, anxious to protect their exposure. Provided they have the resources and expertise it is hard to argue against them. The big lenders are also more likely to be close to the company, with knowledge of its business and confidence of its management. This can improve their ability to get off to a quick start.

Where all this is true, it is right to choose banks with big exposure. But it is not always true. Sometimes a lender is smaller because he has recognised the borrower's weakness earlier. Or sometimes the large lender is so embittered by the loss that he cannot work sensibly with the management. Or larger lenders may already be tied up in too many other situations, or have a policy against serving, and so on. So size of exposure is not a critical factor in the choice of members. What matters is their dedication of resources and skill.

Banks sometimes claim an automatic right to be on the Committee, for various reasons. It will often be best to accept them, but any suggestion that they are there by right should be stamped on at once. The only reason any bank is on the Committee is to assist all banks. And the only way to decide which members are acceptable is a majority view of the banks.

For similar reasons, lenders will often be wise to prefer a bank which is reluctant to serve, but has all the other attributes, to one which is keen, or even claims that it has a right.

Shadow Director and Similar Risk

All banks must be aware of the shadow director risk. This is the English term, and the details differ under the law of each country, but most countries have something. The risk in its simplest form is that banks interfere in the company's management, or support it when it is no longer solvent. This can make them liable for losses of other creditors. Or there may be penalties on either the bank or individual bankers. The Committee is most at risk but since it acts on behalf of all the banks, the liability may cover them as well.

This is not usually as great a risk as the more scarifying lawyers can make it sound. Banks must, however, be aware of it and be scrupulous in how they approach it. Generally, the directors of the company will bear the same risks – personally – as the banks, and much more directly. If the directors are heeding good legal advice, this goes some way towards answering the questions. Nevertheless, it behooves each bank on the Committee, and the lead bank most of all, to be conscious of the risks and to minimise them.

Lead banks and Committees also risk being sued by the other banks. If these blame their losses on failure or negligence by the lead bank or Committee, they may claim for damages. In practice, this too is a minor risk for banks that act diligently and in good faith – as any bank on a steering committee should. Proving that a judgement taken in good faith was so wrong as to be negligent, and that it caused the loss is difficult. Moreover, most banks will recognise the difficulties, and will not sue lightly. But no bank will forgive gross negligence, so banks on committees can minimise this risk by acting diligently and in good faith, but can never eliminate it altogether.

IF YOU WANT TO TAKE THE LEAD

A bank which is inclined to take an active role needs to focus on external factors as well as those internal factors which cause it to consider the role initially.

An obvious external factor is its confidence, or lack of it, in the Chairman and potential members of the Steering Committee. Clearly, if a bank doubts the Chairman's competence, integrity or ability to see the view of all banks, it will want to vote against him. If there is no alternative, it will want a strong committee. Unless it can see other members playing that role it may want to join the committee itself.

This is an extreme expression of a feeling many banks have in a milder and less coherent form. In more general terms, a bank with a large exposure must weigh the cost disadvantages of joining the Committee, or acting as Chairman, against the need, and its own ability, to influence the negotiations. In reaching this balance, some of the factors it may wish to consider are discussed below.

The Number and Attitude of Banks

The difficulty involved in being Chairman grows with the number of banks involved, but even more with their attitude. Some banks feel they have been badly treated, even deceived, by the company. They resist any concession to management, require every point to be double-checked by lawyers and accountants, and resent any suggestion from the Chairman that this adds unnecessary cost. Indeed, some of them transfer their dislike to the Chairman, and treat him as if he were in some way to blame for the problem. In this situation, the Chairman's task is harder than it need be, and can be unpleasant and stressful. If new management performs well, it may be able to dissipate the resentment and even generate trust over time, which can gradually make the Chairman's position easier.

The number of banks matters for two reasons. One is sheer volume of work; more faxes to send out, more telephone calls to make, larger meeting rooms needed, and more banks who call in with questions or demands. This may be compounded if the number of banks includes different nationalities, who need different treatment for tax or regulatory reasons; or who perhaps have to be visited in their own countries.

The more banks there are, the more likely it is that some will either have irrational attitudes, or think that their position is special and requires different treatment.

How Well Do They Know the Borrower?

One difficulty which became more common in the 1980s was that banks lent to borrowers without knowing much about them; or failed to update their knowledge. Some banks made one- or two-week loans just before the borrower declared a moratorium. This failure to analyse borrowers often contributed to the feelings of betrayal discussed above; but even without that, sheer ignorance can make the initial and subsequent briefing of the banks harder than it needs to be. Rene Poisson of J. P. Morgan has likened the reaction of banks in these situations to the classic reaction to bereavement. The first stage is denial, and until the bereaved leaves that stage, he cannot deal effectively with the pain. Banks who know little about a borrower can be hard to move out of the denial stage.

Apart from specific knowledge of the borrower, banks must often absorb sophisticated and unpalatable concepts. Accepting that nothing palatable is available, and selling it to credit committees in distant head offices calls for competence, not only in the account officer, but in both the approval system, and the people operating it. Too many banks are very slow; or come back with an answer which contains conditions which are unworkable – or even against the banks' interests and unacceptable to other banks. Some banks require their people to answer repetitive questions which often have been answered in the original presentations, or have no bearing on the decision, or both.

Incompetent banks can be very wearing to a chairman and the committee; they push banks in the direction of letting someone else do the work.

Size and Complexity of the Situation

A complex situation is made more so by many banks, but the complexity is more apt to draw in many banks than the other way round. It may be a question of the sheer size of the borrower, but is more likely to relate to structure. A company with many overseas subsidiaries, each with their own banking arrangements; or one which has borrowed partly on a corporate basis, partly on a project basis, with a mixture of secured and unsecured lenders; or a company with different layers of public debt, and perhaps even quasi equity; all these and other factors can complicate the task and make a sensible bank even more reluctant to take it on.

It can also affect the decision as to whether to use a single leader or a committee. A single leader in a straightforward situation gives focus and decisiveness. There is no doubt that a committee gives the leader more work; he has to manage it, call meetings and communicate with it. Different members may react differently to the initial proposals from the company, or have ideas of their own which have to be discussed. This aspect is more often a time-saver than appears, because it is likely that other banks will have the same reactions, and the committee should reduce the risk that any good ideas are overlooked, and make it easier to explain why the bad ones will not fly.

The positive reasons for having a committee centre around the committee's ability to reduce the chairman's workload, and/or add a dimension to his response to the problem. Both are more likely to apply in a complex situation. There may be banks which have special knowledge – of a country, of securitisation or other capital issues; or of tax. Or one bank on the committee may be able to lend in a country where the borrower has a key subsidiary; sometimes it is impossible to keep local facilities in place, if the provider is not also a lender to the parent.

Or there may simply be too much for any one bank to do and a need to split the workload. Often the banks will not know this at first; the committee will be established for other reasons. But even then it is vital to ensure that the membership consists of competent banks who can and will work if required. The negative aspects of a committee must be offset by positive aspects.

Whether a bank is considering serving, or merely considering which banks it would like to see serve, these points are relevant.

Remuneration

At one time it was accepted that committees at least, and often chairmen, would act to protect their own exposure without specific payment. This situation is no longer viable though some banks are slow to recognise the fact.

Only a few banks have both the skills and the willingness to take on a major chairmanship. Even these have limited such resources, in great demand. Most banks have more bad loans than they used to, so that their resources are often severely stretched. They cannot take the lead in all, and while fees will never be the only factor they will be decisive in marginal cases. Banks with less bad debts may be doubly in demand as advisers. Few banks will up give advisory fees elsewhere to act free as chairman of a steering committee. Furthermore, the skills developed in restructuring problem loans have much in common with those needed to structure complex new loans, either for fees alone, or for fees and a profitable loan. The same comments apply, though with less strength, to membership of a committee. So provided the committee really shares the load, it too needs to be paid.

More banks are willing to accept the idea of paying a chairman, even if inadequately, than a committee. There was some justice in this, and may still be in some cases, where the committee left most of the work to the chairman. This is to be avoided and it is fair, if impractical, for the committee's payment to be approved only when the banks are satisfied that its members will contribute.

If a good steering committee reduces the net workload of a chairman, it may reduce the chairman's claim. Since it is difficult to assess in advance who will do what, there is an argument for one fee for chairman and committee combined. They can decide who gets what.

A fee can cause genuine difficulties. An immediate fee in cash may aggravate cash flow shortages. If there is any question of new money a cash fee may add to the amount needed. Even where there is no immediate cash problem, the final pay-out to all creditors will be reduced unless the restructuring avoids any loss, which is rare.

However, this is equally true of other fees; lawyers and accountants, for instance, much of whose work is done for the banks, even though paid for by the company. Banks which are most vocal about the committee's fee are often most demanding on minor points, regardless of cost. It is not clear why every labourer is worthy of hire except the committee.

However, banks can adjust the method of payment to reduce the impact. They may take all or part in equity; all or part as a success fee; or defer payment until the cash squeeze is over.

Banks which resist payment of any fee may lose far more if the best chairman refuses to serve; or does not put its best team on the case. It is, however, reasonable for the banks to know the size of the fee being asked, whether as part of this negotiation or as part of the mandate discussed below.

OUTSIDE THE COMMITTEE WHAT ROLE IS THERE?

Influence Choices of Leader and Committee?

Banks which do not take lead roles still have to decide how active to be; and how far they wish to influence the committee's actions rather than just vote yes or no.

Banks may wish to influence the choice of chairman or committee because of specific knowledge of, or relationships with, the banks concerned. Clearly, nobody else can advise on this. Where their decision reflects their views of the specific case, and the candidate's attributes in that context, there are some pointers. Some have been outlined above; but the most important is to avoid the bank with the ulterior motive. Even where it is not clear that there is a specific motive, beware the bank that is too keen to be on the committee. Another reason for distrusting a bank is that it is too close to the company, and may favour it in the negotiations, or may put its relationship ahead of the interests of the bank group.

This can be a real risk but rarely is. The leader needs the best effort of management, so that an easy working relationship is an important aid to success. To reject this aid out of ill-judged suspicion is rarely in the interest of the banks as a whole.

Indeed whether the leader, and/or the committee, is too close to the management is a continuing concern to many banks, usually for the wrong reasons. One function of a leader or committee is to avoid duplication of effort, and to avoid taking up management's time explaining the same points over and over; to let one or a few banks grind through all the detail, and then provide a clear summary of the final plan and the arguments for an against. Or to put it another way, to get to know the company and its management better than the banks as a whole can hope to do, and to use that knowledge to the advantage of all.

The right management will be honest, competent and working in the banks' interest. It is then natural that the banks who know it best and see its work should support it. A good management will consider the interests of other constituencies than just the banks: shareholders, workers, customers, suppliers. But this is not merely a duty; it is usually in the banks' interest as well. A company whose workers are unnecessarily demoralised; which is losing customers and suppliers; whose shareholders have written of their investment and the management, is hardly likely to do a good job for its banks.

Thus, a leader or committee can be too close to the management but this is rare. More often the apparent closeness is just a sound working relationship; the apparent support of management's 'unreasonable' position reflects the committee's understanding of management's reasons.

Influencing the Mandate

Where banks accept the Committee with reluctance, they may try to control the features they dislike by setting a tight mandate. Even without this spur, it is good practice to look closely at the mandate. First, few committees will carry out an unclear mandate well, and may quarrel among themselves as to what they are trying to achieve. Secondly, banks may have different ideas as to how far they want the committee to go without referring back. Thirdly, in deciding a mandate the banks can also begin to give the committee an idea as to what sort of settlement they can accept. And fourthly, a clear mandate can strengthen the committee's hand in dealing with difficult or demanding banks as well as with the company.

The mandate should require the committee to work with the management to control legal and other costs; it should prevent individual banks running up unnecessary legal and accounting costs for self-centred or trivial reasons; it may extend to the company's legal, accounting or investment banking costs, since in many cases the banks are indirectly paying these. At the very least these should be disclosed to the banks, where possible in advance.

The mandate should also identify what the committee is entitled to do or approve, and what needs reference back to the banks as a whole. This will be most important if the committee remains in being after the restructuring is signed. It may well be contentious during the moratorium period, when banks usually want to tie the company very closely. Given the slow decision process in many banks, a requirement for the banks to approve too much can mean that nothing major gets done. The company may lose an opportunity from which all would gain, such as the profitable sale of an asset, or a securitisation to take advantage of a market window.

Banks are usually reluctant to give much leeway to the company during the moratorium, when they have the minimum knowledge: of what is happening; of the competence of the committee; of the integrity and capacity of the management. Nevertheless, even a competent committee and management can do little with their hands tied.

The committee should get, and keep up to date, an accurate feeling of what is likely to be acceptable. Some banks are fairly relaxed as long as there is no new money required; others, if reluctantly, are prepared to provide new money, but only exactly pro rata; yet others will put up new money for more than their fair share, but expect to have some of their old debt given some priority in return. Some like the idea of some equity, as a fee, in return for new money, or even for forgiving old; others regard the suggestion as so painful that it may take months to convince them of the need. The more the committee knows of these likes and dislikes, the better its chance of persuading the company to tailor a proposal which meets all or most of them.

Influencing the Level of Information

Banks always thirst for information. The chairman is often reluctant to take the time to brief banks individually; nor does management have much time at such a difficult period. Moreover, it is a period of negotiation, changing perceptions of the underlying situation and developing ideas as to how to deal with it. Much that the banks might like to know would be irrelevant by the time they learned it. Finally, a leader obtains detailed information and preliminary ideas, which with a quoted borrower may be price-sensitive. There is a highly regrettable tendency for bank syndicates to leak, and severe criminal penalties exist in some countries for misuse of confidential information. Public companies will therefore only provide this type of information to the committee in strict confidence.

For all these reasons, banks cannot be told everything. However, banks both need and have a right to information in two main areas. If they do not get it, this will make the final solution harder to reach.

First, a general update on progress in the company, in the negotiations, and in factors which are critical to those negotiations, such as preparation of budgets and forecasts, valuation of assets, assessment of collateral value, etc. Some of this information may come out automatically, as when a requirement for monthly P&L, cash flow and other figures provides pointers as to general progress.

Secondly, specific factors for each case on which banks need at least general information. These may include possible securitisation issues or asset sales; negotiations with other creditors, often bondholders; negotiations with unions, government or both; or a ream of other things.

It is good practice, too, to try to keep the banks aware of at least the general thinking about the final outcome. This may not be possible where there is insider risk. But the steering committee may begin to believe that a proposal will allow full repayment, but with a long delay; or that full principal can only be recovered if the banks give up interest for several years; or that new money will be necessary; or that banks must convert some debt into equity; or worst of all a combination of these last two. If a final plan containing some of these features comes like a bolt from the blue it will probably fail. Equally, if the plan is likely to be more favourable to the banks than they originally expected, it can make life easier if the banks start to get that idea before the final plan is presented.

The question then is how best to distribute the sensitive information. There is no hard and fast answer, but there are some ways which are better than others.

One way is for different members of the committee to brief different groups of banks: by nationality; by agents briefing their syndicates; or based on the committee members' own contacts with the various banks. There can be advantages to this approach. Each bank can feel that it has a friend in court and provide better feedback than banks usually do in larger meetings. And it can spread the load from the company or the chairman while ensuring that all banks get the full attention they need.

The drawbacks usually outweigh these advantages, unless this method is only a part of the mechanism. The worst drawback is that some members of the committee communicate better than others. They may be more accurate and detailed or just more active. Too often some banks are dissatisfied with the attention they are getting, perhaps being told less than other banks, perhaps something different. Sometimes they feel that their feedback is not being carried to full committee or is being distorted. And sometimes they are right. This is bad enough when the reason is incompetence or misunderstanding, worse if the committee contains dissidents. They may never have left the denial stage themselves, or may not be convinced of the committee's approach. They can use their briefings to try to undermine it, or even report back what they want to believe the banks feel, rather than what they say. On one occasion several Canadian banks wrote to a Steering Committee repudiating a position put forward in their name by their 'representative'. The less extreme cases may be almost as dangerous because less obvious.

Probably the best method of general communication is for the chairman to write periodically to all the banks. This can be a fairly general update and commentary, just to provide a progress report; in the early and tense days of the moratorium, this might be as often as every week or ten days, while later it might be as infrequent as every month or six weeks. Or it can be a more specific description of a particular event or proposal. If the latter is highly complex, or too sensitive to be described in full detail, the chairman may supplement it with face-to-face briefings; if there are too many banks for the chairman to manage alone, then the use of members of the committee in this limited way avoids most of the drawbacks.

A meeting of all the banks is often essential to communicate the plan itself, and subsequent modifications. Where the bank group is small, a meeting may also be an effective method of continuing communication, but a large group, particularly if widespread geographically, may make frequent meetings impractical.

Whatever the method, the chairman must give communication high priority and must find the right balance.

Banks not on the committee have the greatest interest in good communication, and should make it a factor in their choice of chairman. They can use the discussion of the mandate to stress what they want and include it in the mandate. They can also show that they use the information effectively, respond quickly to requests for approval, or ask intelligent questions where appropriate. Almost equally important is to avoid the tendency of some banks to over-analyse and over-question the information. The result of good communication may then be countless hours spent answering questions already answered, or where the answer is obvious or unimportant. Apart from the additional cost and diversion of attention from the task in hand, this tends to discourage chairmen from the effort to communicate well.

Just as the chairman has to find a balance in the information he provides, so the recipients need to use it in a balanced way. Any chairman or active committee member will recognise the problem. Unfortunately, too few banks who have not served do likewise. And too few ask intelligent questions and make constructive points helpful to the company and committee.

VIEWS REQUIRED – WHETHER PASSIVE OR ACTIVE

There are several areas where all banks have to reach a view sooner or later. Sometimes early information leaves too many unanswered questions to decide at once. Even then banks should be thinking on these points and moving towards a clear decision as new information becomes available. Some points are specific to each case, but some justify a general discussion.

The Principle of Equal or Equitable Treatment

The view of banks generally, which this author strongly supports, is that all creditors in a restructuring should be treated equitably. Unfortunately, there is ample room to interpret what is equitable.

The starting point most often used, but sometimes more implicitly than explicitly, is the situation if the company were allowed to enter insolvency proceedings. Allowing this is always an alternative option, and often the only realistic one, to a rescue or restructuring. The aim therefore is to improve everybody's position over that in insolvency, without causing anybody to lose relatively. This means, for instance, recognising a secured lender's position or that of a lender with a guarantee from a strong subsidiary.

Inevitably, there are doubts and difficulties. It may not always be clear what would happen in insolvency; it may not be certain that a charge would stand up; the value of guarantees may depend on whether the borrower's or guarantor's assets are realised first and how many other guarantees the guarantor has given. Or accepting a secured lender's prior claim may make the restructuring impossible. Moreover, banks cannot compel other creditors to behave equitably.

The basic principle of equitable treatment is thus critically important, but also requires attention to the facts. The most important point is that the purpose of restructuring is to improve everybody's recovery. The risks involved should be shared and so should the reward; and no creditor, however small, should be allowed to hold the others to ransom. On the other hand, if senior lenders push too hard, a lower ranking creditor may not find it worthwhile to accept the restructuring and everybody else loses more than they otherwise would. It may be wise to bend the principle a little rather than lose it altogether to insolvency.

Some examples from real life may help illustrate the point.

In one case, some lenders to a holding company had obtained upstream guarantees from all the key subsidiaries; some from just a few; some had no upstream guarantees at all. To give each a priority which exactly matched the guarantee position was impossible. Nobody knew how much each company would raise in liquidation, which guarantees would be paid out first, and what this would mean for the value of other guarantees. The solution was to divide the loans into two groups: those with at least one guarantee from a key subsidiary; and those with no guarantees. The guaranteed accounted for about 60% of the debt, but were to receive 75% of payments until 50% of total debt was repaid; after that, payments would be pro rata to the remaining debt. This recognised that the guaranteed banks would do better, but by an unquantifiable amount, than in liquidation; it still allowed the unguaranteed banks to make some recovery even if the company collapsed more completely than expected, and to hope to recover everything (as eventually they did). At worst, they would be no worse off than in liquidation. In an early insolvency, all would have lost money, although the unguaranteed banks much more than the guaranteed.

In another case, one bank had cross-guarantees from all the UK subsidiaries of the borrower, covering their pooled operating overdrafts. Unless it gave these up, no restructuring could succeed. In return for the bank conceding this, the others agreed that, up to a fixed level, proceeds from the sale of any of those subsidiaries should go first to the conceding bank.

The Question of New Money

One of the hardest decisions is whether to lend new money; it is also one where banks are most likely to disagree. This is partly because the decision is so difficult, but partly because of different attitudes to the underlying concept. These in turn may reflect each bank's philosophy, the size of its exposure in the particular case, or the overall state of its loan book. However, wherever a company needs new money, it is critical to iron out the differences and come to a decision.

Broadly, a bank can agree to provide new money, even if not all banks do; or only if all banks do so pro rata; or it may allow others to supply the new money and to take some priority in return. Or it may believe so strongly that new money is wrong that it refuses to allow it at all.

The decision depends first on the bank's view of the facts of each case. New money either allows time for longer term reforms to bear fruit; or it allows the recovery, short term, of specific assets; or the latter leading to the former. Either way the bank expects it to improve the overall recovery. To lend the last ten per cent of the cost of a major construction project, for instance, may allow the borrower to collect the full price.

The short-term decision may also help preserve a long-term future, but need not depend on that. Where there is no clear short-term return, the risk involved in new money is greater, and the argument against it stronger. Some banks are naturally reluctant to increase their exposure. Banks which know the situation well and have most at risk may provide more than their share to keep the company alive, but will expect to safeguard the new money. They may expect some extra benefit, since the banks which do not share still benefit if the new money succeeds. Most banks which refuse new money accept that it should have priority over the old money; only occasionally do they consider that it has so little chance of success that giving it priority reduces their own recovery unacceptably. The new money banks may want to go a stage further, however, and take some priority on their old money as well. This is sometimes known as sharing the pain and pleasure.

The argument relates back to that about equitable treatment in the previous section; that relates to the recovery, this to the effort needed to secure the recovery. In neither case is exact equality practical; equitable treatment is essential. Exactly what is equitable in both cases can be a matter of judgement and therefore dispute. The priority in return for new money should therefore be set at a level where the argument is reasonably balanced; 'If you think new money is getting too good a deal, join us' should be credible.

The difficulty of this situation emphasises the need for the committee to communicate well, and to be seen to act for the banks as a whole. Only if banks trust what they are being told will those who are naturally opposed to new money be prepared to provide it themselves or allow others to provide it. Banks may feel that the new money is wholly damaging – as it can be if it allows the company to go on losing money with no ultimate improvement; or that its benefits are so doubtful that they prefer not to take the risk. To change that view will be hard; to change it enough to cede priority will be harder if they also feel isolated. Even where banks are more inclined to believe that new money is beneficial but reluctant to provide it themselves, allowing priority on old money to the providers takes trust.

The View on Security

It is normal and right to take security, where not already held, as part of the restructuring. However, the cost of taking some types of security can outweigh the benefits. This is particularly so with people businesses; just as you cannot sell people, so you cannot take a charge over them. Thus the cost of a charge over shares in subsidiaries whose main asset is people can be excessive.

Security over polluted land or polluting plant can be more costly than writing off the loan; and there are other drawbacks to some kinds of security, such as patents to goods which carry product liability.

Unless it covers new money, and perhaps even then, the security may be subject to challenge if the borrower goes into liquidation within a period which varies from six months to two years, depending on the country and circumstances. This can restrict the banks' flexibility if the rescue appears not to be working.

None of these are reasons against taking security when it is appropriate, as it is in most cases. They are arguments for considering the point carefully, rather than taking security reflexively.

Part V

The Other Factors

15 Training

Training has never been more important in credit control than currently. The bad debt record of so many different banks in the late 1980s and early 1990s is evidence of this need. The new trends and products add to it. The case is strengthened by greater competition and the emphasis on marketing. For many reasons banks are under pressure to take credit risk – not only in lending. Many parts of the bank require it to take credit risk to support their profits, but take no interest in credit control. To resist or reduce this pressure banks need more focused and continuous training in credit than ever before.

THE ESSENCE OF CREDIT TRAINING

Credit judgement is 75% applied common sense. There are techniques which help, and experience is vital. Some techniques, such as financial analysis or knowledge of basic legal principles, are used in many aspects of banking; only their application is different in credit. So an important part of credit training is the instillation of attitudes to risk as well as specific techniques. This is particularly important where credit is not the main preoccupation, but the risk is still there.

Traditional bankers obviously need credit training. They usually are trained formally early in their careers but receive most of their deeper training on the job. This background has too often tended to set the pattern for credit training for others where it is less appropriate.

THE RECIPIENTS OF CREDIT TRAINING

In today's banks there are broadly four types of people who need credit training, apart from traditional bankers. Some of these categories can be further subdivided.

Credit Specialists

Credit specialists need training in risk, decision-making, the importance of structure and covenants, and how to apply them to different situations.

They need to understand documentation and legal concepts; the techniques and legal concepts involved in security; and at least something about insolvency law. In an international bank, they need to know where to look for differences in practice and how to adapt to them. And they need to negotiate internally and with the client where it is a part of their function. All this in addition to basic financial analytical skills, understanding of accounting, ability to adjust requirements to the nature of the business, which are important in, but not unique to, credit.

This is broadly similar to the skills required of a traditional senior banker. However, he came to those skills over a long period as a banker, working under close supervision. Only fairly late in his career did he gain authority to make major decisions. This training has largely disappeared in many banks. Credit specialists are either specialists from the beginning of their careers, or they come to the position with little credit experience. Either way, they need a well thought out initial training, and continuous follow-up, to make sure that their skills are, and remain, adequate.

There may need to be two or more such programmes. Many of the principles of corporate credit are the same as those of counterparty credit, but the details are not. Where banks have separate credit specialists dealing with commercial and financial clients – or divided by product – they may need to have separate career structures and training for the two types of specialist. Or where banks serve widely different sizes and strengths of client, they may need separate training. Lending to hundreds of small business clients through a retail branch network calls for different skills to assessing the credit of multibillion pound companies for fifteen-year swaps or private placements.

Indeed, training requires continuous updating. Take swaps, for instance. There are techniques for reducing the risk, of which the best known is to mark to market. The implications of some forms of this are not always crystal clear to the lender when the idea is first presented to him. After working through the theory and when satisfied that it can work, he still has to explain any requirements to whoever negotiates with the company, and ensure that the swap is clearly documented in a way that works for up to fifteen years.

Credit Analysts

The analysis of large corporates, small corporates and banks also require different knowledge and skills. Given basic understanding, an analyst can obtain most of the training needed on the job, under supervision. Nevertheless, if the analysis is to be of highest quality continuous formal training is needed too.

High-quality credit analysis requires proper instruction in accounting and the ways in which accounting can be manipulated. The trainer needs to be careful not to teach analysts to believe that all accounts are designed to deceive; balance between suspicion and constructive belief is as important as excessive naivety or distrust is dangerous.

Equally a credit analyst needs to understand the implications of different types of company; this is easier for an industry specialist, but a general analyst needs to recognise the difference between asset-based companies and cash flow companies, between manufacturing and service, people-based companies. The attention to a second way out; the recognition, for instance, that service companies rarely borrow heavily because they do not need to in the normal course of business; that a borrowing means something unusual has happened and the analyst must understand what; that they have no tangible assets and that this restricts the recovery in liquidation and therefore the ability to threaten insolvency; these are only examples of the features analysts must recognise if they are to apply the correct techniques to each type of borrower.

The Relationship Manager

Even a relationship manager (or account officer) with no lending authority needs to understand credit, for several reasons.

First, he has the widest contact with the client, is most likely to glean information relevant to credit, and has the best opportunity to probe if necessary. A banker who does not recognise credit value robs the bank of a major resource for monitoring credit; a better banker still needs to be trained to probe in a way that supports his role rather than undermines it. And however received, the banker must pass such information on to those who can use it to monitor the borrower more effectively.

Secondly, much of the advice banks give clients relates to credit. If a company has a borrowing need, the banker must know about credit to advise whether to seek: a bank loan, bilateral or syndicated; commercial paper; private placement; FRN; domestic bond or Eurobond; or even an exotic convertible. More important still, he must be able to advise when the company's credit will not stand more debt and it needs equity.

The relationship manager must also know enough about the market's view of credit to assess whether theoretical options are all available in practice. But to understand the market's view without understanding what drives it is difficult. Equally, to advise the company, as it will sometimes be right to do, that the market has misunderstood the credit, and the either to ignore the market's perception or to try to change it, requires a confident banker. And however much he may rely on expert colleagues, if he cannot understand and present the main arguments, the advice loses credibility.

Finally, where his own bank is not the lender, and in some banks even where it is, the relationship manager must be able to advise the client on the terms; not just price, but maturity, amortisation, covenants and other structural matters.

The banker therefore needs training in most of the same areas as the credit specialist, including analysis. He may not need it in the same depth as the specialist, and the best way to give it may be to share some but not all the specialist training, rather than devise a separate training to cover many of the same points.

However, the banker is a marketer and will need to market credit just as much as any other product. This will require a different focus to the specialist's in some areas. For instance, a specialist should know the arguments as to why covenants are necessary to the bank, and should be able to present these convincingly to a reluctant borrower in the context of a loan request. The banker has to remove what is often a deeply held prejudice before the client will even discuss a loan. To do this, he needs to believe firmly that well-designed covenants actually help the borrower; and that a positive approach to covenants helps the borrower to ensure that it accepts only well-designed ones. The banker must also know enough about covenant design to save the borrower from badly designed ones. These two points are not well understood even by many bankers or credit specialists, and come as a surprise to many borrowers. For all of these reasons, the banker needs to be well trained in the theory as well as practice of covenants.

This is only one example of a point which is poorly understood by many bankers and clients. Much of what goes into 'tough credit standards' is seen as being tough on the client. In many cases, however, it helps to put borrowing on a sound basis and is as much in the borrower's interest as in the lender's. We have only to recall the number of borrowers who, when things go wrong, blame the banks for lending too much, too easily. Sometimes banks are indeed sloppy in their lending decisions. More often, the client has insisted on borrowing more than the bank advised or has rejected the safeguards the bank proposed. Here the blame is often mostly the borrower's although the bank may bear some contributory blame, at least if it lent. If the borrower refused the terms and went off and borrowed from a more complaisant bank, they must bear the main blame; the original bank can only be blamed for failing to demonstrate clearly enough that its view was sound.

Banker training is thus one of the key requirements if banks are to avoid repetitions of the appalling bad debt problems of the late 1980s and 1990s.

The Product Specialist

The exact nature of the product specialist's involvement in credit and need for training depends on the nature of the product. Broadly, they fall into two categories, which we will call the strategic and the transactional. The strategic products have a long life and react with the client's credit standing. The transactional products are much shorter term; the credit risk is of failure to complete a transaction, although if the counterparty does enough business with the bank around the world, the total exposure may be enormous. We discuss the needs for the main products below; however, new products, or new variants of old products, are being introduced so fast that it is more important to train people in the principles and the way to recognise credit risk and deal with it, than to lay down elaborate training – or rules – for each product.

Merger and acquisition

This covers the whole financial advisory area, including capital structure, debt capacity and other aspects. To advise on debt capacity requires a clear understanding of credit. To advise on an acquisition requires an understanding of credit in three aspects: the credit of the target, to ensure that it is not already borrowing more than it can handle; that it would not do so under the proposal; or that if it would in either case, the burden is allowed for in the proposal. Advisers need to assess their own client's credit too, to ensure that it can absorb the risk of the target, and also to advise on how best to finance it. Most of all, they need to satisfy themselves that the combined entities, at the proposed price, can be financed soundly, and that the proposed method of financing works.

Of course most of the information needed to make this judgement will be the same as that needed to advise that the purchase is sound in other ways; in particular, that it represents sound value for the client and its shareholders. Nevertheless, the lending banker has a different viewpoint to the shareholder; the adviser needs therefore to apply a credit spin to his information or views. This is particularly important in a fast moving negotiation, where terms can change rapidly. A change that makes good sense to the shareholders may damage credit worthiness. This is particularly so if the idea is to enhance return on equity by increasing debt.

The M&A specialist therefore needs roughly the same level of credit understanding as the non-lending banker. If he works for a bank which also lends, he may be able to consult with his lending colleagues, but it is not safe to assume this. There may be confidentiality considerations which prevent it.

The M&A banker needs to understand how the market thinks even more than his colleagues. There can be nothing more embarrassing than confidently telling a client that a particular financing package is the best and then finding that the market will not accept it. This is more embarrassing still if your own bank refuses to lend. So that one thing M&A needs to learn is to check the credit potential early.

Bond underwriter, salesman

The bond underwriter needs broadly the same training as the M&A specialist, although he uses it in a different context. The focus is narrower; is a bond of a particular type the appropriate financing for this client? Will the market accept the credit at a reasonable price? Can the client service the interest and principle without strain or doubt?

Depending on the type of bond, and the market in which it is being sold, some knowledge may be needed of security; or of covenants, occasionally both.

The bond salesman is more concerned with market perception and interest, or sometimes currency, factors than with credit. Nevertheless, if he does not have a sound basic understanding of credit, he will flounder if the investor asks questions about it. And his reputation and future sales potential will both suffer if the credit rapidly deteriorates after selling the bond; or if an event which he should have foreseen would weaken the credit occurs, even some time later, and this has not been mentioned in his sales pitch.

Both underwriters and salespeople need a much more intensive knowledge of credit if they handle junk or high-yield bonds. Here the analysis needs to cover not just the credit, but the position in insolvency. This is now a real possibility, and the bond may even be selling well below par in anticipation. Particularly with a subordinated bond, the analysis should cover the chance of recovery in an early liquidation, the rules in Administration, Chapter 11, or the local equivalent.

All this requires intensive training closer to that the credit specialist receives, although perhaps not as wide ranging.

Swap and related products

Swaps require credit judgement in two ways. One is similar to that in making a loan. The swap has a life of anywhere from a few months to ten years; indeed swaps against bond issues go longer, with fifteen years almost common, and swaps out to thirty years sought, though rarely granted without at least a strong government involvement. They have one risk that a loan does not have, which is that there is no way of knowing the exact credit risk when the bank decides to do the swap. While each bank should have its own way of calculating loan equivalent, there must always be a risk that the assumptions on which it was based are wrong – or change. If this happens in a sick case, Murphy's law says the loss will be above the expected level. So it is important for swappers to have a feel for credit; not to be expert, but to recognise that the credit risk is as real as the market risk in which they are expert and which they take seriously.

The other aspect is that they should recognise the nature and importance to credit of the specific risk against which their swap – or cap, collar or other variation – protects. They need to be trained in the impact of currency or interest fluctuations on credit standing, and when the risk is greatest or least. They also need to be trained to recognise cases where a swap or other product could actually improve the credit risk.

Transactional Products

Traders and others

The great temptation for traders and salesmen of a wide range of products is to ignore credit risk. For most of them it mainly takes the form of settlement or counterparty risk, where each individual transaction is relatively small and short term; indeed much of it is classic self-liquidating risk. They need to understand how the risk accumulates. A major international bank, active throughout the world may do business with securities firms such as Goldman Sachs or Morgan Stanley in ten or more areas, each in eight or ten products. Even with their smaller, weaker competitors the volume may run into billions of dollars, with the larger names it may be tens of billions. However unlikely it may be that these firms will fail, and however short-term each transaction may be, it is critical to control the amount and nature of the exposure. A cardinal principle of credit risk is that if one risk could break the bank, then however unlikely it may be, you watch it like a hawk. This requires those generating the risk to understand it, understand the workings of the bank, the setting of lines, where to go to get them established or increased.

Training in these aspects of credit is very different to training in financial analysis and medium-term lending. It is, in its way, just as important.

Global custody and related

Global custody may appear to carry little or no credit risk, since the bank acts for the client who takes the risk. Sometimes this is true, but only if the bank takes great care to make it so. To eliminate credit risk altogether in global custody probably makes a bank uncompetitive. Perhaps the risk can be secured but only if the bank knows the legal requirements in the particular market, and follows precisely whatever steps the law requires to maintain the charge. Moreover, a lucrative part of global custody is often security lending which definitely gives rise to credit risk. So do clearing or cash management services which may go naturally to the bank that holds most of the company's cash, but need not be the best foreign exchange bank, to give one example.

Settlement

Some of global custody risk is settlement, but banks also run settlement risk in many other areas, whether in providing a client service or acting as principle.

The essence of settlement risk falls into two parts, one of which can be eliminated by delivery versus payment (DVP), but only if it meets strict criteria. Some definitions distinguish between the two as settlement and market risk. This book believes that they are two facets of the same risk rather than two separate risks as the distinction suggests.

The first risk is that when a bank pays for the delivery of an asset – bonds, perhaps – it does not receive them. This is the part that can be avoided by DVP; any system which ensures simultaneous transfer of asset and cash, with no possibility of one passing without the other. It may be physical transfer, or computerised book entry, but it must be completely sure; otherwise it is not properly called DVP. Many settlement systems reduce the risk to a low level, but only if they eliminate it altogether are they DVP.

The other aspect of risk is that of market movement before the bank can replace the transaction. If the bank expects 1000 bonds to be delivered at a price of 100, and the delivery fails, it has to buy more bonds. If the price is now 103, it has lost money, and has a claim against the failing party; in most cases the reason for failure is credit, and the risk a credit risk.

There are many types of settlement; security, currency, commodity, derivative and so on. Each has its own peculiarities, but they revolve around the simple features outlined above.

Training

The credit training required for traders, global-custody workers and settlement clerks revolves around three things:

- ensuring that they are conscious of the type of credit risk they run and of how to mitigate it;

- ensuring that they know the bank's requirements for dealing with it and the procedures for fulfilling those requirements;

- ensuring that they know how to recognise new credit risks as the bank evolves new products and that they know where in the bank to go to get them evaluated.

To train its people properly, the bank must first have effective systems and cross-functional cooperation. It is no good training the global custody people to ask for approval if the people they ask do not understand what they want and why; or for other reasons do not respond, or refuse permission for no sound reason.

16 Credit and Marketing

Credit and marketing are too often seen as opposed to each other, which they are not. Marketing information is among the most valuable forms of credit information there is; credit, properly used, is a key marketing tool for any lending bank, and even for some that do not lend.

Earlier chapters argued that it is critical for credit decision-makers to be seen to take a positive view. The link between credit and marketing should be more than that, however. The ability to meet a client's borrowing requirements is a marketing tool; even when he does not need to borrow the knowledge and interest shown in learning about the business is flattering to management and can impress favourably. Most of all though, there is a two-way connection between the information gained in marketing products which helps to understand the credit, and information gleaned analysing the credit which helps to generate marketing ideas. Some of these ideas can improve the borrower's credit.

The credit side and the marketing side should therefore work hand in glove. Unfortunately the marketer often avoids credit topics for fear, usually misguided, of upsetting the client; or is ignorant of the sort of information about credit he can and should glean in his marketing. He therefore fails either to steer the conversation the right way or to pass on valuable information gleaned. When a need for credit arises, the bank must generate information from scratch, which it too often does by asking a long list of questions. Direct questions are not usually the best way to gather information, and they may suggest an attitude which contrasts sharply with the impression previously given. The borrower may think the bank has started to worry about credit and take offense. This may then cause the marketer to be even more reluctant to raise credit issues in future.

Marketers should be trained to market credit standards even before they market individual products. A bank should recognise that to serve the client fully it will have to take credit risk (even if not always lending risk). To do this, or to advise the borrower on credit, it will need to be fully informed. To say so early establishes a sounder basis for a relationship than to duck the issue until faced with a specific credit request. If the client is reluctant to give information, at least the bank has laid the groundwork. When he wants credit, the client has no excuse for surprise or for believing that the bank has suddenly changed its view. If the client is permanently unable or unwilling to provide information then the sooner the bank recognises the impact on the relationship, the better.

The same argument applies to credit standards, although perhaps more selectively. Many companies, for example, resist covenants in medium-term loan agreements, often for invalid reasons. If the bank believes that covenants are vital to it and beneficial to the company, it should raise the idea as early as possible.

The argument can be more convincing when made consistently over time, than in the heat of negotiation. It avoids the client feeling that the bank is using the borrowing need to impose covenants on it against its interest. And it allows the bank to judge whether the borrower has a legitimate dislike for certain types of covenant as opposed to a knee-jerk reaction against any covenants. In the former case the bank can, when the need arises, design its covenant package to meet the borrower's legitimate requirements.

Best Source of Information

The relationship manager talks, sometimes as often as weekly, with a range of officials in the client. Depending on the nature of the relationship, and the size of the client, this may include the chief executive, finance director, treasurer, project finance director, their counterparts in subsidiaries and many others. The subject-matter can range over: corporate strategy, acquisition or disposal plans, capital raising; new product introduction, competitive advantages or fears; import or export plans and the currency exposures involved; debt structure and the risks of short-term interest rates; concentration of business with too few customers or suppliers; overseas business; and many other subjects.

Almost inevitably in each of these subjects, there will be credit implications. Often, they will be clearly stated and the banker will not need to steer the conversation towards them. Where the banker does need to, it is much easier to do this effectively than to ask a list of questions; he is also much more likely to get the answer than a list of questions would do.

This is most true if the banker is alert to credit and willing to note the various credit points that arise, and when appropriate, steer the conversation. This emphasises the importance of having bankers trained in credit even when it is not their prime responsibility.

Credit as a Marketing Tool and a Source of Information

The ability to respond positively and promptly to a request for credit does not need stressing. If it applies in unusual cases so much the better. For instance, a willingness to commit several hundred million pounds or dollars at short notice to fund an acquisition may be critically important; even more so the ability to support in a temporary difficulty. Both of these require a close understanding of the company, are easier if the approach to terms is understood in advance, and are probably more profitable than normal loans. Most importantly they create an impression on the client which should boost the relationship and ensure a fair share of the client's other business in future.

The less obvious advantages of credit to marketing lie elsewhere. Analysis of the credit can show areas of weakness which marketing can help to fill. Examples are discussed below.

1. Swap possibilities. Analysis may show that the client is unduly exposed to short-term interest rate movements, or currency movements or both. This gives an opportunity for the marketer to recommend the appropriate swaps or other hedge to the client. The result may be to improve the credit modestly, an additional bonus if the bank is already lending.

2. Foreign currency lending or exchange business. The client may be a major importer or exporter, but with fluctuating requirements which do not suit the swap market. If it is borrowing in domestic currency to finance exports, the answer may be to fund the foreign currency receivables by short-term borrowing in the buyer's currency. Or the forward exchange market may be more appropriate. Either way, the analysis draws attention to the need; the marketer in filling the need also improves the client's credit.

3. Capital structure. Analysis may show the company either needs more equity or needs to replace short-term with longer-term debt. The marketer may introduce the equity people to the client, or the bond underwriters or private placement group, or possibly loan syndication. Again, good business and an improved credit.

4. M&A. Analysis may show either that the company has an ill-focused business and needs to divest some companies, or that it has a hole in its strategy which could best be filled by an acquisition; in fact the two points quite often go together. If M&A can either find a buyer for the surplus assets, or an appropriate acquisition, the bank again has done good business and improved the credit.

There are many other possible examples. Of course they rarely run as smoothly as the above might suggest, but the underlying principle is sound.

The reverse process works equally well. If the banker or swap marketer, to take the first example, sees the swap opportunity, he also sees a credit risk, which should be reported. If the client agrees to do the swap, or has already done it with another bank, or refuses to hedge at all, this too is useful credit information. The same basic point applies, *pari passu* to all examples.

In all cases, cooperation between marketing and credit improves both. While the improvement may be greater on one side in some cases and on the other in others, the net improvement to the bank's position is beyond argument.

Understanding Credit as an Aid to Marketing

As already argued, there is a general sense in which understanding the credit impresses the client and makes a marketing approach more credible. There are also more specific ways in which a knowledge of credit is critical to good marketing.

A company may ask for advice on its capital structure or debt capacity; or may need advice but not recognise the fact. In the latter case, only a banker who understands credit will recognise the need, and can hope to convince the client. In either case, to give sound advice the banker needs to know enough credit to understand, first, whether the present structure is sound; secondly, if it is not, in what way and how seriously it is unsound; thirdly, what solution to propose. Whether the company needs more equity, whether it needs to stretch or smoothe the maturity profile of its debt, has too much floating rate debt, foreign currency debt or both. These may not be solely decided on credit grounds; the shareholders' interest may be different to that of lenders, for instance. Nevertheless, if the solution proposed damages the borrower's credit standing, the banker needs to know this to judge how serious the damage is, and whether the gain to shareholders outweighs the extra risk and cost of a weaker credit standing.

Sometimes the capital structure is not so much the disease as the symptom of an operating weakness which is undermining the finances. The need for credit judgement, as a basis for persuasive advice, is then even greater.

Much the same is true for a bond underwriting. If the client wants it, the bank may not have the option to advise whether it is the best route.

But before underwriting it must satisfy itself on the credit for several main reasons:

1. If it is completely the wrong solution, the bank should advise against it and refuse to participate, however insistent the borrower.
2. By underwriting the bank commits to buy the bonds. However confident it may be that it can sell them, it runs the risk of having to hold them. This is a credit risk, and should be assessed as such.
3. If it sells them, and the issuer collapses shortly thereafter, it may be liable to buy them back; in a less extreme case, the investor will be less likely to buy future issues. A reputation for selling only creditworthy paper is valuable but easily lost.

Similar arguments apply to private placements and *pari passu* to most other products. In essence, a bank either takes credit risk itself, advises on what credit risk the client can sensibly assume or sells credit risk to an investor. To do any of these soundly, and to be able to continue to do so at a profit, requires credit judgement along with other skills.

Probably M&A requires the greatest combination of the three. To advise a buyer properly, the banker needs to understand the buyer's credit standing, the impact on it of any financing structure proposed for the acquisition, the strength or weakness the acquired company will bring to the credit. It may also need to assess the market's reaction to a bond issue or syndicated loan if these form part of the financing package.

Indeed, one aspect that comes up in marketing many products is the market's view of the credit. This can affect advice the bank gives its customer on the availability of credit, the best market to tap, and its price. And although understanding the market's view of credit may not be exactly the same as understanding credit, the connection is close, and the basic understanding is an essential first step.

Of course, in each case the marketer can bring in an expert, just as in selling derivatives or other products. But if the marketer has established the right relationship with the client, it will be his advice they trust. He must know enough about the subject to assimilate the basis for the expert opinion, base his own judgement on it and be able to explain and support the advice.

Gleaning Information

The best credit information comes in a steady stream, not in occasional big chunks or answers to long lists of questions. Credit relates to the overall standing of the business, not just its finances, and therefore almost anything about the business is useful in assessing credit. One of the most important, and hardest, aspects to assess is the quality of management. This is rarely possible at a single meeting, when management is aware it is on parade. On the other hand, over the range of contacts in the normal course of business, the relationship manager will meet a variety of people, or with a small company see the same people in different roles. He will see the type of problems and opportunities they face, and how they react to them; see how well they know their business; how much depth there is in the management as a whole and the various sections.

A product marketer will tend to have a deeper knowledge of a narrower section of management. The swap marketer should develop a feel for how sophisticated the hedging policies and systems are, for instance, and the ability of the people running them. Product specialists may also get an idea of whether the company is running smoothly or whether there is friction or disaffection in the middle management ranks.

But marketers do not only have the chance to appraise – or provide information to allow others to appraise – the management. They are at the source of what can be a steady stream of information. Often all they have to do to get it is listen. Occasionally, they may need to follow up on a later visit something that came up at an earlier one. For instance, finance directors sometimes talk about the launch of a major new product. It might require particular financing, or it might just be that its success was important to the company. Either way, it would be natural at the next meeting to ask how the launch had gone. Or the company might ask for advice about a country or currency, because it planned to sell into that market for the first time; or because it was encountering competition and was thinking of billing in local currency or acquiring a distributor to help it to fight off the competition. Again, a follow-up question at the next meeting would be natural; equally, a further request for a larger line, or its cancellation, might be pointers to how successful the attempt had been.

These are only two examples. Almost any aspect of the business may come up at some time. The marketer needs to do four things:

1. Listen with a credit slant, so that he recognises the value of the information.
2. Follow up on points which can be expected to develop over time, such as shown in the examples above.
3. Where necessary, steer the conversation in the right direction, if possible avoiding direct questions. One method which is quite useful in some cases is to say something which you are not sure is true; the urge to put you right may overcome reticence.
4. Check usage on any facility granted in connection with a specific product or project, and use it as a benchmark of success, or a basis for asking further questions – tactful ones.

Recording the Information

The marketer is not always the person most likely to appraise the credit, and the product specialists are even less able to do so. They must therefore record what they learn, in some central place. Only then can the credit specialist pull together all the comments and impressions gained by the bank over the years, see whether the view of management has changed, and draw a valid overall conclusion.

This requires two things, in addition to the awareness of credit already discussed. One is that everybody record the conversations in which they learn any useful information or from which they derive any views. The second is that the written record be put in a credit file to which everybody with a legitimate interest has access.

This should be – and used to be – standard procedure, and it still is in some banks. Even in those banks, it probably is only in certain parts of the bank, and some of the best information goes unrecorded, or lies hidden in a desk file, unknown to those who could make most use of it.

Banks should encourage, browbeat, train their people to write memos recording the substance of their conversations, their impressions as to the competence of individual managers, but more important as to whether management overall is in control, knows where it is going and why, and works together well. Impressions of this sort, and of the success or otherwise of product or projects, as well as factual information are invaluable in assessing credit, but too often do not reach the people who have to make the assessment. They should.

17 Computers and Credit

THE ROLE OF COMPUTERS

Computers are useful in credit in three broad areas: control of usage; monitoring; and analysis. In all of them there is a danger that they become the master not the tool, although the danger arises in different ways.

To ensure that the bank remains in charge of the computer, rather than the other way round is a major management task, most of which applies to much more than just credit.

CONTROL OF USAGE

Banks have always needed to control usage of facilities, but this has become immensely more complicated in recent years. This is a factor of three things: the international spread of business, so that a facility may be used in several different offices of the bank; the speed and volume of transactions, particularly in trading exposures; and the complexity of products, which can make it difficult to calculate exactly what exposure a given usage involves.

These complexities make a computer desirable in most cases, but essential in a growing number. It may be possible, for instance, to keep track of an advance facility that can be used in three different offices without a computer, but it is easier with one. To keep track of a trading line which may be used several times in an hour is an altogether different matter, and begins to need not just a computer but one with real-time capabilities. And to keep track of swap lines, where the usage depends on complex formulae and changes over time in interest or currency rates, requires a sophistication which few banks yet have.

Banks must decide whether to have different but connected facilities under one limit. If they put interest and currency swaps under one line, and add caps, floors, collars, swaptions and perhaps some other items, there are advantages and disadvantages. Balancing them can be difficult; worse still, unless the bank has identical systems in all branches it may find that the best solution for the larger offices does not work in the smaller ones. Or head office, which sets the rules, may not realise for years that it is imposing unworkable requirements on some overseas offices.

The advantages of putting a group of facilities under one line are:

1. It reduces costs, since setting up lines is expensive.
2. It avoids overstating exposure. If the bank needs to establish separate lines for each product, even though their usage is linked, the full amount of the line will show as exposure. Since it is rare for all products to be heavily used at the same time, there will often be large unused lines.
3. It assists in allocation and pricing. If the client is so active that total exposure is a constraint, it may be essential to reduce exposure in this way. Where capital rather than the client is the constraint, the bank may want to limit the capital used in an area such as hedging, and to measure the capital and the return on it in deciding priorities. Only if the bank can see how much capital is tied up in a product group, and what the returns are, can it be sure the business is a sound one for it; either overall, or with the particular client, given its pattern of business, the returns available in other products for that client, and so on.

The disadvantages are:

1. Again, cost. Computer systems of this level are expensive to buy and to run.
2. Compatibility. Even if the bank has that level in head office, does it have it bank-wide and if not, how do the smaller branches cope?
3. Credibility/reliability. Reliable information requires input from traders and bankers. The trend tends to reinforce itself. If bankers/traders believe the information on the system is reliable and useful, they will take trouble to feed in accurate details of their deals promptly; if they do not, they will ignore the requirement or take little care over the details.

MONITORING

The computer is valuable in monitoring in two broad ways. One basically helps the analytical side of monitoring, and will be discussed under analysis. The other monitors outstandings, and such things as concentration.

Knowing outstandings, average and peak usage all help to monitor facilities and to see whether the pattern of usage is appropriate to the intent of the facility; or whether a change in pattern suggests a change in the credit which requires investigation.

With traditional facilities such as advances or term loans the amount in use changes infrequently. Tracking usage is thus fairly simple and does not need a computer, although even here it is helpful.

With facilities which are heavily used, fluctuate frequently, or where the loan equivalent changes with interest or other rates or shortening maturity, a computer is critical. Even then for a major bank with many branches, the complexity and expense of the systems required may make it hard to get fully adequate and up-to-date information. It is, nevertheless, worth the effort.

Information on outstandings is an important monitoring tool in several different ways. The obvious example is a short-term advance or overdraft line that is supposed to fluctuate to meet seasonal or other needs. Reviewing the pattern of outstandings shows whether, in fact, the borrowings reduce at the proper season, or whether the borrower is tending to use the line more fully in a way that suggests a pending liquidity shortage. There is little need for a computer to gather this information, if there is only one line. If, however, the borrower is a large group with lines in eight or ten subsidiaries in four or five countries, only a computer can keep track of the overall usage to make sure that each line fluctuates, and that the total does too. The same is true of a trading line, where usage is tied to particular aspects of the company's business.

Monitoring outstandings can also show whether the line is being used to excess, and whether it needs to be increased, or suggests overtrading.

Where the bank is concerned about the credit of a group or country, the ability to call up outstandings on all facilities can be critical. If Iraq invades Kuwait, the bank needs to know what exposure it has to all Kuwaiti and Iraqi clients, down to which foreign exchange transaction is due to settle today in which currency and which centre. This may not be pure credit; if the government forbids banks to pay any funds to Kuwaiti or Iraqi residents, banks need to identify quickly those payments which would break the regulations if not stopped. Even where this is not an issue, the ability to identify and stop payments may be invaluable.

Portfolio review

Banks should monitor their portfolios as well as individual names. A computer always makes it easier, but for a large bank with many branches it is essential. Only a computer can gather information on all aspects of the portfolio and then sort it in the various ways needed to check that the portfolio is balanced in all the ways in which it needs to be.

For instance, where there is an internal credit rating system, the computer can sort by credit rating. The bank can see the average credit rating of the portfolio; how much is concentrated at the lower end of the ratings, or in the middle, both in amounts of money and numbers of names; and whether the balance has changed, for better or worse, during the last three, six or twelve months or other period. It can sort in the same way by branch or region, as well as for the whole bank.

It can sort by industry, helping the bank to identify those industries where it has peak exposure; satisfy itself that they are the industries to which it wants to be most exposed; and by credit rating within industry to assess whether the quality of the individual exposures offsets or adds to the concern about concentration. If the computer is programmed to do so, it could also pick out all names vulnerable to specific events, such as changes in the price of copper, or interest or currency rates. This is less likely in practice, but banks should at least consider whether it might not be worth inclusion.

Similarly, it can sort by country risk, by currency of facility, type of facility or product, by maturity and any other way which the bank requires. Provided, that is, that the bank identified the need when the program was being prepared and ensured that the software either specifically built in the ability or was genuinely flexible enough to sort that way when the bank later identified the need.

In the sense that many banks have gone for years without some of this information, it may not appear crucial. However, even in the past it could probably have helped banks avoid the worst excesses, especially of concentration, and perhaps in other areas as well. As banks and products grow more complex the computer will become more important in these areas.

Analysis

The computer can help in some of the more routine aspects of analysis, and in some of the more advanced.

Spreading figures

A critical tool of analysis, whether initial analysis or for monitoring, is a quick and reliable method of spreading the figures and calculating ratios. While it may be possible to buy the information on public companies from services such as Extel, none cover all countries nor the smaller private companies which make up by far the largest number of borrowers from banks. Nor will the services provide monthly or quarterly spreads, let alone adjust the ratios for the different periods.

Yet the ability to see the development of key figures and ratios over five years or more is a vital element of financial analysis. The ability to compare the most recent year with the trends; or the most recent month or quarter with the previous one, or for a seasonal company with the same period in each of the past several years; these are an essential part of monitoring. With a healthy company indeed, they may be for much of the year the only form of financial monitoring; a quick glance may be all that is needed to satisfy an experienced banker that the company remains healthy.

Banks should make more use of the computer for this purpose than many do. With the proper software, the figures can be input rapidly by junior clerical staff; the computer calculates the ratios and the working capital or other reconciliations. The value of the output is therefore much greater than the input cost of the figures. Of course, the program itself is more expensive, but the cost can be spread over thousands of companies, making the per company cost negligible.

Domestic banks – the big four clearing banks in the UK and their equivalents elsewhere – ought to be particular fans of computer spreads. They lend to hundreds of thousands of small companies, which fall like flies in a recession, and often go very fast. Banks should insist on receiving monthly figures for most of these, perhaps quarterly for a few. The prompt receipt is itself desirable, if only to ensure that the company can produce them; but the ability to look at comparative figures and spot changes in trends within a few weeks of their starting to happen is most important with small companies.

Once the raw material is in the program, banks can use it to make comparisons, check industry-wide or country-wide trends – for instance, in receivable turnover. These enable them to put companies into a better context and assess how far change is in the economic environment rather than in the company.

Forecasting and sensitivity analysis

The need to forecast and the value of sensitivity analysis was discussed in an earlier chapter.

The computer makes it immensely easier. It is faster and more detailed than forecasting by hand – educational though that is – so that analysts can review the results at their leisure, rather than spending hours calculating each figure and ratio. Even more important, it allows many scenarios. If the bank needs to forecast by division as well as consolidated, the computer makes it easy. If the bank needs to try several different sensitivities, it is equally easy.

The computer is also valuable in rescue work, although here the bank may need to develop a model to suit the particular company. In theory, the company should be able to do this itself, but often cannot. The portable personal computer can be an absolute Godsend, which can be taken from the company's offices to the bank, or shown to other banks in their own offices. In a rescue, too, the banks need to model scenarios for the different possible financial structures, allowing for tax and regulatory requirements, as well as the operating outcomes. Or the need is often for cash flow models as well as P&L. Even with modern personal computers and forecasting models, this requires intensive work over long periods. Without them, many imaginative rescues would be impractical; nobody could do the detailed analysis to demonstrate that they work, in the time available.

THE DANGERS OF THE COMPUTER

There is no doubt that the computer, properly used, is a great blessing. But it carries several snags, which can be overcome, or at least greatly reduced, with skill and determination, but will otherwise undermine and sometimes eliminate the value.

Computer Runs Are Not Analysis

The first and subtlest, but arguably most dangerous, weakness is the tendency for users to rely on the computer as a substitute for thought. The analyst who presents the computer run thinking he has analysed the company, but who cannot justify the assumptions used; or who can tell why he used those assumptions but cannot tell what are the risks that they will prove wrong, or in what way they are most likely to prove wrong, or how much it matters if they do. Even analysts who do not fall into these traps unconsciously come to rely on the computer output as if it were gospel. 'Profit after tax in 1995 will be at least £x million', they say, when what they mean is 'If the assumptions used in this model prove exactly correct, which is virtually impossible, the arithmetical result will be a profit after tax of £x million'.

This may sound like semantics; after all, the first phrase is shorter and clearer, and we all know about the qualifications, surely. This may be true in some cases, but too often it is not; or not after a while. Inexperienced analysts and others can easily be lured into forgetting the qualifications. They do not consciously believe the output is infallible, of course, but their thinking uses it as a fact rather than as an arithmetical presentation of an opinion.

The ease of computers is vital in sensitivity analysis, but again, only if people think about the sensitivity they are analysing. The ease of feeding in a 15% per annum compound sales growth in a base case may stop the analyst thinking about whether a more erratic growth would be closer to reality. Having once made the mistake he often repeats it by choosing as a downside a sales growth that is equally smoothe, and arbitrarily lower, say 10% per annum. The analyst does not wonder whether sales are not more volatile, and thus whether 5% growth or even a 5% decline in the first few years might not more accurately portray the risk; or whether, in a cyclical company, the timing of the sales slow-down may not be more critical than its size.

The same sort of point applies to margins if the model is programmed to calculate them rather than costs. This may not be recognised, but if costs are expressed as a percentage of sales the affect is the same. But in companies with high fixed costs, a decline in sales may lead to a much steeper decline in margins. This is just the sort of thing sensitivity analysis should catch. It only will, however, if the analyst escapes the tendency to rely on the computer to do the thinking, and instead thinks through carefully what he should input to it, and sometimes what the underlying model should cover.

In brief, it is not just a question of 'garbage in, garbage out' or GIGO. It may also be that the ease of getting garbage out makes it more likely that bankers will put garbage in.

Rigidity

The flexibility of the personal computer is one of its main advantages. The same is often claimed for the mainframes and systems based on them, but with less justification. The ability of the system to cover a new product, or a modification of an existing product, is held out to be one of the advantages when a new system is being designed. Somehow, though, once it is up and running, the changes promised so easily require man weeks or months of programming and the approval of three or more committees; not quite what the banker had in mind. This seems to arise from several reasons discussed below.

Bankers and Computers Do Not Understand Each Other

There are few bankers who understand computers, and probably fewer computer specialists who understand banking. Those few who exist and are forceful enough to get each point of view across to the other are worth their weight in gold.

There are several reasons for this. One at least should not be permanent. Most senior bankers have come to computers fairly late in their careers, often reluctantly. They probably gave their children computers when they were nine or ten years old. There is therefore a generation of bankers growing up, and increasingly common in lower and middle ranks of the banks, who are wholly at ease with computers. They can understand their limitations and strengths, work with specialists, who may have been in the same computer class at school, and so on.

Another problem is jargon. Both banker and computer specialists use it, but computer specialists seem to use it to an unacceptable extent. Certainly much that is written by specialists about computers requires a previous level of knowledge which it is unreasonable to expect non-specialists to have.

One result of this lack of communication is that computer specialists are usually effectively in charge of any changes to the form of output. Often, therefore, changes are made for their convenience which are of no help to the banker for whom it is supposed to constitute 'management information'. Conversely the banker finds it very difficult to get changes to reflect his needs, including those of new products. These may therefore not be managed within the banks' overall systems for some time, making it harder for credit managers to ensure that the procedures established cover credit requirements adequately. Sometimes indeed, the rigidity of the computer may prevent the bank developing a new product because the system cannot handle it.

These weaknesses can directly affect the quality of the data in the system. If bankers, traders, salesmen feel that the information or other value of the computer output is low, they will take less care to input complete and accurate details of their business. The general lack of credibility will then be further undermined by a feeling that the information is not only in an unhelpful format, it is inaccurate too. This will lead to a vicious spiral.

There can be a virtuous spiral too. If the bankers believe that the output is relevant and useful to them, they will input accurate and complete detail, thus improving the value further.

This again is a case where initial garbage in can cause garbage out, which makes the input even worse garbage, and so on.

18 Pricing and Return on Equity

To price facilities correctly, banks need three types of information: their target return on equity; what capital each facility uses, to calculate that return; and for products other than loans, what loan equivalent to use to allocate capital on a comparable basis. Before going into these, however, we need to see some reasons why accurate pricing is necessary.

PRICING AS A DEFENCE AGAINST BAD DECISIONS

There are two ways in which pricing affects the quality of decisions. One is the reduced chance of individual bad decisions; the other is the collective benefit of a sound return on overall risk.

Accurate Pricing Reduces Individual Losses

The level of pricing of all instruments which include credit risk should reflect that risk. In loans, it is the major factor in the risk and therefore in the pricing. The level of pricing of loans is therefore the most important aspect of credit pricing, but the principles are valid in other instruments.

For each loan, there is a level of pricing which accurately reflects the risk. There is no certain way of assessing that level, however, and banks may legitimately disagree on where it is. There are three components to the decision: risk assessment, required return on risk (and through it capital), and value of the loan in obtaining other business. The first and the last are largely subjective, and many banks give no clear guidance as to the returns they require, so that this aspect carries lower priority in many banks than it should.

In all markets, but particularly in competitive phases, some banks will stretch for business. This can take various forms, but in the loan business it usually leads to lower pricing and to an erosion of the price differential between stronger and weaker credits. In extreme cases, as in the late 1980s, competition becomes so fierce that no sensible pricing is available. Here banks which price accurately may still have to make loans at uneconomic prices, for general business rather than pure credit reasons. In that case, it is even more important than usual to lend only to the best credits. If the price is the same for AAA names as for A names, why lend to A names?

More generally a bank which prices accurately will find it misses out on the weaker loans. In most conditions, but particularly in highly competitive ones, there will be banks willing to lend at prices which do not fully reflect the credit risk. To refuse to do this may look, particularly to the marketing people, as it the bank is throwing away opportunities for good business. In a prolonged period of competitive excess – i.e. a boom – this can generate intense pressure to lend. To resist it, the bank must have three things:

● an approach to risk assessment that the marketers can trust;

● an approach which makes clear the need for higher pricing to compensate for higher risk;

● The cooperative attitude of credit decision makers described in earlier chapters. Marketers must see the market's permissive attitude as a problem for the bank, which all parties work to overcome, rather than as a problem caused by an over-conservative approach to credit.

If some banks price on a better assessment of risk than the market, they will miss some business which, in hindsight, they may regret. They will miss more which subsequently turn into problems. Equally important, they will have kept their powder dry. Over-competitive markets in the end lead to excess and grief; the debacle of the late 1980s and early 1990s is the most recent and one of the worst demonstrations of this, but by no means the only one. The outcome is often a violent swing in the availability and price of credit. As banks cut back volume and raise margins, and perhaps tie up their best people in rescue work, the opportunity to lend to good borrowers at sensible prices grows. And although the bottom of a recession is a good place to lend, few people see it that way. The willingness to lend in bad times at generous but not outrageous pricing builds much better relationships than meeting the opposition on the last half basis point on a facility the borrower can get from tens if not hundreds of banks.

Although credit is a much smaller element in other products, the same point is broadly valid in them. The swap book, for instance, requires capital to cover the market risk, but if the book is largely matched, this requirement is quite small. If, however, a number of swaps fail for credit reasons, and the return built into the book does not match the credit risk, the overall return will diminish and may turn into a loss if the swap margins have been allowed to shrink too far.

The Need for a Sound Return

Banks make their money, in lending, from earning enough on the bulk of their loans to cover with a secure margin those that default, in a way that causes them losses.

The losses can be divided into two types: expected and unexpected. The expected loss is the statistically likely loss on a portfolio of given standards. The only public basis for the statistics is the loss record on rated bond issues. Moody's provides statistics and analysis of the default record on bonds they rate, by rating, thus showing the difference between say AAA three-year bonds and BBB for ten years; this includes an element of recovery. The problem is that bonds are a different instrument to bank debt, issuers are not necessarily typical of bank borrowers, and too few companies outside the US have been rated long enough to provide statistically valid data. There is no solid evidence that the default and recovery rates would, over a long enough period, be very different for other nationalities than they are for US companies. Nor, however, is there any proof that they are the same.

Banks with an internal rating system can develop statistics based on their own experience. Others may use the Moody's statistics with whatever reservations their own experience justifies. (For one example, Moody's uses a recovery rate of 40%, i.e. suggesting that on average, lenders lose 60% of the value of each defaulted bond. Banks may well feel that overall, or in certain areas, their experience justifies a higher recovery rate. This would reduce the expected rate of loss.)

Whatever the basis of calculation, or even if the bank does not calculate it, expected loss sets the credit cost of being a lender. Unless pricing covers this, as well as other costs, the bank is running its business at a loss. This is unsustainable in the long run – and indeed in the short run unless the bank has enough capital or profitable non-credit business to absorb the loss.

The unexpected loss has two components. One is fluctuations in the expected loss. If the statistical basis for calculating it is even slightly wrong, the loss may be greater than expected. Even where the statistical base is accurate, it predicts the average level of loss over an economic cycle; inevitably in some years the loss will be greater, and in others less. Nevertheless, when it peaks, the bank must be able to meet it.

The other cause of unexpected loss relates to losses which either:

- were not included in the statistical base; or

- increase to such an extent as to change the previous statistical prediction to a permanently higher level. This will require higher pricing which, however, will only become available gradually, as existing loans mature and are replaced by higher yielding ones.

The Latin American crisis could be considered an example of the first, and the combined LBO and property losses of the late 1980s and early 1990s of the second.

Unexpected loss thus requires capital protection. The capital may be partly retained earnings, but some must be paid up. Whatever the source, the shareholders expect a return. Pricing which does not provide it is thus doubly mistaken. Not only does it make it probable that the bank will take on loans it will regret; it means that even where the basic credit judgement is correct, the loans will be ill-judged. A loan whose return does not allow a bank to make an adequate profit is bad in a different sense to the one where the bank loses principal, but it is bad just the same.

Competitive Pressures Inhibit a Sound Return

Competition is desirable in lending as in all other economic activities, but can become too severe. Unlike most companies, banks are rarely put out of business by cutthroat competition; they are seen, rightly or wrongly, as too important to the economy. While a few small banks may collapse, or be discreetly merged into stronger competitors, this rarely happens to big banks; mergers raise monopoly fears unless they are totally incapable of surviving in any other way. The result is that cutthroat competition can last as long as governments keep the money supply plentiful, and sometimes longer.

This is a major argument against a policy of growth in the portfolio, discussed in earlier chapters. It also, however, presents a real problem to banks which rely on credit earnings for survival. They can, of course, try to develop other products; this is one reason why so many commercial banks have branched into the securities business in various forms. Or they can try to compensate for their unwillingness to follow the market down by better service. This can be difficult in lending; it is hard to argue that one bank's money is better than another's. And while understanding of, and loyalty to, the borrower in times of trouble are invaluable, it is hard to convince clients of that during a boom; it is even harder when other banks of comparable standing offer the borrower exactly what he wants. Corporate treasurers who run into trouble through too much borrowing may later blame those banks for lending too freely, rather than themselves for borrowing too much, but by then it is too late.

So what can banks do? The answer is a mixture: keep the standards up where possible; find other products, including specialised forms of lending which keep their margins up for a while at least; lead transactions, but take a small enough stake that the fees give a good return (not an option all banks can take); allow the book to run down somewhat, and perhaps buy bonds until the boom peaks; or build relationships around lending so that although the pricing on the loan may be unattractive, the overall return on the relationship is acceptable (see below).

None of these are easy; few banks manage to get the right mixture. Those that do will be called 'over conservative', 'unimaginative', or even 'declining', 'lacking direction or vision' or similar phrases. Or at least they will while the boom lasts; when it ends and they suddenly are among the few banks not writing off large amounts, the terminology changes. The danger then is that the praise is so extravagant that it goes to the bank's head, and it starts to think it is infallible. But that is a management problem pure and simple, not a credit problem, and thus beyond the scope of this book.

DIFFERENT WAYS OF ASSESSING CAPITAL AND RETURNS

Some banks years ago worked out methods of calculating return on capital after allowing for risk (risk adjusted returns). Most did not. They did not know what capital they needed against different levels of credit risk; many had no way of categorising credit risk. Moreover, each country had different rules as to the level of capital, and sometimes liquidity, banks needed for a given volume of assets. This lead to claims of unfair treatment and a desire for a 'level playing-field'.

BIS, its Strengths and Weaknesses

The central bank governors meeting at the Bank for International Settlements (BIS) were the first to make a serious attempt at a standard for the amount of capital required for various types of risk. They set up a committee under the chairmanship of Peter Cooke of the Bank of England to develop a set of guidelines as to the capital required against different types of risk. While mainly concerned with credit risk it did contain some allowance for interest rate risk on government bonds.

The BIS capital adequacy rules (also known in their early days as the Cooke or Basle rules) were a great step forward. If followed, they undoubtedly will prevent banks going quite so far overboard in the next boom as they did in the 1980s. Banks which have not developed any alternative approach certainly do better to follow the Basle rules than nothing.

However, the Basle rules are deeply flawed, in that they assess risk on political rather than economic or commercial grounds. The basic principle is to require banks to maintain a minimum level of capital against credit risk. Banks must keep 8% of adjusted risk in combined Tier 1 and Tier 2 definitions of capital. The method of adjusting for risk is the most flawed part of the requirement. Banks must apply a rating of 100% to all corporate loans, regardless of the quality of the borrower. However, they need only keep 20% against any bank in an OECD country, either 20% or 50% against various government and quasi-government bodies, and no capital at all against governments of OECD countries. Given the weakness of many banks and of some government entities it is clearly nonsense to argue, as the BIS rules do, that they are all lower risk than corporates rated AAA, AA or even A. This will clearly tend to divert lending away from corporates towards banks and government institutions, and towards those private sector loans, such as mortgages, which have less than 100% capital requirement.

The worst feature though is that it tends to push banks towards lending more to weaker credits within the corporate sector. If the capital a bank has to keep is the same for a AAA and a BBB name, but the price on the BBB is higher, many banks will go for the higher yield, even though on a properly risk adjusted basis it might give a lower return.

Certain other features of BIS have distorting effects, but at a less important level. For example, unused committed facilities carry a 50% capital weighting, unless the commitment is for less than one year, in which case there is no requirement. This has given rise to the 364-day commitment. There is also a requirement for swaps which uses rather crude methods of valuation. If this method is badly wrong in either direction, it will distort the balance of capital and pricing between loans and swaps. Until someone comes up with a guaranteed correct way of calculating the loan equivalent of swaps, however, we will not know whether it is in fact distorted or not.

Nevertheless, BIS remains, despite these weaknesses, a step forward. Also, it is hard to see how BIS could lay down standards for different treatment of strong and weak corporates, given the lack of public ratings for the great majority of borrowers.

The most important aspect of BIS is that it compels banks to meet minimum capital requirements on almost all their loans, and swaps. This in turn has made banks concentrate more on pricing. There are after all two ways of meeting a capital ratio. Banks can reduce their assets or increase their capital. Higher pricing will do both; it will turn away some loans; and it will increase the earnings. These may increase capital by being retained, or by making it easier to raise new capital or both.

Other Approaches

Banks affected by Basle have to pay attention to the Basle requirements. If, however, banks believe as the author does that the Basle rules incorrectly weight the risk and therefore misstate the capital required for different loans, they can develop their own. Where this shows that Basle understates the risk and therefore capital requirement, the bank can attach a higher requirement to such loans. Moreover, a bank is not bound by politics; if it believes that Corporate Borrower A is a better credit than Bank B, or Local Government Entity C, it can apply a higher capital requirement and therefore charge a higher price to the latter than the former.

To make this assessment, of course, it needs a method of comparing the credit risk in widely different entities. The arguments in favour of an internal rating system are discussed in the next section. But whatever the method, if the bank has no reliable way of comparing widely differing credits, it is hard to see how it can do anything very sophisticated. It might divide banks into broad strands – by size and likelihood of government support, for instance. Or companies on some basis such as net worth, or perhaps the product of factors such as net worth, leverage, and average pre-tax profits over the past three years. All of these however amount to a rough, ready and sometimes inaccurate form of rating.

However the bank differentiates between borrowers, it also needs some method of allocating capital to different levels of risk. Here the large banks at least can draw on their own experience to develop default and recovery statistics for various levels of credit risk. If they have only recently installed a rating system, they can still prepare statistics based on size, industry or other criteria and gradually improve them as the experience with the ratings grows more reliable.

The credit of the borrower, however, is the most important but not the only factor affecting default and recovery rates. Banks should factor in the extra risk in longer maturities, perhaps in foreign currency lending or lending in countries where the bank does not have a branch and is less well placed to follow the borrower. Collateral does not affect the default rate but may improve the recovery rate. The bank may want to build in an extra capital requirement for concentration of risk, one factor liable to be outside past statistics and therefore to lead to an unexpected loss.

Each bank should choose its own combination of factors to decide how much capital it needs to keep against each level of risk. The final factor is then the return on capital the bank requires. If a given credit exposure requires $x\%$ capital cover, and the desired return on capital is $y\%$, it is easy to discover what yield makes the credit attractive. This may be paid in some combination of upfront and continuing fees as well as interest margin, but any modern calculator will solve the appropriate levels quite quickly. Or the bank may program the main features onto a floppy disc and distribute it around the bank. It can then include the solution to how much different types of fees add to the yield in the floppy disc.

The critical point is that the bank must have a basis for calculating capital needed and returns on it. Without this it is impossible to price loans accurately; in a competitive market that is a recipe for disaster. Of course, banks have other decisions to make: do they want to follow the Basle 8% rule? Or do they need a higher capital cover overall than Basle requires? Their own calculations may show some borrowers needing more capital than Basle, others needing less. Will they always use the higher, always their own, or some compromise?

Banks also need to recognise that even though the return on equity is critical, it is not the only factor affecting pricing. The two other main ones are relationships, discussed below, and the pricing implications when capital is not fully used. To oversimplify, if a bank has spare capacity to lend (excess capital) then any return is better than none. In these circumstances the bank may well lend short term at a rate below the required rate. By doing so it earns some return now, and keeps open the ability to earn a better return later if demand grows.

The Need for Internal or External Rating Systems

All of the above suggests that some form of rating system is necessary to accurate pricing as well as to credit control in a broader sense. The question is how to have it consistently at reasonable cost?

One way in theory is to use external ratings. For some parts of the business this may be possible. Bond trading or dealing in commercial paper, for instance, can cover only borrowers rated by one or more rating agencies.

For most banks, however, the rating agencies cover only a small proportion of the names in their portfolio. These banks therefore need an internal rating system if they are to have one at all. To have full value, it needs to be applied consistently across the bank, which requires considerable management effort.

First, however, we should be clear on the advantages of such a rating system. Some have been touched on in this and earlier chapters.

Accurate ratings are first a tool in the individual decision, which consists of two parts: do we want to lend to this company at all? If so on what terms? Neither should be answered solely on the basis of the rating; no rating on its own can answer all the questions bankers need to ask about a

---

credit. But the rating does sum up the overall view of the credit and provides an agreed basis from which to start. If the rating is very low, it may make it easier to turn down the proposal without major internal argument. If it suggests a sound but not prime credit – BBB rather than AAA – it helps put the credit proposal in context, and enables specific bank policies to apply. For instance, a policy only to lend for ten years or longer to AA or better names makes it clear why the bank refuses a ten-year loan to a BBB name. The same is true of pricing.

Ratings are also useful in monitoring individual names. Low or declining ratings justify spending more time analysing and monitoring; while a high or improving rating justifies less. Ratings thus help ensure that the monitoring effort is well directed. They also help in monitoring the portfolio, particularly with the help of a computer as described in Chapter 17.

Generating ratings without undue cost is relatively easy, but ensuring consistency in the way they are given is sometimes less so.

Where the bank has a separate analytical unit, it should clearly apply ratings to everything it analyses. If it analyses all names, consistency becomes less of a problem. Where it analyses only some of the names, or where there is no such unit, consistency is more of a problem. The rating then has to be given, or at least proposed, by the marketing banker. If he is too heavily market-oriented, this can be dangerous.

The solution then may be to have a rating committee. Depending on the size of the bank and each branch, this might be in the branch, at regional headquarters or at head office. It would consist of at least the senior credit specialist, the senior analyst and the senior business manager; it might well be expanded beyond this. It would review the ratings proposed, and their justification; it would then either confirm them, adjust them or occasionally send them back to be rethought. A regional or head office committee could impose greater consistency, and if the ratings are set at branch level they should certainly be reviewed further up the ladder.

If the bank uses facility ratings, exclusively or with company ratings, these can be given while approving the facility. Some pressure for consistency can be built in by requiring a discussion whenever the ratings given are more than one notch apart; by requiring the lower to be the one that rules; or, where a credit specialist is one signatory and non-specialists also sign, giving precedence to the specialist's rating. This will usually ensure consistency within branches, but unless most decisions are made at regional or higher level, it may not alone ensure it between them. This may be partly a matter of training, or may require further review of ratings at a higher level to assess whether all areas of the bank are applying the same standards.

Whatever the precise method, it should flow naturally out of the requirements to analyse and approve credit. In this way, the only additional cost is that of recording the ratings as they are given.

Relationship in Pricing

We have argued in earlier chapters that marketing should play no part in the decision whether to lend at all; but that once the bank takes a positive decision, marketing can affect the conditions on which to lend; only under careful control, however.

This is true of pricing in particular. There are cases where the decision to charge a full price on a loan (or other credit facility) can lose the bank existing profitable business. If the profit on that business is taken into account, then the loan may still meet the bank's overall ROE target. This argument needs to be taken with a pinch of salt. The profits on the other business may generate merely an adequate return on the capital and risk involved in doing the business, in which case to apply it to the loan is to double-count it. Only profit above the minimum ROE should be counted.

Or the argument may be that to make the loan is the only way to establish a relationship, which over time will generate more profits. It is certainly true that some companies require, often explicitly, that a bank show 'trust' in them by lending money before they will consider it as a relationship bank; this is particularly common in some European countries, less so in the United States. It is also true, however, that companies will make vague promises of this with no follow through, or that marketers will believe the connection is much stronger than it really is.

It is dangerous to tie the pricing on a loan to a specific piece of business. In the United States this 'linkage' is actually illegal in some cases; even where it is legal, it forces the borrower to do a specific piece of business with a bank which may not offer the best service. This is hardly the best way to start a relationship.

If, instead, the bank sees a number of business opportunities with a client, where it believes it can be competitive, it is fair to price a loan at the market level, to gain the opportunity. It needs to avoid two traps. First, to do this when in fact the borrower is indifferent whether the bank lends is pointless. Secondly, there is a tendency among marketers to count all the fees on the transaction towards the return on the loan, whether or not they are contingent on the loan being made.

Where there is genuine reason to believe that pricing a loan below the bank's required return, but not below the market, will affect the relationship, there is a case for doing so. However, it is vital to ensure follow-up;

the marketer who claims the benefit must produce it, at least in most cases; otherwise the discipline is soon lost. There are two ways of doing this. One is to calculate the shortfall between the actual earnings on the loan and those that would be needed to meet the bank's minimum returns. The marketer then owes that amount to the credit portfolio or credit officer depending on the internal system. If this cannot be produced, the marketer not only loses credibility, but this should be deducted from the revenue with which he is credited in considering his overall performance and perhaps bonus. The other approach is to calculate a return on total capital used by the borrower in all its business, not just credit business, with the bank. If this is above the benchmark, then the lower rates are more acceptable; if not, not. This, of course, requires the bank to have calculated capital needs and returns on every product in its quiver.

Loan Equivalents in Pricing

The concept of loan equivalents was discussed in Chapter 6. It is important in pricing because it gives a basis for comparison. If a five-year swap to a BBB name carries the same credit risk as a $1 million five-year loan, the pricing must allow for the same return on credit-based capital as if the bank had made the loan. It must, of course, allow for profits to cover the market and trading risk the bank bears, and the skill and consequent high salaries of swap dealers.

This can be easier said than done. Swaps are agreed in a dealing atmosphere with the total return depending on negotiation between traders. They must know what credit spread they must charge in advance so that they can include it in their bid. This could mean, and in the early days of swaps usually did, that they must check with the credit officer before dealing. He decides whether the credit is acceptable and what credit spread they should take. With the advent of swap lines this became less practicable even than before. This is another area where ratings are useful. If the trader has a grid showing what spread to charge for each rating level and maturity, all the credit officer has to do is establish the line and say 'Price it as a AA'.

Other types of product are impossible to charge for directly. The settlement risk on government bonds, with DVP, for instance, is too small to break out by transaction. Banks can only ensure that the profits on the business are enough to justify the credit risk involved and give a decent return on the capital required by that risk.

The euphoria of a boom can never be eliminated. It can be controlled; one means is pricing to ensure a sound return on equity. The loan equivalent helps to do that on non-lending credits.

Index